1119

SELECTED POETRY

Hugh MacDiarmid SELECTED POETRY

INTRODUCTION BY ELIOT WEINBERGER

Edited by Alan Riach & Michael Grieve

A NEW DIRECTIONS BOOK

Manufactured in the United States of America
New Directions Books are printed on acid-free paper.
First published clothbound by New Directions in 1993.

Library of Congress Cataloging-in-Publication Data

MacDiarmid, Hugh, 1892–1978
    [Poems. Selections]
    Selected poetry / Hugh MacDiarmid ; introduction by Eliot
Weinberger ; edited by Alan Riach & Michael Grieve.
        p.   cm.
    Includes index.
    ISBN 0–8112–1248–3 : $25.00
    1. Scotland—Poetry. I. Riach, Alan, 1957–   . II. Grieve,
Michael. III. Title.
PR6013.R735A6   1993
821'.912—dc20   93–5312
                                                              CIP

New Directions Books are published for James Laughlin
by New Directions Publishing Corporation,
80 Eighth Avenue, New York 10011

Contents

Acknowledgements

Dating periods of composition is almost impossible with Mac-Diarmid's later work. It is known that a massive amount of material was written in the Shetlands in the 1930s, and that much of this was not published until the '40s, '50s and '60s. In some cases – demonstrably with *In Memoriam James Joyce* for example – material written earlier was supplemented and changed at later periods, so the composition of the work continued over decades and indeed right up to weeks or even days before actual publication. In this selection, I have tried to arrange the poems as much as possible by date of completion of the text or version that was first printed. For help with this arrangement I am very grateful to W.R. Aitken.

In the present selection, the most problematic Scots words have been glossed at the foot of each page so that reading the texts should prove no more difficult than reading Shakespeare. I hope that this will allow the Shakespearian exhilaration in MacDiarmid's language to be more quickly felt. *The Hugh MacDiarmid Anthology*, co-edited by Michael Grieve and the late Alexander Scott, set a valuable precedent for this form of glossary. Further information on Scots vocabulary or the history of the Scots language is readily available in the *Concise Scots Dictionary* (ed. Mairi Robinson, Aberdeen University Press). Except where noted, the footnotes are MacDiarmid's.

The chronology is based on the biography of Hugh MacDiarmid by Alan Bold and the chronology supplied in the MacDiarmid exhibition catalogue (no.7) of the National Library of Scotland. For further details and critical suggestions I am indebted to Edwin Morgan and my colleagues at the University of Waikato, John Jowett and Marshall Walker.

–Alan Riach

Introduction, by Eliot Weinberger

"My job," he wrote, is "to erupt like a volcano, emitting not only flame, but a lot of rubbish." Heat, fireworks, acrid smoke, and tons of dead ash are indeed among his attributes, but a volcano is too small a trope for Hugh MacDiarmid. He occupied—perhaps he was himself—an entire planet.

"Hugh MacDiarmid": the dominant pseudonym among a dozen pseudonyms and one actual birth-name, Christopher Murray Grieve. They wrote about each other, usually in praise, sometimes in disagreement. They were Nietzschean Marxist Christians; supporters of Mussolini and Stalin and Scottish nationalism; followers of Hindu Vedanta. They produced tens of thousands of pages of journalism and commissioned books; edited anthologies and a string of magazines; wrote an autobiography estimated to be four thousand pages, hundreds of pages of fiction and translations, hundreds of letters to editors and thousands to friends and enemies, and, above all, some two thousand pages of poetry, much of it in long lines. They wrote in variations of two languages, with passages in a few dozen others, even Norn. One of the two primary languages, "synthetic Scots," was their own invention. And behind the curtains of this vast collective enterprise was a short, often miserable and alcoholic man, a nationalist who hated his nation, a gregarious misanthrope who spent most of his life in extreme poverty. All of his teeth were extracted at twenty-four; most of his writing was completed by fifty; he died at eighty-six, and never learned to type: MacDiarmid!

The work that will survive begins in 1922, when, at age thirty, Christopher Grieve gave birth to Hugh MacDiarmid. At the time he was a nine-to-five journalist for small-town newspapers and a bad Georgian English poet. Most of the passions of his life were already in place: Scottish nationalism, which was flaring all around him, lit by the Irish and Russian revolutions; Marxism; the Social Credit schemes of Major C. H. Douglas, championed by A. R. Orage and Ezra Pound in the *New Age*. His heroes were Nietzsche and Lenin ("I have no use for anything between genius and the working man"), Dostoyevsky for his nationalist spiritualism, and the Russian philosopher Leo Shestov for his evocation of the limitlessness of the imagination, an imagination beyond all dogmas, and where all contradictions are reconciled. For Scottish writers at the time, the central question was what language to write. Middle Scots, in the fifteenth and sixteenth centuries, had been one of the grand vehicles for poetry: the Great Makars Robert Henrysoun and William Dunbar (whom the English call the "Scottish Chaucerians"), Gawin Douglas' magnificent version of the *Aeneid*, Mark Alexander Boyd's single and perfect sonnet, "Venus and Cupid." After 1603—the death of Queen Elizabeth, the transformation of the Scottish James VI into the English James I, and the subsequent loss of Scottish autonomy in the "United Kingdom"—Scots as a literary language decayed. In the eighteenth century, Allan Ramsay, Robert Fergusson, and finally Robert Burns attempted a revival which never quite caught on. (Their greatest contemporary, David Hume, for one, spoke Scots in private but wrote only in English.) Ironically, it was the success of Burns that strangled the movement: Scots became the domain of the corny songs of his imitators, which in turn led to vaudeville parodies. By the time of Grieve's childhood, kids were punished for speaking Scots in school; it was considered unspeakably vulgar.

There was a new Scots Revival movement, led by the various Burns Societies, which Grieve and his pseudonyms had violently opposed as reactionary and irrelevant to the struggle. But by 1922, the wonder year of Modernism, a conjunction of forces changed his mind. His mentor, the militant nationalist Lewis Spence (now remembered as a historian of Atlantis) suddenly switched sides, and supported Scots. There were the examples of the revival of Gaelic in the Irish Republic, and the invention of Nynorsk, a new language created out of various rural dialects, which became the official second language of Norway. There were the writings by Gregory Smith promoting the idea of a unique Scottish psychological make-up: the Caledonian Antisyzygy, capable of holding "without conflict irreconcilable opinions," "easily passing from one mood to the other," and with a "zest for handling a multiple of details"—a perfect description, in fact, of MacDiarmid himself. Moreover, there was the general belief that this sensibility—anticipating, in a way, Benjamin Lee Whorf's studies of the Navajo—could only be expressed by the Scots language. ("Speakin' o' Scotland in English words," MacDiarmid later wrote, was like "Beethoven chirpt by birds.") And most of all, there were the examples of Charles Doughty and

James Joyce: Doughty, mining his poems from archaic English, and Joyce, opening the gates for all the world's languages to rush in. From them, Grieve believed that one's spoken language was not enough, that one must ransack the dictionaries for precision of expression.

Grieve created MacDiarmid—and kept MacDiarmid's identity secret for years—as an experiment in writing in Scots. His goal was to return not to the folkish Burns, but to the continental and intellectual Dunbar; to "extend the Vernacular to embrace the whole range of modern culture," as well as to delineate the Scottish mind. By doing so, he thought he would help to sever Scotland from England and insert it into Europe as a nation among equals.

His sources were books like John Jamieson's 1808 *Etymological Dictionary of the Scottish Language* and Sir James Wilson's *Lowland Scotch as Spoken in the Lower Strathearn District of Perthshire*. There he found the words like *watergaw* (an indistinct rainbow) and *yow-trummle* (cold weather in July after sheep-shearing) and *peerieweerie* (dwindled to a thread of sound) that would fill the lyrics of his first important books, *Sangschaw* (1925) and *Penny Wheep* (1926). As one stumbles through these poems now, the eyes bouncing between the lines and the glossary below, it is important to remember that this is exactly how most Scottish readers would have had to read them at the time. (Worse, the glossaries in those early editions were in the back.) MacDiarmid's Scots— and later, much of his English—is written in a language foreign to everyone.

From these early short pieces, which he later dismissed as "chocolate boxes," he set out to write the Scots *Ulysses* or *The Waste Land*, a poem that could demonstrate that Scots was not only a medium for lyrics, but also for the rigorous intellect of difficult "modern" works. The result was *A Drunk Man Looks at the Thistle* (1926), a poem five times as long as Eliot's. Like *The Waste Land*, which makes a cameo appearance in the poem, it is written in a variety of styles and meters—though largely interspersed among ballad stanzas—and it collages other texts: translations of whole poems by Alexander Blok and Else Lasker-Schüler, and some forgotten continentals like Zinaida Hippius, George Ramaekers, and Edmond Rocher, to give the poem a European context. Like "Prufrock" it is an interior monologue, though one that continually locates itself. To *Ulysses'* single day, it takes place in a single night; its Molly is Jean, who similarly has the last word. Its narrative comes from Burns' "Tam o' Shanter," who was also on his way home from the taverns at midnight, and its inspiration from Paul Valery's *La Jeune Parque*, which the French poet described as "the transformation of a consciousness in the course of one night."

A Drunk Man is unquestionably the Scots masterpiece of the century, and nearly all of MacDiarmid's critics and acolytes consider it his greatest work. Certainly it is dense with complexities that are still being unravelled in a parade of monographs, most of them written in Scotland. But it is a curious late Symbolist work in the age of High Modernism. The thistle itself is fraught with significant meaning, and would have appalled the Imagists: emblem of Scotland and the Scottish character, sign of the Drunk Man's virility, image of the soul flowering over the thorns of the "miseries and grandeurs of human fate"; it even becomes Ygdrasil, the cosmic tree. And its Nietzschean narrative has dated badly: the triumph of the intellect and the soul over drunkenness, psychological difficulties, cultural inferiorities and doubt; the dream of the transformation of the low-born Drunken Man, the poet, into "A greater Christ, a greater Burns"—an odd pair as models for one's superior self. At the end of a century that has seen what can be wrought by acts of "the beautiful violent will," it is MacDiarmid's Nietzscheism more than his Stalinism—perhaps they are the same—that is most difficult to take.

Though *A Drunk Man* sold poorly, Hugh MacDiarmid became the most famous poet in Scotland, and Grieve and the pseudonyms shrank in his shadow (except of course when writing articles about him). In the 1920s he edited three magazines, including *The Scottish Chapbook*, which is considered to be the greatest Scottish literary review ever, and contributed to dozens of magazines with "Scots" or "Scottish" in their titles; founded the Scottish chapter of PEN; joined and broke with countless political organizations; stood for Parliament a few times; and held posts in local governments like Convener of Parks and Gardens, Hospitalmaster, member of the Water Board. A hero-worshipper, he read the news from Italy and—as many did at the time—mistook National Socialism for socialism and wrote "A Plea for Scottish Fascism." But his continuing loyalty was to Lenin and Major Douglas and Dostoyevsky ("This Christ o' the neist thoosand years"), believing that the combination of Marxist-Leninism and Social Credit would end the struggle for material existence and prepare the world for the struggle for spiritual transcendence.

In 1933, at age forty-one, he went into a kind of exile and a prodigious burst of writing perhaps unmatched by any other writer in the century. With his wife, Valda Trevlyn, and son Michael, he moved to a place called Sodom on the tiny island of Whalsay in the Shetlands, paying two shillings a month for a house without electricity, and water a quarter of a mile away. The family subsisted on gifts of fish and potatoes from their neighbors and gulls' eggs gathered in the cliffs. In his eight years there, MacDiarmid wrote a series of hack-works, with titles like *Scottish Doctors, Scottish Eccentrics, The Islands of Scotland, Scottish Scene;* political tracts like *Red Scotland, or What Lenin Has Meant to Scotland,* and *Scotland and the Question of a Popular Front Against Fascism and War;* and an autobiography estimated to be a million words long, parts of which were later published as *Lucky Poet* and *The Company I've Kept.* He edited a series of books on Scotland and a large anthology of Scottish poetry, translating the Gaelic sections himself, in collaboration with Sorley Maclean. He was expelled from the National Party of Scotland for Communism and from the Communist Party for nationalism. He had a nervous breakdown and was hospitalized for some months. And there was more:

He set out to write, in English, the longest poem ever written by one individual, *Cornish Heroic Song for Valda Trevlyn.* In the two years between 1937 and 1939, he wrote some six or seven hundred pages of it—one-third of the intended whole. This was virtually all of the poetry (with the exception of *The Battle Continues*), largely unrevised, that he was to publish for the next forty years.

The *Cornish Heroic Song* has never been reconstructed. According to MacDiarmid's biographer, Alan Bold, the first part was a 20,000-line section entitled *Mature Art.* MacDiarmid sent a 10,000-line version to T. S. Eliot at Faber and Faber's, which the poet admired (while finding the title "forbidding"), but the publisher rejected. Of the surviving longer poems, "In Memoriam James Joyce" (now 150 pages in the so-called *Complete Poems*) was originally merely a piece of *Mature Art.* "The Kind of Poetry I Want" (now fifty pages) was to run throughout the *Cornish He-*

roic Song, and "Direadh" (now thirty pages) was to be in a later section. It is unclear where all the other poems belonged, and "Cornish Heroic Song for Valda Trevlyn" itself now survives as an eight-page poem. In 1967 MacDiarmid published a book of poetry called *A Lap of Honour,* containing, he claimed, poems that had been omitted from his 1962 *Collected* because he'd forgotten that he'd written them! Rescued by the scholar Duncan Glen, these included some of his greatest works, among them, "Diamond Body" and "Once in a Cornish Garden."

Various forces impel the poems of *Cornish Heroic Song:* First, the attempt to create a "synthetic English," as he had invented a "synthetic Scots," a project inspired by Doughty, but with a vocabulary drawn not, as Doughty had done, from archaicisms, but from the new language of science. It is a poetry of "hard facts," of hundreds of thousands of details ("The universal *is* the particular"), and its ultimate mysticism anticipates the computer age, where the more precisely we have been able to describe and measure the universe, the more mysterious it has become.

Second, MacDiarmid discovered that the way out of the traditional prosody and rhyme he had hitherto employed almost exclusively was to break prose down into long jagged lines. Often this meant transcribing—the current term is "sampling"—other people's prose: long passages from obscure travel and science books, reviews in *The Times Literary Supplement,* Herman Melville's letters, the writings of Martin Buber, Thomas Mann's *Tonio Kröger.* His practice of reproducing these uncredited led to charges of plagiarism later in his life, but plagiarism, to his mind, was besides the point for an epic that was to include everything.

Third, he had come to believe that the poetry of the classless society was not the personal lyric, but an epic without heroes (or with thousands of heroes). And he had taken to heart the words from Lenin's last speech, delivered in 1922 in a prose that sounds like MacDiarmid's, and which are quoted twice in *Lucky Poet:*

> It would be a very serious mistake to suppose that one can become a Communist without making one's own the treasures of human knowledge . . . Communism becomes an empty phrase, a mere façade, and the Communist a mere bluffer, if he has not worked over in his consciousness the whole inheritance of human knowledge—made his own and worked over anew all that was of value in the more than two thousand years [!] of development of human thought.

The result, then, was, in MacDiarmid's words, "an enormous poem,"

> dealing with the interrelated themes of the evolution of world
> literature and world consciousness, the problems of linguis-
> tics, the place and potentialities of the Gaelic genius . . . the
> synthesis of East and West and the future of civilization. It is a
> very learned poem involving a stupendous range of reference,
> especially to Gaelic, Russian, Italian and Indian literatures,
> German literature and philosophy, and modern physics and
> the physiology of the brain, and while mainly in English, uti-
> lizes elements of over a score of languages, Oriental and Occi-
> dental.

There is nothing like it in modern literature, nothing even
close. It is an attempt to return poetry to its original role as
repository for all that a culture knows about itself. Unlike
Pound's *Cantos*, it does not merely allude to its extraordinary
range of referents; it explains everything in a persistent, unor-
ganized stream of erudition to match the Joycean stream of con-
sciousness. Sylvia Townsend Warner described the autobiogra-
phy in words that are more applicable to the poetry: "as though
the pages of two encyclopedias were being turned by a sixty-
mile gale." It is a poetry that wants to raise the standard—both
in the sense of hoisting a battle flag and of educating the world
through unremitting instruction and admonition—and it is a
poetry that, uniquely, keeps reminding us what it wants to be:
"The Kind of Poetry I Want."

Certain poems easily detach themselves—among them, the
earlier "On a Raised Beach," "In the Slums of Glasgow," "The
Glass of Pure Water," "Direadh III," "Diamond Body" and
"Once in a Cornish Garden" (the latter two omitted here)—and
can stand with the poems of the great twentieth-century poets
from the Celtic Isles: Yeats, Basil Bunting, D. H. Lawrence,
David Jones. But to excerpt—as an editor of a *Selected Poems*
must—from the poems of *Cornish Heroic Song* is to destroy the
effect of MacDiarmid's greatly underestimated music. Based on
Scottish piping and Indian ragas, it is dependent on the counter-
point (MacDiarmid would say dialectic) between a continuous
drone and bursts of melody. The pleasures of MacDiarmid are
precisely the explosions of passion, rage, intellectual insight,
aphorism, and spiritual transcendence that occur after pages of

foreign word-lists and arcane bibliographies, catalogues of scientific terms and theories, histories of literature and art and philosophy and music, piling up, as he wrote, like Zouave acrobats. These are the volcanic fireworks amidst the tons of dead ash; out of context there is no contrast, and their power is diminished. Rather like excerpting the magnificent landscapes from the *Cantos*, they are the jewels without the crown.

He is one of the great materialist poets and one of the great mystics; a poet thoroughly immersed in the technicalities of geology, astronomy, and physics who could also write "The astronomical universe is *not* all there is" and "everything I write, of course, / Is an extended metaphor for something I never mention." He was a political animal who believed that the role of the poet is to be a solitary contemplative; a man whose millions of words revolve around a center of absolute stillness: "The word with which silence speaks / Its own silence without breaking it." A Nietzschean Marxist, he thought that the collective, with all its contradictions, could be embodied by one superior man. A Communist from the working-class (unlike his English poet contemporaries), he had no pity for the poor, but honored them for their stoicism and loathed them for their ignorance and spiritual decay, "innumerable meat without minds." He expressed his love, in "Once in a Cornish Garden," one of the great love poems, through an astonishingly detailed celebration of his wife's clothes and cosmetics. He wrote in a style that owed nothing to the modern writers he most admired: Joyce, Pound, Rilke, Brecht, Mayakovsky, Hikmet. He may be the only poet of the century for whom, in the poem, philosophy matters. Science was his mythology.

He believed that the first civilization was Ur-Gaelic, and that it rose in Georgia, birth-place of Stalin. He started a Hugh MacDiarmid Book Club, which offered subscribers a new MacDiarmid book every two months. He envisioned a Celtic Union of Socialist Soviet Republics (Scotland, Wales, Ireland, Cornwall) which would join in an "East-West Synthesis" with the Soviet Union. He listed his hobby in *Who's Who* as "anglophobia." He believed that Cornwall was an outpost of Atlantis. He rejoined the Party after the invasion of Hungary, while simultaneously signing a public letter attacking it. He believed that "there lie hidden in language elements that, effectively combined, can utterly change the nature of man." He read his poems under huge portraits of Blake and Whitman in Peking in 1957. He debated on the same side as Malcolm X at the Oxford Union in defense of extremism. He said that "Of all the men I have known, I loved Ezra Pound," but they only briefly corresponded, and had met only once, in 1970, when Pound had already stopped speaking and MacDiarmid was nearly deaf. In his eighties he was writing television reviews. The words he wanted on his tombstone were: "A disgrace to the community." MacDiarmid:

Recalling *Hugh MacDiarmid* by Michael Grieve

I fight in red for the same reasons
That Garibaldi chose the red shirt
– Because a few men in a field wearing red
Look like many men – if there are ten you will think
There are a hundred; if a hundred
You will believe them a thousand.
And the colour of red dances in the enemy's rifle sights
And his aim will be bad – But, best reason of all,
A man in a red shirt can neither hide nor retreat.
                                    – 'Why I Choose Red'

And that is why my father, from the various tartans he was enti-
tled to wear, chose the red Murray of Tullibardine.

Son of a local postman, he was born in the 'Muckle Toon' of
Langholm on 11 August 1892, and was named Christopher Mur-
ray Grieve. Thirty years later his *alter ego*, Hugh MacDiarmid,
swung into action as the 'cat-fish that vitalizes the other torpid
denizens of the aquarium.'

It was a startling metamorphosis as Dr Grieve and Mr MacDiar-
mid began their herculean task of rescuing Scots poetry from the
kailyard of mediocrity.

As the reporter-editor of the *Montrose Review*, founder and
editor of various influential literary magazines, vitriolic pam-
phleteer, polemical politician, syndicator of articles, and tireless
contributor to many other publications, he took on the pettifog-
ging Establishment to create the Scottish Literary Renaissance.

But it was his poetry, springing 'from the deeps of the
destined', that spear-headed the attack and which, despite a life-
time of poverty, political controversy and publishing neglect, has
given him an international reputation to match that of his friends
and contemporaries, Yeats, Eliot and Pound. The 'golden lyrics'
of *Sangschaw* and *Penny Wheep* culminated in his satiric master-
piece *A Drunk Man Looks at the Thistle*.

It's an ill wund that blaws nae yin ony guid. I owe my existence
to the personal disasters which overtook and almost over-
whelmed him.

He had been invited by Compton Mackenzie to be editor of a
critical magazine he was launching to cover the new-fangled wire-
less. And on 9 September 1929, he took the night-train to London.
It was an ill-fated journey which, in the long run, was almost to

end his life, not to mention his writing career (exactly forty-nine years later to the day he died in Edinburgh, aged eighty-six).

Vox was ahead of its time. His wife, Peggy Grieve, embarked on a well-publicized affair, and at the subsequent divorce he 'took the blame' as was customary in those days. The cruellest blow, perhaps, was his wife breaking her promise and refusing him access to the children of the marriage, Christine and Walter. It was during this time, when he was at a low ebb emotionally and professionally, that he met my mother, a Cornish girl of spirit and remarkable staying power. I was born in 1932.

A few years earlier, in 1928, he had written to his friend, William Jeffrey, a fellow journalist and poet:

> One of the things that has hurt me most all these years... is the fact that for one reason or another none of my friends will openly range themselves alongside me. I grant it isn't easy to do. To maintain my own stand involves me in sacrifices enough. But if instead of having to fight singly I'd half-a-dozen others with me we'd win through. As it is, I'm being frozen out. Scotland is denying me even the barest livelihood...

And he added: 'All I'm concerned about in the last analysis is intellectual status, and artistic worth.'

The bright promise that had lured him to London rapidly became a mind-sapping disaster; and so it was that in 1933, driven by the winds of despair and poverty, we embarked from Aberdeen on a voyage 'to the edge of the world'. 'Wind-blasted Whalsay, sodden with the peat of forgotten centuries where trees grew and none now stand,' I later recalled, was to become home. 'A bucket or two of earth in the chilled lapping bitterness of the North Sea.'

My mother made friends easily but my father, though accepted, remained an oddity in this tight community of sea-going crofters. He didn't seem to work, and we didn't go to church.

> Yet I get on well with the island people when I do meet them, and of this I am sure – that I know of no group of my fellow writers, no group of intellectuals or politicians with whom I would be happier to associate than I am with the entirely unlettered crews of the little sailing boats on which I go to the herring fishing thirty miles beyond the Hamna Stacks on the edge of the main deep.

And it was here that he pulled his life together, saying: 'I owe everything to my wife, Valda. It was her loyalty and help that has carried me over to a new phase of creative writing.'

But at times it all became too much. Exile was hard to bear for a man who had been at the centre of affairs. Frustrations built up, often fuelled by lack of mail from tardy correspondents, or because the *Earl of Zetland* was storm-bound; and he lamented that it was a curious turn of fortune that had sent him to the abandoned fisherman's cottage at Suidheim (on the map it was Sodom) where he could 'go for a week at a time and see no one to exchange a word with, nay, even as much as get a passing glimpse of anyone, except my son and wife.'

The Shetland years were a happy time for me, fishing for sillicks and climbing the cliffs for seagulls' eggs to pickle for winter. I was unaware of any shortages for my mother, with few resources, had created a home that was bright and gay, made friends, and learnt to knit the dazzle of Fair Isle gloves to shop standard. The few shillings they brought were much needed.

Through his omnivorous reading my father kept in touch with the world, recognizing and translating European poets long before their significance had dawned on the English intelligentsia. On the other hand, he had great difficulty in getting his work published.

T.S. Eliot, of Faber & Faber, praised but failed to publish; Jack Kahane, of the *avant-garde* Obelisk Press in the Place Vendôme, had agreed to publish *Mature Art* but he died in the autumn of 1939. His son, Maurice, took up the project but it was finally scuppered by the fall of France. His ill-luck with publishers, some of whom brought out books without an adequate distribution system, plagued him to the end, and has resulted in much public and critical neglect.

And then, of course, there were the political hurdles he set up. One of the founders of the National Party of Scotland (later to merge and become the Scottish National Party), he was expelled for his Communist sympathies, and later expelled from the Communist Party for being a Nationalist. His most extreme step was to rejoin the Communist Party in the wake of the Soviet Union's invasion of Hungary, alienating friends and delighting enemies. Arguments raged between us.

He freely acknowledged that he would never have survived the totalitarian terror that swamped the Soviet Union. Yet he felt he had to make a stand against the re-emergence of capitalist exploitation, believing still in a Socialism where people put the interest of the community before their own. It was not the idea, but human greed, that destroyed the great experiment. I believe he described his fundamental belief in *The Battle Continues*:

> Fools need not trouble to call me a Red,
> A Bolshie, an Anarchist – for none of these terms
> > Really describes my position at all.
> I believe *thoroughly* in the philosophy
> Of equality of opportunity, and know of nothing
> That is more radical.

Utopia has yet to be established.

During the war, despite being unused to hard physical labour, he worked in a Glasgow munitions factory, yet still found enough energy to burn the midnight oil writing, mostly unpaid, for various publications.

The last thirty years were spent in a two-room farm-worker's cottage at Candymill, near Biggar. We had been living in the laundry house on the Duke of Hamilton's Dungavel estate, but the great mansion was about to be converted into a prison and we had to leave.

Although I was recovering from pneumonia, my mother and I left on the back of an open lorry, and finally managed to squeeze all our belongings into Brownsbank, a bleak place then with a cold-water tap and an outside loo. My father was supposed to be safely out of the way, staying with friends while we tried to sort out the chaos. But next morning, as we rose exhausted, he arrived on the doorstep. It was almost the last straw but we ensconced him in a corner, the rich, strong smell of thick black twist swirling through the air, as we got on with the job of creating a home. And a happy place it was to be.

From there he sallied forth to give poetry readings and lectures in many countries, and the world came to him where they found he belied his public ferocity with a kindly benevolence, happy to help all who landed on the doorstep.

In the last year or two of his life he suffered greatly from cancer of the rectum but he largely ignored it, remaining clear-headed and cheerfully optimistic to the end.

After his death on 9 September 1978, *The Scotsman* said in its first leader that Scotland now 'seems a colder and quieter place.' And went on:

For 50 years this man's hot and angry integrity radiated through

Scotland. It burned holes in the blankets of national complacency, and it warmed those who often felt that their own country was a tundra in which the creators must freeze to death...

There is very little written, acted, composed, surmised or demanded in Scotland which does not in some strand descend from the new beginning he made.

In this centenary year, his life's work continues to create controversy, and at times downright hostility but the 'stone among the pigeons' as he once described himself, has fulfilled his original intention 'to keep Scotland on the main march of the world's interests.'

Michael Grieve

SELECTED POETRY

from *Sonnets of the Highland Hills*

The Wind-bags
Gildermorie, November 1920

Rain-beaten stones: great tussocks of dead grass
And stagnant waters throwing leaden lights
To leaden skies: a rough-maned wind that bites
With aimless violence at the clouds that pass,
Roaring, black-jowled, and bull-like in the void,
And I, in wild and boundless consciousness,
A brooding chaos, feel within me press
The corpse of Time, aborted, cold, negroid.

Aimless lightnings play intermittently,
Diffuse, vacant, dully, athwart the stones,
Involuntary thunders slip from me
And growl, inconsequently, hither, thither
– And now converse, see-saws of sighs and groans,
Oblivion and Eternity together!

Well Hung

You shall be, my dear,
One of El Greco's holy figures,
Lithe and undulating
And bluishly spiritual,
And I one of Ribera's
Wrinkled black heads,
Ferocious with torture,
And we shall hang
On opposite walls
Of a small private gallery
Belonging to an obese financier
Forever
And ever.

1

A Moment in Eternity
(To George Ogilvie)

The great song ceased
– Aye, like a wind was gone,
And our hearts came to rest,
Singly as leaves do,
And every leaf a flame.

My shining passions stilled
Shone in the sudden peace
Like countless leaves
Tingling with the quick sap
Of Immortality.

I was a multitude of leaves
Receiving and reflecting light,
A burning bush
Blazing for ever unconsumed,
Nay, ceaselessly,
Multiplying in leaves and light
And instantly
Burgeoning in buds of brightness
– Freeing like golden breaths
Upon the cordial air
A thousand new delights,
– Translucent leaves
Green with the goodness of Eternity,
Golden in the Heavenly light,
– The golden breaths
Of my eternal life,
Like happy memories multiplied,
Shining out instantly from me
And shining back for ever into me,
– Breaths given out
But still unlost,
For ever mine
In the infinite air,
The everlasting foliage of my soul
Visible awhile
Like steady and innumerable flames,
Blending into one blaze

Yet each distinct
With shining shadows of difference.

A sudden thought of God's
Came like a wind
Ever and again
Rippling them as water over stars,
And swiftlier fanning them
And setting them a-dance,
Upflying, fluttering down,
Moving in orderly intricacies
Of colour and of light,
Delaying, hastening,
Blazing and serene,
Shaken and shining in the turning wind,
Lassoing cataracts of light
With rosy boughs,
Or clamouring in echoing unequalled heights,
Rhythmical sprays of many-coloured fire
And spires chimerical
Gleaming in fabulous airs,
And suddenly
Lapsing again
To incandescence and increase.

And again the wind came
Blowing me afar
In fair fantastic fires,
– Ivies and irises invading
The upland garths of ivory;
Queen daisies growing
In the tall red grass
By pools of perfect peace;
And bluebells tossing
In transparent fields;
And silver airs
Lifting the crystal sources in dim hills
And swinging them far out like bells of glass
Pealing pellucidly
And quivering in faery flights of chimes;
Shivers of wings bewildered
In alleys of virgin dream;

Floral dances and revels of radiance
Whirling in stainless sanctuaries;
And eyes of Seraphim,
Shining like sunbeams on eternal ice,
Lifted toward the unexplored
Summits of Paradise.

And the wind ceased.
Light dwelt in me,
Pavilioned there.
I was a crystal trunk,
Columnar in the glades of Paradise,
Bearing the luminous boughs
And foliaged with the flame
Of infinite and gracious growth,
– Meteors for roots,
And my topmost spires
Notes of enchanted light
Blind in the Godhead!
– White stars at noon!

I shone within my thoughts
As God within us shines.

And the wind came,
Multitudinous and light
I whirled in exultations inexpressible
– An unpicturable, clear,
Soaring and glorying,
Swift consciousness,
A cosmos turning like a song of spheres
On apices of praise,
A separate colour,
An essential element and conscious part
Of successive and stupendous dreams
In God's own heart!

And the wind ceased
And like a light I stood,
A flame of glorious and complex resolve,
Within God's heart.

I knew then that a new tree,
A new tree and a strange,
Stood beautifully in Heaven.
I knew that a new light
Stood in God's heart
And a light unlike
The Twice Ten Thousand lights
That stood there,
Shining equally with me,
And giving and receiving increase of light
Like the flame that I was
Perpetually.
And I knew that when the wind rose
This new tree would stand still
Multiplied in light but motionless,
And I knew that when God dreamt
And His creative impulses
Ran through us like a wind
And we flew like clear and coloured
Flames in His dreams,
(Adorations, Gratitudes and Joys,
Plenary and boon and pure,
Crystal and burning-gold and scarlet
Competing and co-operating flames
Reflecting His desires,
Flashing like epical imaginings
And burning virgin steeps
With ceaseless swift apotheoses)
One light would stand unmoved.

And when on pinnacles of praise
All others whirled
Like a white light deeper in God's heart
This light would shine,
Pondering the imponderable,
Revealing ever clearlier
Patterns of endless revels,
Each gesture freed,
Each shining shadow of difference,
Each subtle phase evolved
In the magnificent and numberless
Revelations of ecstasy

Succeeding and excelling inexhaustibly,
– A white light like a silence
Accentuating the great songs!
– A shining silence wherein God
Might see as in a mirror
The miracles that He must next achieve!

Ah, Light,
That is God's inmost wish,
His knowledge of Himself,
Flame of creative judgment,
God's interrogation of infinity,
Searching the unsearchable,
– Silent and steadfast tree
Housing no birds of song,
Void to the wind,
But rooted in God's very self,
Growing ineffably,
Central in Paradise!

When the song ceased
And I stood still,
Breathing new leaves of life
Upon the eternal air,
Each leaf of all my leaves
Shone with a new delight
Murmuring Your name.

O Thou,
Who art the wisdom of the God
Whose ecstasies we are!

The Fool

He said that he was God.
  'We are well met,' I cried,
'I've always hoped I should
  Meet God before I died.'

I slew him then and cast
  His corpse into a pool,
– But how I wish he had
  Indeed been God, the fool!

A Last Song
(Withered Wreaths)

The heavens are lying like wreaths
Of dead flowers breaking to dust
Round the broken column of Time.

Like a fitful wind and a cold
That rustles the withered stars
And the wisps of space is my song.

Like a fitful wind and a cold
That whistles awhile and fails
Round the broken column of Time.

The Dying Earth

Pitmirk the nicht: God's waukrife yet
An' lichtnin'-like his glances flit
An' sair, sair are the looks he gies
The auld earth as it dees.

Pitmirk the nicht: an' God's 'good tell
I' broken thunners to hissel'
A' that he meent the warl' to be
An' hoo his plan gaed jee.

He canna steek his weary lids
But aye anither gey look whids
Frae pole to pole: an's tears doonfa'
In lashin' rain owre a'.

---

pitmirk pitch-black   *waukrife* awake   *gies* gives   *dees* dies
's'good has begun to   *warl'* world   *hoo* how   *gaed jee* went wrong
steek shut   *whids* flies   *an's* and his

The Bonnie Broukit Bairn
(For Peggy)

Mars is braw in crammasy,
Venus in a green silk goun,
The auld mune shak's her gowden feathers,
Their starry talk's a wheen o' blethers,
Nane for thee a thochtie sparin',
Earth, thou bonnie broukit bairn!
– But greet, an' in your tears ye'll droun
The haill clanjamfrie!

The Watergaw

Ae weet forenicht i' the yow-trummle
I saw yon antrin thing,
A watergaw wi' its chitterin' licht
Ayont the on-ding;
An' I thocht o' the last wild look ye gied
Afore ye deed!

There was nae reek i' the laverock's hoose
That nicht – an' nane i' mine;
But I hae thocht o' that foolish licht
Ever sin' syne;
An' I think that mebbe at last I ken
What your look meant then.

---

broukit neglected   *bairn* child   *braw* handsome   *crammasy* crimson
wheen o' blethers pack of nonsense   *greet* weep   *clanjamfrie* collection

watergaw indistinct rainbow   *ae weet* one wet   *forenicht* early evening
yow-trummle cold weather in July after sheep-shearing   *antrin* rare
chitterin' shivering   *on-ding* downpour   *reek* smoke   *laverock* lark
sin' syne since then

9

The Sauchs in the Reuch Heuch Hauch[1]

(For George Reston Malloch)

There's teuch sauchs growin' i' the Reuch Heuch Hauch.
Like the sauls o' the damned are they,
And ilk ane yoked in a whirligig
Is birlin' the lee-lang day.

O we come doon frae oor stormiest moods,
And licht like a bird i' the haun',
But the teuch sauchs there i' the Reuch Heuch Hauch
As the deil's ain hert are thrawn.

The winds 'ud pu' them up by the roots,
Tho' it broke the warl' asunder,
But they rin richt doon thro' the boddom o' Hell,
And nane kens hoo fer under!

There's no' a licht that the Heavens let loose
Can calm them a hanlawhile,
Nor frae their ancient amplefeyst
Sall God's ain sel' them wile.

Ex vermibus

Gape, gape, gorlin',
For I ha'e a worm
That'll gi'e ye a slee and sliggy sang
Wi' mony a whuram.

---

sauchs willow-trees   *teuch* tough   *ilk ane* each one   *hert* heart
thrawn twisted   *a hanlawhile* a little while   *amplefeyst* contrariness

gorlin' fledgling   *slee* sly   *sliggy* cunning   *whuram* crotchet or quaver

[1] A field near Hawick.

Syne i' the lift
Byous spatrils you'll mak',
For a gorlin' wi' worms like this in its wame
Nae airels sall lack.

But owre the tree-taps
Maun flee like a sperk,
Till it hes the haill o' the Heavens alunt
Frae dawin' to derk.

Au Clair de la Lune
(For W.B.)

*. . . She's yellow
An' yawps like a peany.*
                            Anon.

*They mix ye up wi' loony fowk,
Wha are o' stars the mense,
The madness that ye bring to me,
I wadna change't for sense.*
                            W.B.

I

Prelude to Moon Music

Earth's littered wi' larochs o' Empires,
Muckle nations are dust.
Time'll meissle it awa', it seems,
An' smell nae must.

---

syne then   *lift* sky   *byous spatrils* wonderful musical sounds
wame belly   *airels* musical notes   *alunt* alight

loony fowk mad people   *mense* ornament   *larochs* fragments, rubble
meissle crumble   *must* bad, stale or mouldy smell

But wheest! – Whatna music is this,
While the win's haud their breath?
– *The Moon has a wunnerfu' finger*
For the back-lill o' Death!

II

Moonstruck

When the warl's couped soon' as a peerie
That licht-lookin' craw o' a body, the moon,
Sits on the fower cross-win's
Peerin' a' roon'.

She's seen me – she's seen me – an' straucht
Loupit clean on the quick o' my hert.
The quhither o' cauld gowd's fairly
Gi'en me a stert.

An' the roarin' o' oceans noo'
Is peerieweerie to me:
Thunner's a tinklin' bell: an' Time
Whuds like a flee.

III

The Man in the Moon

Oh lad, I fear that yon's the sea
Where they fished for you and me,
And there, from whence we both were ta'en,
You and I shall drown again.

A.E. Housman

---

wheest hush   *back-lill* thumb-hole on bagpipe chanter

couped tilted   *soon'* sound   *peerie* spinning top   *craw* crow
loupit leapt   *quhither* beam   *peerieweerie* dwindled to a thread of sound
whuds flits   *flee* fly

The moonbeams kelter i' the lift,
An' Earth, the bare auld stane,
Glitters beneath the seas o' Space,
White as a mammoth's bane.

An', lifted owre the gowden wave,
Peers a dumfoun'ered Thocht,
Wi' keethin' sicht o' a' there is,
An' bodily sicht o' nocht.

IV

The Huntress and her Dogs

Her luchts o' yellow hair
Flee oot ayont the storm,
Wi' mony a bonny flaught
The colour o' Cairngorm.

Oot owre the thunner-wa'
She haiks her shinin' breists,
While th' oceans to her heels
Slink in like bidden beasts.

So sall Earth's howlin' mobs
Drap, lown, ahint the sang
That frae the chaos o' Thocht
In triumph braks or lang.

---

kelter undulate   *lift* sky   *keethin' sicht* glimpse, as of salmon ripple

luchts locks   *flaught* flame, gleam   *haiks* hoists   *lown* silent   *or* ere

Crowdieknowe

Oh to be at Crowdieknowe
When the last trumpet blaws,
An' see the deid come loupin' owre
The auld grey wa's.

Muckle men wi' tousled beards,
I grat at as a bairn
'll scramble frae the croodit clay
Wi' feck o' swearin'.

An' glower at God an' a' his gang
O' angels i' the lift
– Thae trashy bleezin' French-like folk
Wha gar'd them shift!

Fain the weemun-folk'll seek
To mak' them haud their row
– *Fegs, God's no blate gin he stirs up*
The men o' Crowdieknowe!

The Eemis Stane

I' the how-dumb-deid o' the cauld hairst nicht
The warl' like an eemis stane
Wags i' the lift;
An' my eerie memories fa'
Like a yowdendrift.

Crowdieknowe graveyard near Langholm   *loupin'* leaping   *grat* wept
bairn child   *feck* plenty   *lift* sky   *thae* those   *bleezin'* blazing
gar'd made   *fegs* faith (an exclamation)   *blate* backward   *gin* if

eemis unsteady   *how-dumb-deid* hollow dead silent depth
cauld hairst nicht cold harvest night   *yowdendrift* blizzard

Like a yowdendrift so's I couldna read
The words cut oot i' the stane
Had the fug o' fame
An' history's hazelraw
No' yirdit thaim.

The Innumerable Christ

Other stars may have their Bethlehem, and their Calvary too.
Professor J.Y. Simpson

Wha kens on whatna Bethlehems
Earth twinkles like a star the nicht,
An' whatna shepherds lift their heids
    In its unearthly licht?

'Yont a' the stars oor een can see
An' farther than their lichts can fly,
I' mony an unco warl' the nicht
    The fatefu' bairnies cry.

I' mony an unco warl' the nicht
The lift gaes black as pitch at noon,
An' sideways on their chests the heids
    O' endless Christs roll doon.

An' when the earth's as cauld's the mune
An' a' its folk are lang syne deid,
On coontless stars the Babe maun cry
    An' the Crucified maun bleed.

---

fug moss   *hazelraw* lichen   *yirdit* buried   *thaim* them

kens knows   *whatna* whichever   *'yont* beyond   *een* eyes
unco strange   *lang syne* long since

Wheesht, Wheesht

Wheesht, wheesht, my foolish hert,
For weel ye ken
I widna ha'e ye stert
Auld ploys again.

It's guid to see her lie
Sae snod an' cool,
A' lust o' lovin' by –
Wheesht, wheesht, ye fule!

Focherty

Duncan Gibb o' Focherty's
A giant to the likes o' me,
His face is like a roarin' fire
For love o' the barley-bree.

He gangs through this and the neebrin' shire
Like a muckle rootless tree
– And here's a caber for Daith to toss
That'll gi'e his spauld a swee!

His gain was aye a wee'r man's loss
And he took my lass frae me,
And wi' mony a quean besides
He's ta'en his liberty.

I've had nae chance wi' the likes o' him
And he's tramped me underfit.
– Blaefaced afore the throne o' God
He'll get his fairin' yet.

---

wheesht hush   *auld ploys* old games   *guid* good   *sae snod* so tidy
fule fool

barley-bree whisky   *gangs* goes   *neebrin'* neighbouring
spauld shoulder bone   *swee* jerk   *wee'r* lesser   *quean* lass
blaefaced livid with fear   *fairin'* deserts

He'll be like a bull in the sale-ring there,
And I'll lauch lood to see,
Till he looks up and canna mak' oot
Whether it's God – or me!

The Love-sick Lass

As white's the blossom on the rise
The wee lass was
That 'bune the green risp i' the fu' mune
Cannily blaws.

Sweet as the cushie's croud she sang
Wi' 'r wee reid mou' –
Wha sauch-like i' the lowe o' luve
Lies sabbin' noo!

The Dead Liebknecht
After the German of Rudolf Leonhardt

His corpse owre a' the city lies
In ilka square and ilka street
His spilt bluid floods the vera skies
And nae hoose but is darkened wi't.

The factory horns begin to blaw
Thro' a' the city, blare on blare,
The lowsin' time o' workers a',
Like emmits skailin' everywhere.

And wi' his white teeth shinin' yet
The corpse lies smilin' underfit.

'bune above   *risp* grass   *cushie's croud* song of the dove
sauch-like willow-like   *lowe* hollow aftermath   *sabbin'* sobbing

ilka every   *lowsin'* freeing   *skailin'* scattering

17

Scunner

Your body derns
In its graces again
As the dreich grun' does
In the gowden grain,
And oot o' the daith
O' pride you rise
Wi' beauty yet
For a hauf-disguise.

The skinklan' stars
Are but distant dirt
Tho' fer owre near
You are still – whiles – girt
Wi' the bonnie licht
You bood ha'e tint
– And I lo'e Love
Wi' a scunner in't.

Servant Girl's Bed

The talla spales
And the licht loups oot,
Fegs, it's your ain creesh
Lassie, I doot,
And the licht that reeled
Loose on't a wee
Was the bonny lowe
O' Eternity.

---

scunner disgust   *derns* hides   *dreich* drab   *skinklan'* gleaming
fer owre far too   *bood* should   *lo'e* love   *in't* in it

talla tallow candle   *spales* melts or runs down   *loups* leaps   *creesh* fat
a wee a moment   *lowe* light

Empty Vessel

I met ayont the cairney
A lass wi' tousie hair
Singin' till a bairnie
That was nae langer there.

Wunds wi' warlds to swing
Dinna sing sae sweet,
The licht that bends owre a' thing
Is less ta'en up wi't.

Gairmscoile

Aulder than mammoth or than mastodon
Deep i' the herts o' a' men lurk scaut-heid
Skrymmorie monsters few daur look upon.
Brides sometimes catch their wild een, scansin' reid,
Beekin' abune the herts they thocht to lo'e
And horror-stricken ken that i' themselves
A like beast stan's, and lookin' love thro' and thro'
Meets the reid een wi' een like seevun hells.
...Nearer the twa beasts draw, and, couplin', brak
The bubbles o' twa sauls and the haill warld gangs black.

Yet wha has heard the beasts' wild matin'-call
To ither music syne can gi'e nae ear.
The nameless lo'enotes haud him in a thrall.
Forgot are guid and ill, and joy and fear.
...My bluid sall thraw a dark hood owre my een
And I sall venture deep into the hills
Whaur, scaddows on the skyline, can be seen
– Twinin' the sun's brent broo wi' plaited horns

---

ayont beyond   *cairney* small cairn   *tousie* tousled   *wunds* winds

gairmscoile poets' school   *scaut-heid* disfigured
skrymmorie frightful and terrific   *daur* dare   *scansin'* glinting   *reid* red
beekin' exposing themselves   *abune* above   *haill* whole
scaddows shadows   *brent broo* wrinkled brow

As gin they crooned it wi' a croon o' thorns –
The beasts in wha's wild cries a' Scotland's destiny thrills.

The lo'es o' single herts are strays; but there
The herds that draw the generations are,
And whasae hears them roarin', evermair
Is yin wi' a' that gangs to mak' or mar
The spirit o' the race, and leads it still
Whither it can be led, 'yont a' desire and will.

I

Wergeland, I mind o' thee – for thy bluid tae
Kent the rouch dirl o' an auld Scots strain,
– A dour dark burn that has its ain wild say
Thro' a' the thrang bricht babble o' Earth's flood.
Behold, thwart my ramballiach life again,
What thrawn and roothewn dreams, royat and rude,
Reek forth – a foray dowless herts condemn –
While chance wi' rungs o' sang or silence renshels them.

(A foray frae the past – and future tae
Sin Time's a blindness we'll thraw aff some day!)
...On the rumgunshoch sides o' hills forgotten
Life hears beasts rowtin' that it deemed extinct,
And, sudden, on the hapless cities linked
In canny civilisation's canty dance
Poor herds o' heich-skeich monsters, misbegotten,
...Streets clear afore the scarmoch advance:
Frae every winnock skimmerin' een keek oot
To see what sic camsteerie cast-offs are aboot.

Cast-offs? – But wha mak's life a means to ony end?
This sterves and that stuff's fu', scraps this and succours that?

---

yin one
tae too, also   *rouch dirl* rough thrill   *burn* stream   *ain* own
thrang bricht busy bright   *thwart* across   *ramballiach* tempestuous
thrawn stubborn, perverse   *royat* unmanageable   *dowless* feeble, dismal
rungs cudgels   *renshels* beats   *rumgunshoch* rough   *rowtin'* roaring
canny careful   *canty* happy   *heich-skeich* crazy   *scarmoch* tumultuous
winnock window   *skimmerin'* glittering   *keek* peep   *sic* such
camsteerie disorderly   *sterves* starves   *fu'* full

20

The best survive there's nane but fules contend.
Na! Ilka daith is but a santit need.
...Lo! what bricht flames o' beauty are lit at
The unco' een o' lives that Life thocht deid
Till winnock efter winnock kindles wi' a sense
O' gain and glee – as gin a mair intense
Starn nor the sun had risen in wha's licht
Mankind and beasts anew, wi' gusto, see their plicht.

Mony's the auld hauf-human cry I ken
Fa's like a revelation on the herts o' men
As tho' the graves were split and the first man
Grippit the latest wi' a freendly han'
...And there's forgotten shibboleths o' the Scots
Ha'e keys to senses lockit to us yet
– Coorse words that shamble thro' oor minds like stots,
Syne turn on's muckle een wi' doonsin' emerauds lit.

I hear nae 'hee-haw' but I mind the day
A'e donkey strunted doon a palm-strewn way
As Chesterton has sung; nae wee click-clack
O' hoofs but to my hert at aince comes back
Jammes' Prayer to Gang to Heaven wi' the Asses;
And shambles-ward nae cattle-beast e'er passes
But I mind hoo the saft een o' the kine
Lichted Christ's craidle wi' their canny shine.

Hee-Haw! Click-Clack! And Cock-a-doodle-doo!
– Wull Gabriel in Esperanto cry
Or a' the warld's undeemis jargons try?
It's soon', no' sense, that faddoms the herts o' men,
And by my sangs the rouch auld Scots I ken
E'en herts that ha'e nae Scots'll dirl richt thro'
As nocht else could – for here's a language rings
Wi' datchie sesames, and names for nameless things.

---

santit swallowed up in sand, but also sanctified   *unco' een* strange eyes
coorse coarse   *stots* bullocks   *doonsin' emerauds* dazzling emeralds
strunted strutted   *undeemis* countless   *datchie* secret

II

Wergeland, my warld as thine 'ca' canny' cries,
And daurna lippen to auld Scotland's virr.
Ah, weel ye kent – as Carlyle quo' likewise –
Maist folk are thowless fules wha downa stir,
Crouse sumphs that hate nane 'bies wha'd wauken them.
To them my Pegasus tae's a crocodile.
Whummelt I tak' a bobquaw for the lift.
Insteed o' sangs my mou' drites eerned phlegm.
...Natheless like thee I stalk on mile by mile,
Howk'n up deid stumps o' thocht, and saw'in my eident gift.

Ablachs, and scrats, and dorbels o' a' kinds
Aye'd drob me wi' their puir eel-droonin' minds,
Wee drochlin' craturs drutling their bit thochts
The dorty bodies! Feech! Nae Sassunuch drings
'll daunton me. – Tak' ye sic things for poets?
Cock-lairds and drotes depert Parnassus noo.
A'e flash o' wit the lot to drodlich dings.
Rae, Martin, Sutherland – the dowless crew,
I'll twine the dow'd sheaves o' their toom-ear'd corn,
Bind them wi' pity and dally them wi' scorn.

Lang ha'e they posed as men o' letters here,
Dounhaddin' the Doric and keepin't i' the draiks,
Drivellin' and druntin', wi' mony a datchie sneer
...But soon we'll end the haill eggtaggle, fegs!

---

ca' canny be careful   lippen trust   virr stamina, force   thowless useless
downa dare not   crouse sumphs conceited blockheads   'bies except
whummelt overturned   bobquaw bog   drites drips   eerned clotted
howk'n digging   eident busy   ablachs dwarfs   scrats monstrous midgets
dorbels eyesores   drob pester, annoy   puir eel-droonin' poor ludicrously vain
drochlin' craturs drutling puny creatures piddling   bit thochts slight thoughts
dorty bodies haughty but feeble persons   feech expression of disgust
Sassunuch drings English wretches   daunton intimidate
cock-lairds empty braggarts   drotes upstarts   depert depart from
drodlich a useless mass   dings beats   dowless feeble   dow'd faded
toom-ear'd empty eared
dally stick used in binding sheaves to push in ends of rope
dounhaddin' holding down   the Doric the Scots vernacular
i' the draiks in a slovenly, neglected condition   druntin' whining
datchie sly, crafty eggtaggle act of wasting time in bad company

22

...The auld volcanoes rummle 'neath their feet,
And a' their shoddy lives 'll soon be drush,
Danders o' Hell! They feel th' unwelcome heat,
The deltit craturs, and their sauls are slush,
For we ha'e faith in Scotland's hidden poo'ers,
The present's theirs, but a' the past and future's oors.

---

drush refuse   *danders* cinders   *deltit* pampered   *sauls* souls

A Drunk Man Looks at the Thistle

Vast imbecile mentality of those
Who cannot tell a thistle from a rose.
This is for others....
                    Sacheverell Sitwell

To F.G. Scott

Can ratt-rime and ragments o' quenry
And recoll o' Gillha' requite
Your faburdoun, figuration, and gemmell,
And prick-sangs' delight?

Tho' you've cappilowed me in the reapin'
– And yours was a bursten kirn tae! –
Yet you share your advantage wi' me
In the end o' the day.

And my flytin' and sclatrie sall be
Wi' your fantice and mocage entwined
As the bauch Earth is wi' the lift
Or fate wi' mankind!

---

ratt-rime incantations for killing rats, doggerel
ragments o' quenry odds and ends of reminiscences of dealings with women
recoll memories   *Gillha'* pub of all weathers or hostelry of life
faburdoun, figuration, and gemmell bass-note or drone of the bagpipe, harmony
and musical structure, and two-part harmony
prick-sangs written songs, compositions   *cappilowed* outdistanced
a bursten kirn a difficult harvest, an overflowing churn or a bursting imagination
flytin' and sclatrie railing and poetic abuse and obscenities, scolding, intemperate
language   *fantice and mocage* imagination, whimsicality, and sardonic humour
bauch sorry, pathetic, dull   *lift* sky

25

I amna' fou' sae muckle as tired – deid dune.
It's gey and hard wark coupin' gless for gless
Wi' Cruivie and Gilsanquhar and the like,
And I'm no' juist as bauld as aince I wes.

The elbuck fankles in the coorse o' time,
The sheckle's no' sae souple, and the thrapple
Grows deef and dour: nae langer up and doun
Gleg as a squirrel speils the Adam's apple.

Forbye, the stuffie's no' the real Mackay.
The sun's sel' aince, as sune as ye began it,
Riz in your vera saul: but what keeks in
Noo is in truth the vilest 'saxpenny planet'.

And as the worth's gane doun the cost has risen.
Yin canna thow the cockles o' yin's hert
Wi' oot ha'en' cauld feet noo, jalousin' what
The wife'll say (I dinna blame her fur't).

It's robbin' Peter to pey Paul at least . . .
And a' that's Scotch aboot it is the name,
Like a' thing else ca'd Scottish nooadays
– A' destitute o' speerit juist the same.

(To prove my saul is Scots I maun begin
Wi' what's still deemed Scots and the folk expect,
And spire up syne by visible degrees
To heichts whereo' the fules ha'e never recked.

25   But aince I get them there I'll whummle them
And souse the craturs in the nether deeps,
– For it's nae choice, and ony man s'ud wish
To dree the goat's weird tae as weel's the sheep's!)

---

fou' drunk   *deid dune* exhausted   *gey* extremely   *coupin'* upending
aince once   *elbuck fankles* elbow becomes clumsy   *sheckle* wrist
thrapple gullet   *deef* unimpressionable   *gleg* lively   *speils* climbs
forbye besides   *keeks* peeps   *thow* thaw   *jalousin'* suspecting
spire soar   *whummle* overturn   *craturs* creatures   *dree* endure
weird tae fate also

Heifetz in tartan, and Sir Harry Lauder!
Whaur's Isadora Duncan dancin' noo?
Is Mary Garden in Chicago still
And Duncan Grant in Paris – and me fou'?

Sic transit gloria Scotiae – a' the floo'ers
O' the Forest are wede awa'. (A blin' bird's nest
Is aiblins biggin' in the thistle tho'? . . .
And better blin' if'ts brood is like the rest!)

You canna gang to a Burns supper even
Wi'oot some wizened scrunt o' a knock-knee
Chinee turns roon to say, 'Him Haggis – velly goot!'
And ten to wan the piper is a Cockney.

No' wan in fifty kens a wurd Burns wrote
But misapplied is a'body's property,
And gin there was his like alive the day
They'd be the last a kennin' haund to gi'e –

Croose London Scotties wi' their braw shirt fronts
And a' their fancy freen's, rejoicin'
That similah gatherings in Timbuctoo,
Bagdad – and Hell, nae doot – are voicin'

Burns' sentiments o' universal love,
In pidgin English or in wild-fowl Scots,
And toastin' ane wha's nocht to them but an
Excuse for faitherin' Genius wi' *their* thochts.

A' *they've* to say was aften said afore
A lad was born in Kyle to blaw aboot.
What unco fate mak's *him* the dumpin'-grun'
For a' the sloppy rubbish they jaw oot?

Mair nonsense has been uttered in his name
Than in ony's barrin' liberty and Christ.
If this keeps spreedin' as the drink declines,
Syne turns to tea, wae's me for the *Zeitgeist*!

50

---

wede awa' vanished   *aiblins biggin'* perhaps building   *scrunt* mite
kennin' knowing   *croose* conceited   *braw* fine   *wae's* woe is

27

Rabbie, wad'st thou wert here – the warld hath need,
And Scotland mair sae, o' the likes o' thee!
The whisky that aince moved your lyre's become
A laxative for a' loquacity.

O gin they'd stegh their guts and haud their wheesht
I'd thole it, for 'a man's a man,' I ken,
But though the feck ha'e plenty o' the 'a' that,'
They're nocht but zoologically men.

I'm haverin', Rabbie, but ye understaun'
It gets my dander up to see your star
A bauble in Babel, banged like a saxpence
'Twixt Burbank's Baedeker and Bleistein's cigar.

There's nane sae ignorant but think they can
Expatiate on *you*, if on nae ither.
The sumphs ha'e ta'en you at your wurd, and, fegs!
The foziest o' them claims to be a – Brither!

Syne 'Here's the cheenge' – the star o' Rabbie Burns.
Sma' cheenge, 'Twinkle, Twinkle.' The memory slips
As G.K. Chesterton heaves up to gi'e
'The Immortal Memory' in a huge eclipse,

Or somebody else as famous if less fat.
You left the like in Embro' in a scunner
To booze wi' thieveless cronies sic as me.
I'se warrant you'd shy clear o' a' the hunner

Odd Burns Clubs tae, or ninety-nine o' them,
And haud your birthday in a different kip
Whaur your name isna ta'en in vain – as Christ
Gied a' Jerusalem's Pharisees the slip

75

---

stegh stuff   *haud their wheesht* be quiet   *thole* endure   *feck* majority
haverin' rambling   *dander* temper   *sumphs* fools   *fegs* faith
foziest most stupid   *scunner* disgust   *thieveless* powerless, immoral
kip brothel

28

– Christ wha'd ha'e been Chief Rabbi gin he'd lik't! –
Wi' publicans and sinners to forgether,
But, losh! the publicans noo are Pharisees,
And I'm no' shair o' maist the sinners either.

But that's aside the point! I've got fair waun'ert.
It's no' that I'm sae fou' as juist deid dune,
And dinna ken as muckle's whaur I am
Or hoo I've come to sprawl here 'neth the mune.

That's it! It isna me that's fou' at a',
But the fu' mune, the doited jade, that's led
Me fer agley, or 'mogrified the warld.
100   – For a' I ken I'm safe in my ain bed.

Jean! Jean! Gin *she*'s no' here it's no' *oor* bed,
Or else I'm dreamin' deep and canna wauken,
But it's a fell queer dream if this is no'
A real hillside – and thae things thistles and bracken!

It's hard wark haud'n by a thocht worth ha'en'
And harder speakin't, and no' for ilka man;
Maist Thocht's like whisky – a thoosan' under proof,
And a sair price is pitten on't even than.

As Kirks wi' Christianity ha'e dune,
Burns Clubs wi' Burns – wi' a'thing it's the same,
The core o' ocht is only for the few,
Scorned by the mony, thrang wi'ts empty name.

And a' the names in History mean nocht
To maist folk but 'ideas o' their ain,'
The vera opposite o' onything
The Deid 'ud awn gin they cam' back again.

---

shair sure   *waun'ert* confused   *doited* foolish   *fer agley* far astray
fell exceedingly   *ocht* anything   *thrang* busy
'ud awn would own (up to)   *gin* if

A greater Christ, a greater Burns, may come.
The maist they'll dae is to gi'e bigger pegs
To folly and conceit to hank their rubbish on.
They'll cheenge folks' talk but no' their natures, fegs!

I maun feed frae the common trough ana'
Whaur a' the lees o' hope are jumbled up;
While centuries like pigs are slorpin' owre't
Sall my wee 'oor be cryin': 'Let pass this cup'?

125   In wi' your gruntle then, puir wheengin' saul,
Lap up the ugsome aidle wi' the lave,
What gin it's your ain vomit that you swill
And frae Life's gantin' and unfaddomed grave?

I doot I'm geylies mixed, like Life itsel',
But I was never ane that thocht to pit
An ocean in a mutchkin. As the haill's
Mair than the pairt sae I than reason yet.

I dinna haud the warld's end in my heid
As maist folk think they dae; nor filter truth
In fishy gills through which its tides may poor
For ony *animalcula* forsooth.

I lauch to see my crazy little brain
– And ither folks' – tak'n' itsel' seriously,
And in a sudden lowe o' fun my saul
Blinks dozent as the owl I ken't to be.

I'll ha'e nae hauf-way hoose, but aye be whaur
Extremes meet – it's the only way I ken
To dodge the curst conceit o' bein' richt
That damns the vast majority o' men.

---

hank fasten   *slorpin' owre't* slobbering over it   *gruntle* snout
puir wheengin' saul poor complaining soul   *ugsome aidle* repulsive slop
lave remainder   *gantin'* yawning   *doot* suspect   *geylies* pretty well
haill's whole is   *poor* pour   *lauch* laugh   *lowe* blaze
dozent stupefied   *ken't* know it

I'll bury nae heid like an ostrich's,
Nor yet believe my een and naething else.
My senses may advise me, but I'll be
Mysel' nae maitter what they tell's . . .

150   I ha'e nae doot some foreign philosopher
Has wrocht a system oot to justify
A' this: but I'm a Scot wha blin'ly follows
Auld Scottish instincts, and I winna try.

For I've nae faith in ocht I can explain,
And stert whaur the philosophers leave aff,
Content to glimpse its loops I dinna ettle
To land the sea serpent's sel' wi' ony gaff.

Like staundin' water in a pocket o'
Impervious clay I pray I'll never be,
Cut aff and self-sufficient, but let reenge
Heichts o' the lift and benmaist deeps o' sea.

Water! Water! There was owre muckle o't
In yonder whisky, sae I'm in deep water
(And gin I could wun hame I'd be in het,
For even Jean maun natter, natter, natter) . . .

And in the toon that I belang tae
– What tho'ts Montrose or Nazareth? –
Helplessly the folk continue
To lead their livin' death! . . .

> [1]*At darknin' hings abune the howff*
> *A weet and wild and eisenin' air.*
> *Spring's spirit wi' its waesome sough*
> *Rules owre the drucken stramash there.*

---

een eyes   *ettle* aspire   *lift* sky   *benmaist* inmost   *het* hot
natter nag   *hings abune* hangs above   *howff* tavern   *eisenin'* yearning
waesome sough woeful sigh   *drucken stramash* drunken uproar

[1] From the Russian of Alexander Blok.

31

And heich abune the vennel's pokiness,
Whaur a' the white-weshed cottons lie;
The Inn's sign blinters in the mochiness,
And lood and shrill the bairnies cry.

The hauflins 'yont the burgh boonds
Gang ilka nicht, and a' the same,
Their bonnets cocked; their bluid that stounds
Is playin' at a fine auld game.

And on the lochan there, hauf-herted
Wee screams and creakin' oar-locks soon',
And in the lift, heich, hauf-averted,
The mune looks owre the yirdly roon'.

And ilka evenin', derf and serious
(Jean ettles nocht o' this, puir lass),
In liquor, raw yet still mysterious,
A'e freend's aye mirrored in my glass.

Ahint the sheenin' coonter gruff
Thrang barmen ding the tumblers doun;
'In vino veritas' cry rough
And reid-een'd fules that in it droon.

But ilka evenin' fey and fremt
(Is it a dream nae wauk'nin' proves?)
As to a trystin'-place undreamt,
A silken leddy darkly moves.

Slow gangs she by the drunken anes,
And lanely by the winnock sits;
Frae'r robes, atour the sunken anes,
A rooky dwamin' perfume flits.

---

vennel's pokiness lane's congestion   *cottons* small cottages   *blinters* gleams
mochiness moist air   *bairnies* children   *hauflins 'yont* lads beyond
ilka every   *stounds* throbs   *lochan* small lake   *yirdly* earthly
derf taciturn   *ettles* suspects   *a'e freend's aye* one friend is always
ahint behind   *sheenin' coonter* shining counter   *thrang* busy   *ding* dash
fey fated   *fremt* lonely   *winnock* window   *frae'r* from her
atour around   *rooky dwamin'* misty swooning

Her gleamin' silks, the taperin'
O' her ringed fingers, and her feathers
Move dimly like a dream wi'in,
While endless faith aboot them gethers.

I seek, in this captivity,
To pierce the veils that darklin' fa'
– See white clints slidin' to the sea,
And hear the horns o' Elfland blaw.

I ha'e dark secrets' turns and twists,
A sun is gi'en to me to haud,
The whisky in my bluid insists,
And spiers my benmaist history, lad.

And owre my brain the flitterin'
O' the dim feathers gangs aince mair,
And, faddomless, the dark blue glitterin'
O' twa een in the ocean there.

My soul stores up this wealth unspent,
The key is safe and nane's but mine.
You're richt, auld drunk impenitent,
I ken it tae – the truth's in wine!

The munelicht's like a lookin'-glass,
The thistle's like mysel',
But whaur ye've gane, my bonnie lass,
Is mair than I can tell.

225   Were you a vision o' mysel',
Transmuted by the mellow liquor?
Neist time I glisk you in a glass,
I'se warrant I'll mak' siccar.

---

clints cliffs   *haud* hold   *spiers* inquires of   *benmaist* inmost
neist next   *glisk* glimpse   *mak' siccar* make sure

A man's a clean contrairy sicht
Turned this way in-ootside,
And, fegs, I feel like Dr Jekyll
Tak'n' guid tent o' Mr Hyde . . .

Gurly thistle – hic – you canna
Daunton me wi' your shaggy mien,
I'm sair – hic – needin' a shave,
That's plainly to be seen.

But what aboot it – hic – aboot it?
Mony a man's been that afore.
It's no' a fact that in his lugs
A wund like this need roar! . . .

> [1]*I ha'e forekent ye! O I ha'e forekent.*
> *The years forecast your face afore they went.*
> *A licht I canna thole is in the lift.*
> *I bide in silence your slow-comin' pace.*
> *The ends o' space are bricht: at last – oh swift!*
> *While terror clings to me – an unkent face!*

> *Ill-faith stirs in me as she comes at last,*
> *The features lang forekent . . . are unforecast.*
> *O it gangs hard wi' me, I am forspent.*
250 > *Deid dreams ha'e beaten me and a face unkent,*
> *And generations that I thocht unborn*
> *Hail the strange Goddess frae my hert's-hert torn! . . .*

Or dost thou mak' a thistle o' me, wumman? But for thee
I were as happy as the munelicht, withoot care,
But thocht o' thee – o' thy contempt and ire –
Turns hauf the warld into the youky thistle there,

---

tak'n' guid tent paying close attention to   *gurly* savage   *daunton* frighten
sair badly   *lugs* ears   *forekent* foreknown   *thole* endure   *lift* sky
youky itchy, disgusting and sexually aroused

[1] Freely adapted from the Russian of Alexander Blok.

34

Feedin' on the munelicht and transformin' it
To this wanrestfu' growth that winna let me be.
The munelicht is the freedom that I'd ha'e
But for this cursèd Conscience thou hast set in me.

It is morality, the knowledge o' Guid and Ill,
Fear, shame, pity, like a will and wilyart growth,
That kills a' else wi'in its reach and craves
Nae less at last than a' the warld to gi'e it scouth.

The need to wark, the need to think, the need to be,
And a'thing that twists Life into a certain shape
And interferes wi' perfect liberty –
These feed this Frankenstein that nae man can escape.

For ilka thing a man can be or think or dae
Aye leaves a million mair unbeen, unthocht, undune,
Till his puir warped performance is,
To a' that micht ha' been, a thistle to the mune.

It is Mortality itsel' – the mortal coil,
Mockin' Perfection, Man afore the Throne o' God
275   He yet has bigged himsel', Man torn in twa
And glorious in the lift and grisly on the sod! ...

There's nocht sae uobei as a man blin' drunk.
I maun ha'e got an unco bellyfu'
To jaw like this – and yet what I am sayin'
Is a' the apter, aiblins, to be true.

This munelicht's fell like whisky noo I see't.
– Am I a thingum mebbe that is kept
Preserved in spirits in a muckle bottle
Lang centuries efter sin' wi' Jean I slept?

---

wanrestfu' restless   *will* uncontrolled but wilful
wilyart obstinate, headstrong   *scouth* scope   *bigged* built
unco unusual   *aiblins* perhaps   *fell* extremely

– Mounted on a hillside, wi' the thistles
And bracken for verisimilitude,
Like a stuffed bird on metal like a brainch,
Or a seal on a stump o' rock-like wood?

Or am I just a figure in a scene
O' Scottish life AD one-nine-two-five?
The haill thing kelters like a theatre claith
Till I micht fancy that I was alive!

I dinna ken and nae man ever can.
I micht be in my ain bed efter a'.
The haill damned thing's a dream for ocht we ken
– The Warld and Life and Daith, Heaven, Hell ana'.

We maun juist tak' things as we find them then,
And mak' a kirk or mill o' them as we can
– And yet I feel this muckle thistle's staun'in'
300   Atween me and the mune as pairt o' a Plan.

It isna there – nor me – by accident.
We're brocht thegither for a certain reason,
Ev'n gin it's naething mair than juist to gi'e
My jaded soul a necessary *frisson*.

I never saw afore a thistle quite
Sae intimately, or at sic an 'oor.
There's something in the fickle licht that gi'es
A different life to't and an unco poo'er.

> [1]*'Rootit on gressless peaks, whaur its erect*
> *And jaggy leafs, austerely cauld and dumb,*
> *Haud the slow scaly serpent in respect,*
> *The Gothic thistle, whaur the insect's hum*
> *Soon's fer aff, lifts abune the rock it scorns*
> *Its rigid virtue for the Heavens to see.*
> *The too'ering boulders gaird it. And the bee*
> *Mak's honey frae the roses on its thorns.'*

---

kelters ripples   *a kirk or mill* the best or worse

[1] From the Belgian poet, Georges Ramaekers.

But that's a Belgian refugee, of coorse.
This Freudian complex has somehoo slunken
Frae Scotland's soul – the Scots aboulia –
Whilst a' its *terra nullius* is *betrunken*.

And a' the country roon' aboot it noo
Lies clapt and shrunken syne like somebody wha
Has lang o' seven devils been possessed;
Then when he turns a corner tines them a',

325   Or like a body that has tint its soul,
Perched like a monkey on its heedless kist,
Or like a sea that peacefu' fa's again
When frae its deeps an octopus is fished.

I canna feel it has to dae wi' me
Mair than a composite diagram o'
Cross-sections o' my forbears' organs
– And mine – 'ud bring a kind o' freen'ly glow.

And yet like bindweed through my clay it's run,
And a' my folks' – it's queer to see't unroll.
My ain soul looks me in the face, as 'twere,
And mair than my ain soul – my nation's soul!

And sall a Belgian pit it into words
And sing a sang to't syne, and no' a Scot?
Oors is a wilder thistle, and Ramaekers
Canna bear aff the gree – avaunt the thocht!

To meddle wi' the thistle and to pluck
The figs frae't is *my* metier, I think.
Awak', my muse, and gin you're in puir fettle,
We aye can blame it on th' inferior drink.

T.S. Eliot – it's a Scottish name –
Afore he wrote 'The Waste Land' s'ud ha'e come
To Scotland here. He wad ha'e written
A better poem syne – like this, by gum!

---

aboulia pathological indecision   *clapt* pressed down   *tines* loses
tint lost   *kist* chest   *syne* then   *bear aff the gree* win the prize

Type o' the Wissenschaftsfeindlichkeit,
Begriffsmüdigkeit that has gar't
Men try Morphologies der Weltgeschichte,
And mad Expressionismus syne in Art.

[1]*A shameless thing, for ilka vileness able,*
It is deid grey as dust, the dust o' a man.
I perish o' a nearness I canna win awa' frae,
Its deidly coils aboot my buik are thrawn.

A shaggy poulp, embracin' me and stingin',
And as a serpent cauld agen' my hert.
Its scales are poisoned shafts that jag me to the quick
– And waur than them's my scunner's fearfu' smert!

O that its prickles were a knife indeed,
But it is thowless, flabby, dowf, and numb.
Sae sluggishly it drains my benmaist life
A dozent dragon, dreidfu', deef, and dumb.

In mum obscurity it twines its obstinate rings
And hings caressin'ly, its purpose whole;
And this deid thing, whale-white obscenity,
This horror that I writhe in – is my soul!

Is it the munelicht or a leprosy
That spreids aboot me; and a thistle
Or my ain skeleton through wha's bare banes
A fiendish wund's begood to whistle?

The devil's lauchter has a *hwyl* like this.
My face has flown open like a lid
– And gibberin' on the hillside there
Is a' humanity sae lang has hid! . . .

Wissenschaftsfeindlichkeit hostility to scientific knowledge
Begriffsmüdigkeit weariness of different ideas   *gar't* prompted, made
Morphologies der Weltgeschichte coherent structures of world history   *buik* body
thrawn twisted   *poulp* octopus   *waur* worse   *scunner* disgust
thowless impotent   *dowf* inert   *begood* begun   *hwyl* howl (Welsh)

[1] Adapted from the Russian of Zinaida Hippius.

My harns are seaweed – when the tide is in
They swall like blethers and in comfort float,
But when the tide is oot they lie like gealed
And runkled auld bluid-vessels in a knot!

The munelicht ebbs and flows and wi't my thocht,
Noo movin' mellow and noo lourd and rough.
I ken what I am like in Life and Daith,
But Life and Daith for nae man are enough . . .

And O! to think that there are members o'
St Andrew's Societies sleepin' soon',
Wha to the papers wrote afore they bedded
On regimental buttons or buckled shoon,

Or use o' England whaur the UK's meent,
Or this or that anent the Blue Saltire,
Recruitin', pedigrees, and Gude kens what,
Filled wi' a proper patriotic fire!

Wad I were them – they've chosen a better pairt,
The couthie craturs, than the ane I've ta'en,
Tyauvin' wi' this root-hewn Scottis soul;
A fer, fer better pairt – except for men.

Nae doot they're sober, as a Scot ne'er was,
Each tethered to a punctual-snorin' missus,
Whilst I, puir fule, owre continents unkent
400   And wine-dark oceans waunder like Ulysses . . .

> [1]*The Mune sits on my bed the nicht unsocht,*
> *And mak's my soul obedient to her will;*
> *And in the dumb-deid, still as dreams are still,*
> *Her pupils narraw to bricht threids that thrill*
> *Aboot the sensuous windin's o' her thocht.*

---

harns brains   *blethers* bladders   *gealed* congealed
runkled auld wrinkled old   *lourd* heavy   *anent* concerning
Blue Saltire Scottish Flag   *Gude kens* God knows   *couthie craturs* smug creatures
tyauvin' struggling   *dumb-deid* middle of the night

[1] Suggested by the German of Else Lasker-Schüler.

39

But ilka windin' has its coonter-pairt
— The opposite 'thoot which it couldna be —
In some wild kink or queer perversity
O' this great thistle, green wi' jealousy,
That breenges 'twixt the munelicht and my hert . . .

Plant, what are you then? Your leafs
Mind me o' the pipes' lood drone
— And a' your purple tops
Are the pirly-wirly notes
That gang staggerin' owre them as they groan.

Or your leafs are alligators
That ha'e gobbled owre a haill
Company o' Heilant sodgers,
And left naethin' but the toories
O' their Balmoral bonnets to tell the tale.

Or a muckle bellows blawin'
Wi' the sperks a' whizzin' oot;
Or green tides sweeshin'
'Neth heich-skeich stars,
Or centuries fleein' doun a water-chute.

Grinnin' gargoyle by a saint,
Mephistopheles in Heaven,
Skeleton at a tea-meetin',
Missin' link — or creakin'
Hinge atween the deid and livin' . . .

(I kent a Terrier in a sham fecht aince,
Wha louped a dyke and landed on a thistle.
He'd naething on ava aneth his kilt.
Schönberg has nae notation for his whistle.) . . .

425

---

breenges plunges forward   *pirly-wirly notes* grace notes   *gang* go
owre over   *toories* pom-poms   *heich-skeich* irresponsible
Terrier Territorial soldier   *fecht* fight   *louped a dyke* jumped a wall
ava aneth at all beneath

(Gin you're surprised a village drunk
Foreign references s'ud fool in,
You ha'ena the respect you s'ud
For oor guid Scottish schoolin'.

For we've the maist unlikely folk
Aye braggin' o' oor lear,
And, tho' I'm drunk, for Scotland's sake
I tak' my barrowsteel here!

Yet Europe's faur eneuch for me,
Puir fule, when bairns ken mair
O' th' ither warld than I o' this
– But that's no' here nor there!) . . .

Guid sakes, I'm in a dreidfu' state.
I'll ha'e nae inklin' sune
Gin I'm the drinker or the drink,
The thistle or the mune.

I'm geylies feart I couldna tell
Gin I s'ud lay me doon
The difference betwixt the warld
And my ain heid gaen' roon'! . . .

Drums in the Walligate, pipes in the air,
Come and hear the cryin' o' the Fair.

A' as it used to be, when I was a loon
On Common-Ridin' Day in the Muckle Toon.

The bearer twirls the Bannock-and-Saut-Herrin',
The Croon o' Roses through the lift is farin',

The aucht-fit thistle wallops on hie;
In heather besoms a' the hills gang by.

450

---

lear learning   *tak' my barrowsteel* co-operate   *faur eneuch* far enough
geylies feart very much afraid   *loon* boy   *Muckle Toon* Langholm
Bannock-and-Saut-Herrin' flat oatmeal cake nailed to a salted herring
aucht-fit eight-foot   *wallops on hie* dances on high   *besoms* brooms

But noo it's a' the fish o' the sea
Nailed on the roond o' the Earth to me;

Beauty and Love that are bobbin' there;
Syne the breengin' growth that alane I bear;

And Scotland followin' on ahint
For threepenny bits spleet-new frae the mint.

Drums in the Walligate, pipes in the air,
The wallopin' thistle is ill to bear.

But I'll dance the nicht wi' the stars o' Heaven
In the Mairket Place as shair's I'm livin'.

Easy to carry roses or herrin',
And the lave may weel their threepenny bits earn.

475   Devil the star! It's Jean I'll ha'e
Again as she was on her weddin' day . . .

Nerves in stounds o' delight,
Muscles in pride o' power,
Bluid as wi' roses dight
Life's toppin' pinnacles owre,
The thistle yet'll unite
Man and the Infinite!

Swippert and swith wi' virr
In the howes o' man's hert
Forever its muckle roots stir
Like a Leviathan astert,
Till'ts coils like a thistle's leafs
Sweep space wi' levin sheafs.

---

breengin' bursting   *ahint* behind   *spleet-new* brand new   *lave* rest
stounds astonishments   *dight* coloured   *swippert* agile
swith wi' virr quick with vigour   *howes* hollows   *astert* on the move
levin lightning

Frae laichest deeps o' the ocean
It rises in flight upon flight,
And 'yont its uttermaist motion
Can still set roses alight,
As else unreachable height
Fa's under its triumphin' sight.

Here is the root that feeds
The shank wi' the blindin' wings
Dwinin' abuneheid to gleids
Like stars in their keethin' rings,
And blooms in sunrise and sunset
Inowre Eternity's yett.

Lay haud o' my hert and feel
Fountains ootloupin' the starns
Or see the Universe reel
Set gaen' by my eident harns,
Or test the strength o' my spauld
The wecht o' a' thing to hauld!

— The howes o' Man's hert are bare,
The Dragon's left them for good,
There's nocht but naethingness there,
The hole whaur the Thistle stood,
That rootless and radiant flies
A Phoenix in Paradise! . . .

Masoch and Sade
Turned into ane
Havoc ha'e made
O' my a'e brain.

Weel, gin it's Sade
Let it be said
They've made me mad
— That'll dae instead.

500

---

laichest lowest   *shank* stem
dwinin' abuneheid to gleids dwindling overhead to sparks
keethin' rings rings on water made by fish   *inowre* into and over   *yett* gate
starns stars   *eident harns* eager brains   *spauld* shoulder
wecht o' a' thing to hauld weight of everything to hold   *a'e* single   *gin* if

But it's no' instead
In Scots, but insteed.
– The life they've led
In my puir heid.

525   But aince I've seen
In the thistle here
A' that they've been
I'll aiblins wun clear.

> *Thistleless fule,*
> *You'll ha'e nocht left*
> *But the hole frae which*
> *Life's struggle is reft! . . .*

Reason ser's nae end but pleasure,
Truth's no' an end but a means
To a wider knowledge o' life
And a keener interest in't.

We wha are poets and artists
Move frae inklin' to inklin',
And live for oor antrin lichtnin's
In the haingles atweenwhiles,

Laich as the feck o' mankind
Whence we breenge in unkennable shapes
   – *Crockats up, hair kaimed to the lift,*
   And no' to cree legs wi'! . . .

We're ootward boond frae Scotland.
Guid-bye, fare-ye-weel; guid-bye, fare-ye-weel.
– A' the Scots that ever wur
Gang ootward in a creel.

---

aiblins wun perbaps get   *reft* torn   *ser's* serves   *in't* in it
antrin lichtnin's rare lightnings
haingles atweenwhiles states of boredom in-between   *laich* low   *feck* majority
crockats up proud   *hair kaimed to the lift* on the go, ready for anything
no' to cree legs wi' not safe to be meddled with   *wur* were
creel state of confusion, but also a fish basket

We're ootward boond frae Scotland.

Guid-bye, fare-ye-weel; guid-bye, fare-ye-weel.
The cross-tap is a monkey-tree
That nane o' us can spiel.

We've never seen the Captain,
But the first mate is a Jew.
We've shipped aboord Eternity.
Adieu, kind freends, adieu! . . .

In the creel or on the gell
O' oor coutribat and ganien.
What gin ithers see or hear
Naething but a gowkstorm?

Gin you stop the galliard
To teach them hoo to dance,
There comes in Corbaudie
And turns their gammons up! . . .

You vegetable cat's melody!
Your *Concert Miaulant* is
A triumph o' discord shairly,
And suits my fancy fairly
– I'm shair that Scott'll agree[1]
He canna vie wi' this . . .

Said my body to my mind,
'I've been startled whiles to find,
When Jean has been in bed wi' me,
A kind o' Christianity!'

575 To my body said my mind,
'But your benmaist thocht you'll find
Was "Bother what I think I feel

---

cross-tap mizzen-mast   *spiel* climb   *gell* go   *coutribat* struggle
ganien boasting talk   *gowkstorm* foolish fuss   *galliard* dance
Corbaudie Difficulty   *gammons* hoofs

[1] F.G. Scott, the composer, to whom the poem is dedicated – Eds.

–Jean kens the set o' my bluid owre weel,
And lauchs to see me in the creel
O' my courage-bag confined."' ...

I wish I kent the physical basis
O' a' life's seemin' airs and graces.

It's queer the thochts a kittled cull
Can lowse or splairgin' glit annul.

Man's spreit is wi' his ingangs twined
In ways that he can ne'er unwind.

A wumman whiles a bawaw gi'es
That clean abaws him gin he sees.

Or wi' a movement o' a leg
Shows'm his mind is juist a geg.

I'se warrant Jean 'ud no' be lang
In findin' whence this thistle sprang.

Mebbe it's juist because I'm no'
Beddit wi' her that gars it grow! ...

A luvin' wumman is a licht[1]
That shows a man his waefu' plicht,
Bleezin' steady on ilka bane,
Wrigglin' sinnen an' twinin' vein,
Or fleerin' quick an' gane again,
And the mair scunnersome the sicht
The mair for love and licht he's fain
Till clear and chitterin' and nesh
Move a' the miseries o' his flesh ...

600

---

courage-bag scrotum *kittled cull* tickled testicle *lowse* loosen
splairgin' glit splattering slime *spreit* spirit *ingangs* entrails
bawaw scornful glance *abaws* abashes *geg* deception *gars* makes
waefu' woeful *bleezin'* blazing *bane* bone *sinnen* sinew
twinin' twisting *fleerin'* flaring *scunnersome* disgusting
chitterin' shivering *nesh* alertly, aware

[1] Suggested by the French of Edmond Rocher.

O lass, wha see'est me
As I daur hardly see,
I marvel that your bonny een
Are as they hadna seen.

Through a' my self-respect
They see the truth abject
    – Gin you could pierce their blindin' licht
    You'd see a fouler sicht! . . .

O wha's the bride that cairries the bunch
O' thistles blinterin' white?
Her cuckold bridegroom little dreids
What he sall ken this nicht.

For closer than gudeman can come
And closer to'r than hersel',
Wha didna need her maidenheid
Has wrocht his purpose fell.

O wha's been here afore me, lass,
And hoo did he get in?
    – A man that deed or I was born
    This evil thing has din.

And left, as it were on a corpse,
625   Your maidenheid to me?
    – Nae lass, gudeman, sin' Time began
    'S hed ony mair to gi'e.

But I can gi'e ye kindness, lad,
And a pair o' willin' hands,
And you sall ha'e my breists like stars,
My limbs like willow wands,

And on my lips ye'll heed nae mair,
And in my hair forget,
The seed o' a' the men that in
My virgin womb ha'e met . . .

---

blinterin' gleaming   *dreids* dreads, suspects   *gudeman* husband
to'r to her   *deed or* died ere   *din* done

Millions o' wimmen bring forth in pain
Millions o' bairns that are no' worth ha'en.

Wull ever a wumman be big again
Wi's muckle's a Christ? Yech, there's nae sayin'.

Gin that's the best that you ha'e comin',
Fegs but I'm sorry for you, wumman!

Yet a'e thing's certain. – Your faith is great.
Whatever happens, you'll no' be blate! . . .

Mary lay in jizzen
As it were claith o' gowd,
But it's in orra duds
Ilka ither bairntime's row'd.

Christ had never toothick,
Christ was never seeck,
But Man's a fiky bairn
Wi' bellythraw, ripples, and worm-i'-the-cheek! . . .

Dae what ye wull ye canna parry
This skeleton-at-the-feast that through the starry
Maze o' the warld's intoxicatin' soiree
Claughts ye, as micht at an affrontit quean
A bastard wean!

Prood mune, ye needna thring your shouder there,
And at your puir get like a snawstorm stare,
It's yours – there's nae denyin't – and I'm shair
You'd no' enjoy the evenin' much the less
Gin you'd but openly confess!

---

blate bashful   *jizzen* childbed   *claith o' gowd* cloth of gold
orra duds shabby clothes
ilka ither bairntime's row'd every other woman's lying-in is rolled   *seeck* sick
fiky bairn troublesome child   *bellythraw* colic   *ripples* diarrhoea
worm-i'-the-cheek toothache   *claughts* clutches   *quean* young woman
wean child   *thring your shouder* shrug your shoulder
puir get poor offspring

48

Dod! It's an eaten and a spewed-like thing,
Fell like a little-bodies' changeling,
And it's nae credit t'ye that you s'ud bring
The like to life – yet, gi'en a mither's love,
– Hee, hee! – wha kens hoo't micht improve? . . .

Or is this Heaven, this yalla licht,
And I the aft'rins o' the Earth,
Or sic's in this wanchancy time
May weel fin' sudden birth?

The roots that wi' the worms compete
Hauf-publish me upon the air.
The struggle that divides me still
Is seen fu' plainly there.

675   The thistle's shank scarce holes the grun',
My grave'll spare nae mair I doot.
– The crack's fu' wide; the shank's fu' strang;
A' that I was is oot.

My knots o' nerves that struggled sair
Are weel reflected in the herb;
My crookit instincts were like this,
As sterile and acerb.

My self-tormented spirit took
The shape repeated in the thistle;
Sma' beauty jouked my rawny banes
And maze o' gristle.

I seek nae peety, Paraclete,
And, fegs, I think the joke is rich
– Pairt soul, pairt skeleton's come up;
They kentna which was which! . . .

---

spewed-like vomit-like   *little-bodies'* fairies   *hoo't* how it
aft'rins remains   *sic's* such as   *wanchancy* unfortunate   *shank* stem
jouked avoided   *rawny* prominent   *kentna* did not know

Thou Daith in which my life
Sae vain a thing can seem,
Frae whatna source d'ye borrow
Your devastatin' gleam?

Nae doot that hidden sun
'Ud look fu' wae ana',
Gin I could see it in the licht
That frae the Earth you draw!...

Shudderin' thistle, gi'e owre, gi'e owre!
A'body's gi'en in to the facts o' life;
The impossible truth'll triumph at last,
And mock your strife.

Your sallow leafs can never thraw,
Wi' a' their oorie shakin',
Ae doot into the hert o' life
That it may be mistak'n...

O Scotland is
THE barren fig.
Up, carles, up
And roond it jig.

Auld Moses took
A dry stick and
Instantly it
Floo'ered in his hand.

Pu' Scotland up,
And wha can say
It winna bud
And blossom tae.

A miracle's
Oor only chance.
Up, carles, up
And let us dance!

700

---

whatna what kind of   *fu' wae ana'* extremely sad as well   *oorie* weird, chilly
carles fellows

Puir Burns, wha's bouquet like a shot kail blaws
– Will this rouch sicht no' gi'e the orchids pause?
725   The Gairdens o' the Muses may be braw,
But nane like oors can breenge and eat ana'!

And owre the kailyaird-wa' Dunbar they've flung,
And a' their countrymen that e'er ha'e sung
For ither than ploomen's lugs or to enrichen
Plots on Parnassus set apairt for kitchen.

Ploomen and ploomen's wives – shades o' the Manse
May weel be at the heid o' sic a dance,
As through the polish't ha's o' Europe leads
The rout o' bagpipes, haggis, and sheep's heids!

The vandal Scot! Frae Brankstone's deidly barrow
I struggle yet to free a'e winsome marrow,
To show what Scotland micht ha'e hed instead
O' this preposterous Presbyterian breed.

(Gin Glesca folk are tired o' Hengler,
And still need breid and circuses, there's Spengler,
Or gin ye s'ud need mair than ane to teach ye,
Then learn frae Dostoevski and frae Nietzsche.

And let the lesson be – to be yersel's,
Ye needna fash gin it's to be ocht else.
To be yersel's – and to mak' that worth bein',
Nae harder job to mortals has been gi'en.

To save your souls fu' mony o' ye are fain,
But de'il a dizzen to mak' it worth the daein'.
I widna gi'e five meenits wi' Dunbar
750   For a' the millions o' ye as ye are).

---

shot kail sprouted cabbage   rouch rough   kailyaird-wa' kitchen-garden wall
kitchen vegetable plots   ha's halls   Brankstone Flodden   marrow mate
fash trouble   fu' mony a great many   de'il a dizzen not a dozen

I micht ha'e been contentit wi' the Rose
Gin I'd had ony reason to suppose
That what the English dae can e'er mak' guid
For what Scots dinna – and first and foremaist should.

I micht ha'e been contentit – gin the feck
O' my ain folk had grovelled wi' less respec',
But their obsequious devotion
Made it for me a criminal emotion.

I micht ha'e been contentit – ere I saw
That there were fields on which it couldna draw,
(While strang-er roots ran under't) and a'e threid
O't drew frae Scotland a' that it could need,

And left the maist o' Scotland fallow
(Save for the patch on which the kail-blades wallow),
And saw hoo ither countries' genius drew
Elements like mine that in a rose ne'er grew . . .

Gin the threid haud'n us to the rose were snapt,
There's no' a'e petal o't that 'ud be clapt.
A' Scotland gi'es gangs but to jags or stalk,
The bloom is English – and 'ud ken nae lack! . . .

O drumlie clood o' crudity and cant,
Obliteratin' as the Easter rouk
That rows up frae the howes and droons the heichs,
And turns the country to a faceless spook.

775   Like blurry shapes o' landmarks in the haar
The bonny idiosyncratic place-names loom,
Clues to the vieve and maikless life that's lain
Happit for centuries in an alien gloom . . .

Eneuch! For noo I'm in the mood,
Scotland, responsive to my thoughts,
Lichts mile by mile, as my ain nerves
Frae Maidenkirk to John o' Groats!

---

feck majority   *clapt* shrunken   *drumlie* dreary   *rouk* mist   *howes* hollows
haar mist   *vieve* vivid   *maikless* matchless   *happit* covered
Maidenkirk to John o' Groats from one end of Scotland to the other

What are prophets and priests and kings,
What's ocht to the people o' Scotland?
Speak – and Cruivie'll goam at you,
Gilsanquhar jalouse you're dottlin!

And Edinburgh and Glasgow
Are like ploomen in a pub.
They want to hear o' naething
But their ain foul hubbub . . .

The fules are richt; an extra thocht
Is neither here nor there.
Oor lives may differ as they like
– The self-same fate we share.

And whiles I wish I'd nae mair sense
Than Cruivie and Gilsanquhar,
And envy their rude health and curse
My gnawin' canker.

Guid sakes, ye dinna need to pass
Ony exam. to dee
– Daith canna tell a common flech
Frae a performin' flea! . . .

It sets you weel to slaver
To let sic gaadies fa'
– *The mune's the muckle white whale*
I seek in vain to kaa!

The Earth's my mastless samyn,
The thistle my ruined sail.
– Le'e go as you maun in the end,
And droon in your plumm o' ale! . . .

800

___

goam gape stupidly   *jalouse* imagine   *dottlin* going crazy   *flech* flea
slaver slobber   *gaadies fa'* howlers fall   *kaa* drive   *samyn* deck
plumm deep pool

Clear keltie aff an' fill again
Withoot corneigh bein' cryit,
The drink's aye best that follows a drink.
Clear keltie aff and try it.

Be't whisky gill or penny wheep,
Or ony ither lotion,
We bood to ha'e a thimblefu' first,
And syne we'll toom an ocean! . . .

'To Luna at the Craidle-and-Coffin
To sof'n her hert if owt can sof'n: –

Auld bag o' tricks, ye needna come
And think to stap me in your womb.

You needna fash to rax and strain.
Carline, I'll *no'* be born again

In ony brat you can produce.
Carline, gi'e owre – O what's the use?

You pay nae heed but plop me in,
Syne shove me oot, and winna be din

– Owre and owre, the same auld trick,
Cratur withoot climacteric!' . . .

'Noo Cutty Sark's tint that ana',
And dances in her skin – Ha! Ha!

I canna ride awa' like Tam,
But e'en maun bide juist whaur I am.

I canna ride – and gin I could,
I'd sune be sorry I hedna stude,

For less than a' there is to see
'll never be owre muckle for me.

825

---

keltie bumper   corneigh enough   whisky gill dram of whisky
penny wheep light beer   bood intend   toom empty   owt anything
stap stuff   fash trouble   rax stretch   carline old woman   brat child
winna be din won't be finished

54

Cutty, gin you've mair to strip,
Aff wi't, lass – and let it rip!' . . .

Ilka pleesure I can ha'e
Ends like a dram ta'en yesterday.

And tho' to ha'e it I am lorn
– What better 'ud I be the morn? . . .

My belly on the gantrees there,
The spigot frae my cullage,
And wow but how the fizzin' yill
In spilth increased the ullage!

850

I was an anxious barrel, lad,
When first they tapped my bung.
They whistled me up, yet thro' the lift
My freaths like rainbows swung.

Waesucks, a pride for ony bar,
The boast o' barleyhood,
Like Noah's Ark abune the faem
Maun float, a gantin' cude,

For I was thrawn fu' cock owre sune,
And wi' a single jaw
I made the pub a blindin' swelth,
And how'd the warld awa'! . . .

What forest worn to the back-hauf's this,
What Eden brocht doon to a bean-swaup?
The thistle's to earth as the man
In the mune's to the mune, puir chap.

---

lorn longing   *the morn* tomorrow   *gantrees* wooden stand for barrels
cullage genitals   *yill* ale   *spilth* overflow
ullage deficiency of the contents   *freaths* plumes of foam   *waesucks* alas
barleyhood drunkenness   *gantin' cude* gaping barrel
thrawn fu' cock owre sune thrown full cock (completely on) too soon   *jaw* spurt
swelth whirlpool   *how'd* washed   *back-hauf* completely out
bean-swaup bean-husk, nothing of value

The haill warld's barkin' and fleein',
And this is its echo and aiker,
A soond that arrears in my lug
Herrin'-banein' back to its maker,

A swaw like a flaw in a jewel
Or nadryv[1] jaloused in a man,
Or Creation unbiggit again
To the draucht wi' which it began . . .

Abordage o' this toom houk's nae mowse.
It munks and's ill to lay haud o',
As gin a man ettled to ride
On the shouders o' his ain shadow.

I canna biel't; tho' steekin' an e'e,
Tither's munkie wi' munebeam for knool in't,
For there's nae sta'-tree and the brute's awa'
Wi' me kinkin' like foudrie ahint . . .

Sae Eternity'll buff nor stye
For Time, and shies at a touch, man;
Yet aye in a belth o' Thocht
Comes alist like the Fleein' Dutchman . . .

As the worms'll breed in my corpse until
It's like a rice-puddin', the thistle
Has made an eel-ark o' the lift
Whaur elvers like skirl-in-the-pan sizzle,

875

---

barkin' and fleein' on the verge of ruin   aiker movement of water (by fish)
arrears goes backwards   herrin'-banein' zig-zagging   swaw ripple
jaloused suspected   unbiggit unbuilt   draucht draught
abordage embarking   toom houk empty hulk   nae mowse no joke
munks swings away   ettled attempted   canna biel't cannot secure it
steekin' an e'e shutting one eye   tither's munkie the other is a rope-loop
knool peg   sta'-tree tethering pole   kinkin' twisting
foundrie ahint lightning behind   buff nor stye neither one thing nor the other
belth sudden swirl   comes alist recovers   eel-ark breeding ground for eels
elvers young eels   skirl-in-the-pan fried oatmeal

[1] Tragical crack (Dostoevski's term).

Like a thunder-plump on the sunlicht,
Or the slounge o' daith on my dreams,
Or as to a fair forfochen man
A breedin' wife's beddiness seems,

Saragossa Sea, St Vitus' Dance,
A *cafard* in a brain's despite,
Or lunacy that thinks a' else
Is loony – and is dootless richt! . . .

Gin my thochts that circle like hobby-horses
'Udna loosen to nightmares I'd sleep;
For nocht but a chowed core's left whaur Jerusalem lay
900   Like aipples in a heap! . . .

It's a queer thing to tryst wi' a wumman
When the boss o' her body's gane,
And her banes in the wund as she comes
Dirl like a raff o' rain.

It's a queer thing to tryst wi' a wumman
When her ghaist frae abuneheid keeks,
And you see in the licht o't that a'
You ha'e o'r's the cleiks . . .

What forest worn to the back-hauf's this,
What Eden brocht doon to a bean-swaup?
– A' the ferlies o' natur' spring frae the earth,
And into't again maun drap.

Animals, vegetables, what are they a'
But as thochts that a man has ha'en?
And Earth sall be like a toom skull syne.
– Whaur'll its thochts be then? . . .

---

thunder-plump heavy rain after thunder   *slounge* sudden splash
fair forfochen completely exhausted   *beddiness* sexual demand
boss o' her body front part of her torso   *dirl* rattle   *raff* flurry
abuneheid keeks overhead peers
ha'e o'r's the cleiks have of her is the merest shadow of what's left
ferlies marvels   *toom* empty

57

The munelicht is my knowledge o' mysel',
Mysel' the thistle in the munelicht seen,
And hauf my shape has fund itsel' in thee
And hauf my knowledge in your piercin' een.

E'en as the munelicht's borrowed frae the sun
I ha'e my knowledge o' mysel' frae thee,
And much that nane but thee can e'er mak' clear,
Save my licht's frae the source, is dark to me.

925 Your acid tongue, vieve lauchter, and hawk's een,
And bluid that drobs like hail to quicken me,
Can turn the mid-day black or midnicht bricht,
Lowse me frae licht or eke frae darkness free.

Bite into me forever mair and lift
Me clear o' chaos in a great relief
Till, like this thistle in the munelicht growin',
I brak in roses owre a hedge o' grief . . .

I am like Burns, and ony wench
Can ser' me for a time.
Licht's in them a' – in some a sun,
In some the merest skime.

I'm no' like Burns, and weel I ken,
Tho' ony wench can ser',
It's no' through mony but through yin
That ony man wuns fer . . .

I weddit thee frae fause love, lass,
To free thee and to free mysel';
But man and wumman tied for life
True can be and truth can tell.

Pit ony couple in a knot
They canna lowse and needna try,
And mair o' love at last they'll ken
– If ocht! – than joy'll alane descry.

---

vieve vivid *drobs* stings *eke* else *skime* gleam *wuns fer* gets far
fause false

For them as for the beasts, my wife

950 A's fer frae dune when pleesure's owre,
And coontless difficulties gar
Ilk hert discover a' its power.

I dinna say that bairns alane
Are true love's task – a sairer task
Is aiblins to create oorsels
As we can be – it's that I ask.

Create oorsels, syne bairns, syne race.
Sae on the cod I see't in you
Wi' Maidenkirk to John o' Groats
The bosom that you draw me to.

And nae Scot wi' a wumman lies,
But I am he and ken as 'twere
A stage I've passed as he maun pass't,
Gin he grows up, his way wi' her! . . .

A'thing wi' which a man
Can intromit's a wumman,
And can, and s'ud, become
As intimate and human.

And Jean's nae mair my wife
Than whisky is at times,
Or munelicht or a thistle
Or kittle thochts or rhymes.

He's no' a man ava',
And lacks a proper pride,

975 Gin less than a' the warld
Can ser' him for a bride! . . .

Use, then, my lust for whisky and for thee,
Your function but to be and let me be
And see and let me see.

---

gar compel   *sairer* more difficult   *aiblins* perhaps   *cod* pillow
intromit engage   *kittle* exciting, tricky   *ava'* at all

If in a lesser licht I grope my way,
Or use't for ends that need your different ray
Whelm't in superior day.

Then aye increase and ne'er withdraw your licht.
– Gin it shows either o's in hideous plicht,
What gain to turn't to nicht?

Whisky mak's Heaven or Hell and whiles mells baith,
Disease is but the privy torch o' Daith,
– But sex reveals life, faith!

I need them a' and maun be aye at strife.
Daith and ayont are nocht but pairts o' life.
– Then be life's licht, my wife! . . .

Love often wuns free
In lust to be strangled,
Or love, o' lust free,
In law's sairly tangled.

And it's ill to tell whether
Law or lust is to blame
When love's chokit up
– It comes a' to the same.

1000   In this sorry growth
Whatna beauty is tint
That freed o't micht find
A waur fate than is in't? . . .

Yank oot your orra boughs, my hert!

God gied man speech and speech created thocht,
He gied man speech but to the Scots gied nocht
Barrin' this clytach that they've never brocht
To onything but sic a Blottie O
As some bairn's copybook micht show,

---

mells baith mixes both   *orra* worthless   *barrin'* except   *clytach* nonsense
Blottie O a school game

A spook o' soond that frae the unkent grave
In which oor nation lies loups up to wave
Sic leprous chuns as tatties have
That cellar-boond send spindles gropin'
Towards ony hole that's open,

Like waesome fingers in the dark that think
They still may widen the ane and only chink
That e'er has gi'en mankind a blink
O' Hope – tho' ev'n in that puir licht
They s'ud ha'e seen their hopeless plicht.

This puir relation o' my topplin' mood,
This country cousin, streak o' churl-bluid,
This hopeless airgh 'twixt a' we can and should,
This Past that like Astarte's sting I feel,
This arrow in Achilles' heel.

1025   *Yank oot your orra boughs, my hert!*

Mebbe we're in a vicious circle cast,
Mebbe there's limits we can ne'er get past,
Mebbe we're sentrices that at the last
Are flung aside, and no' the pillars and props
O' Heaven foraye as in oor hopes.

Oor growth at least nae steady progress shows,
Genius in mankind like an antrin rose
Abune a jungly waste o' effort grows,
But to Man's purpose it mak's little odds,
And seems irrelevant to God's . . .

Eneuch? Then here you are. Here's the haill story.
Life's connached shapes too'er up in croons o' glory,
Perpetuatin', natheless, in their gory
Colour the endless sacrifice and pain
That to their makin's gane.

---

loups leaps   *chuns* sprouts   *tatties* potatoes   *waesome* woeful
airgh gap   *sentrices* scaffolding   *foraye* forever   *antrin* rare
connached spoiled

61

The roses like the saints in Heaven treid
Triumphant owre the agonies o' their breed,
And wag fu' mony a celestial heid
Abune the thorter-ills o' leaf and prick
In which they ken the feck maun stick.

Yank oot your orra boughs, my hert!

A mongrel growth, jumble o' disproportions,
Whirlin' in its incredible contortions,
Or wad-be client that an auld whore shuns,
1050   Wardin' her wizened orange o' a bosom
Frae importunities sae gruesome,

Or new diversion o' the hormones
Mair fond o' procreation than the Mormons,
And fetchin' like a devastatin' storm on's
A' the uncouth dilemmas o' oor natur'
Objectified in vegetable maitter.

Yank oot your orra boughs, my hert!

And heed nae mair the foolish cries that beg
You slice nae mair to aff or pu' to leg,
You skitin' duffer that gars a'body fleg,
– What tho' you ding the haill warld oot o' joint
Wi' a skier to cover-point!

Yank oot your orra boughs, my hert!

There *was* a danger – and it's weel I see't –
Had brocht ye like Mallarmé to defeat: –
'Mon doute, amas de nuit ancienne, s'achève
En maint rameau subtil, qui, demeuré les vrais
Bois mêmes, prouve, hélas! que bien seul je m'offrais
Pour triomphe la faute idéale de roses.'[1]

---

treid tread   *thorter-ills* paralytic seizures   *skitin'* capering   *gars* makes
fleg afraid   *ding* knock

[1] The line which precedes these in Mallarmé's poem is 'Aimai-je un rêve?' and
Wilfred Thorley translates the passage thus:
        'Loved I Love's counterfeit?
        My doubts, begotten of the long night's heat,
        Dislimn the woodland till my triumph shows
        As the flawed shadow of a frustrate rose.'

Yank oot your orra boughs, my hert! . . .

I love to muse upon the skill that gangs
To mak' the simplest thing that Earth displays,
The eident life that ilka atom thrangs,
And uses it in the appointit ways,
1075   And a' the endless brain that nocht escapes
That myriad moves them to inimitable shapes.

Nor to their customed form or ony ither
New to Creation, by man's cleverest mind,
A' needfu' particles first brocht thegither,
Could they wi' timeless labour be combined.
There's nocht that Science yet's begood to see
In hauf its deemless detail or its destiny.

Oor een gi'e answers based on pairt-seen facts
That beg a' questions, to ebb minds' content,
But hoo a'e feature or the neist attracts,
Wi' millions mair unseen, wha kens what's meant
By human brains and to what ends may tell
– For naething's seen or kent that's near a thing itsel'!

Let whasae vaunts his knowledge then and syne
Sets up a God and kens His purpose tae
Tell me what's gart a'e strain o' maitter twine
In sic an extraordinary way,
And what God's purpose wi' the Thistle is
– I'll aiblins ken what he and his God's worth by this.

I've watched it lang and hard until I ha'e
A certain symp'thy wi' its orra ways
And pride in its success, as weel I may,
In growin' exactly as its instinct says,
Save in sae fer as thwarts o' weather or grun'
1100   Or man or ither foes ha'e'ts aims perchance fordone.

---

eident eager   *thrangs* crowds   *begood* begun   *deemless* countless
whasae whosever   *twine* unite   *thwarts* obstructions   *grun'* ground
fordone frustrated

But I can form nae notion o' the spirit
That gars it tak' the difficult shape it does,
Nor judge the merit yet or the demerit
O' this detail or that sae fer as it goes
T' advance the cause that gied it sic a guise
As maun ha'e pleased its Maker wi' a gey surprise.

The craft that hit upon the reishlin' stalk,
Wi'ts gausty leafs and a' its datchie jags,
And spired it syne in seely flooers to brak
Like sudden lauchter owre its fousome rags
Jouks me, sardonic lover, in the routh
O' contrairies that jostle in this dumfoondrin' growth.

What strength 't'ud need to pit its roses oot,
Or double them in number or in size,
He canna tell wha canna plumb the root,
And learn what's gar't its present state arise,
And what the limits are that ha'e been put
To change in thistles, and why – and what a change
        'ud boot . . .

I saw a rose come loupin' oot[1]
Frae a camsteerie plant.
O wha'd ha'e thocht yon puir stock had
Sic an inhabitant?

For centuries it ran to waste,
Wi' pin-heid flooers at times.
O'ts hidden hert o' beauty they
Were but the merest skimes.

Yet while it ran to wud and thorns,
The feckless growth was seekin'
Some airt to cheenge its life until
A' in a rose was beekin'.

1125

---

reishlin' rustling   *gausty* ghastly   *datchie* sly, hidden
spired it made it soar   *seely* innocent and pleasant   *fousome* disgusting
jouks dodges   *routh* plenty   *boot* profit   *camsteerie* perverse
wud wood   *airt* way   *beekin'* showing, shining

[1] The General Strike (May 1926).

64

'Is there nae way in which my life
Can mair to flooerin' come,
And bring its waste on shank and jags
Doon to a minimum?

'It's hard to struggle as I maun
For scrunts o' blooms like mine,
While blossom covers ither plants
As by a knack divine.

'What hinders me unless I lack
Some needfu' discipline?
– I wis I'll bring my orra life
To beauty or I'm din!'

Sae ran the thocht that hid ahint
The thistle's ugsome guise,
'I'll brak' the habit o' my life
A worthier to devise.

'My nobler instincts sall nae mair
This contrair shape be gi'en.
I sall nae mair consent to live
1150   A life no' fit to be seen.'

Sae ran the thocht that hid ahint
The thistle's ugsome guise,
Till a' at aince a rose loupt oot
– I watched it wi' surprise.

A rose loupt oot and grew, until
It was ten times the size
O' ony rose the thistle afore
Hed heistit to the skies.

And still it grew till a' the buss
Was hidden in its flame.
I never saw sae braw a floo'er
As yon thrawn stock became.

---

scrunts stunted things   *wis* know   *ugsome* ugly   *hed heistit* had hoisted
buss bush   *thrawn* obstinate

And still it grew until it seemed
The haill braid earth had turned
A reid reid rose that in the lift
Like a ball o' fire burned.

The waefu' clay was fire aince mair,
As Earth had been resumed
Into God's mind, frae which sae lang
To grugous state 'twas doomed.

Syne the rose shrivelled suddenly
As a balloon is burst;
The thistle was a ghaistly stick,
As gin it had been curst.

1175 Was it the ancient vicious sway
Imposed itsel' again,
Or nerve owre weak for new emprise
That made the effort vain,

A coward strain in that lorn growth
That wrocht the sorry trick?
– The thistle like a rocket soared
And cam' doon like the stick.

Like grieshuckle the roses glint,
The leafs like farles hing,
As roond a hopeless sacrifice
Earth draws its barren ring.

The dream o' beauty's dernin' yet
Ahint the ugsome shape.
– Vain dream that in a pinheid here
And there can e'er escape!

The vices that defeat the dream
Are in the plant itsel',
And till they're purged its virtues maun
In pain and misery dwell.

---

grugous ugly *grieshuckle* embers *farles* ash filaments *dernin'* hiding

Let Deils rejoice to see the waste,
The fond hope brocht to nocht.
The thistle in their een is as
A favourite lust they've wrocht.

The orderin' o' the thistle means
1200   Nae richtin' o't to them.
Its loss they ca' a law, its thorns
A fule's fit diadem.

And still the idiot nails itsel'
To its ain crucifix,
While here a rose and there a rose
Jaups oot abune the pricks.

Like connoisseurs the Deils gang roond
And praise its attitude,
Till on the Cross the silly Christ
To fidge fu' fain's begood!

Like connoisseurs the Deils gang roond
Wi' ready platitude.
It's no' sae dear as vinegar,
And every bit as good!

The bitter taste is on my tongue,
I chowl my chafts, and pray
'Let God forsake me noo and no'
Staund connoisseur-like tae!' . . .

The language that but sparely flooers
And maistly gangs to weed;
The thocht o' Christ and Calvary
Aye liddenin' in my heid;
And a' the dour provincial thocht
That merks the Scottish breed
1225   – These are the thistle's characters,
To argie there's nae need.

Deils Devils   *jaups* splashes
fidge fu' fain's begood has begun to move anxiously
chowl my chafts distort my jaws, grind my teeth   *liddenin'* moving to and fro

Hoo weel my verse embodies
The thistle you can read!
– But will a Scotsman never
Frae this vile growth be freed? . . .

O ilka man alive is like
A quart that's squeezed into a pint
(A maist unScottish-like affair!)
Or like the little maid that showed
Me into a still sma'er room.

What use to let a sunrise fade
To ha'e anither like't the morn,
Or let a generation pass
That ane nae better may succeed,
Or wi' a' Time's machinery
Keep naething new aneth the sun,
Or change things oot o' kennin' that
They may be a' the mair the same?

The thistle in the wund dissolves
In lichtnin's as shook foil gi'es way
In sudden splendours, or the flesh
As Daith lets slip the infinite soul;
And syne it's like a sunrise tint
In grey o' day, or love and life
That in a cloody blash o' sperm
Undae the warld to big't again,
Or like a pickled foetus that
Nae man feels ocht in common wi'
– But micht as easily ha' been!
Or like a corpse a soul set free
Scunners to think it tenanted
– And little recks that but for it
It never micht ha' been at a',
Like love frae lust and God frae man!

1250

---

kennin' recognition, knowledge   *blash* spurt   *big't* build it
scunners feels disgusted

The wasted seam that dries like stairch
And pooders aff, that micht ha' been
A warld o' men and syne o' Gods;
The grey that haunts the vievest green;
The wrang side o' the noblest scene
We ne'er can whummle to oor een,
As 'twere the hinderpairts o' God
His face aye turned the opposite road,
Or's neth the flooers the drumlie clods
Frae which they come at sicna odds,
As a' Earth's magic frae a spirt,
In shame and secrecy, o' dirt!

Then shak' nae mair in silly life,
Nor stand impossible as Daith,
Incredible as a' thing is
Inside or oot owre closely scanned.
As mithers aften think the warld
O' bairns that ha'e nae end or object,
Or lovers think their sweethearts made
Yince-yirn – wha ha'ena waled the lave,
Maikless – when they are naebody,
Or men o' ilka sort and kind
Are prood o' thochts they ca' their ain,
That nameless millions had afore
And nameless millions yet'll ha'e,
And that were never worth the ha'en,
Or Cruivie's 'latest' story or
Gilsanquhar's vows to sign the pledge,
Or's if I thocht maist whisky *was*,
Or failed to coont the cheenge I got,
Sae wad I be gin I rejoiced,
Or didna ken my place, in thee.

O stranglin' rictus, sterile spasm,
Thou stricture in the groins o' licht,
Thou ootrie gangrel frae the wilds

1275

---

seam semen   stairch starch   *vievest* most vivid   *whummle* overturn
drumlie dull   sicna such great   *yince-yirn* especially
waled the lave tried the rest   *maikless* matchless   *ootrie gangrel* outré wanderer

O' chaos fenced frae Eden yet
By the unsplinterable wa'
O' munebeams like a bleeze o' swords!

Nae chance lunge cuts the Gordian knot,
Nor sall the belly find relief
1300 In wha's entangled moniplies
Creation like a stoppage jams,
Or in whose loins the mapamound
Runkles in strawns o' bubos whaur
The generations gravel.
The soond o' water winnin' free,
The sicht o' licht that braks the rouk,
The thocht o' every thwart owrecome
Are in my ears and een and brain,
In whom the bluid is spilt in stour,
In whom a' licht in darkness fails,
In whom the mystery o' life
Is to a wretched weed bewrayed.

But let my soul increase in me,
God dwarfed to enter my puir thocht
Expand to his true size again,
And protoplasm's look befit
The nature o' its destiny,
And seed and sequence be nae mair
Incongruous to ane anither,
And liquor packed impossibly
Mak' pint-pot an eternal well,
And art be relevant to life,
And poets mair than dominies yet,
And ends nae langer tint in means,
1325 Nor forests hidden by their trees,
Nor men be sacrificed alive
In foonds o' fates designed for them,

---

wha's whose   *moniplies* intestines   *mapamound* map of the world
runkles wrinkles   *strawns o' bubos* chains of swellings
gravel collect in confusion   *rouk* mist   *thwart* hindrance   *stour* clouds
bewrayed distorted, betrayed   *dominies* schoolmasters or ministers
foonds foundations

Nor mansions o' the soul stand toom
Their owners in their cellars trapped,
Nor a' a people's genius be
A rumple-fyke in Heaven's doup,
While Calvinism uses her
To breed a minister or twa!

A black leaf owre a white leaf twirls,
A grey leaf flauchters in atween,
Sae ply my thochts aboot the stem
O' loppert slime frae which they spring.
The thistle like a snawstorm drives,
Or like a flicht o' swallows lifts,
Or like a swarm o' midges hings,
A plague o' moths, a starry sky,
But's naething but a thistle yet,
And still the puzzle stands unsolved.
Beauty and ugliness alike,
And life and daith and God and man,
Are aspects o't but nane can tell
The secret that I'd fain find oot
O' this bricht hive, this sorry weed,
The tree that fills the universe,
1350   Or like a reistit herrin' crines.

Gin I was sober I micht think
It was like something drunk men see!

The necromancy in my bluid
Through a' the gamut cheenges me
O' dwarf and giant, foul and fair,
But winna let me be mysel'
– My mither's womb that reins me still
Until I tae can prick the witch
And 'Wumman' cry wi' Christ at last,
'Then what hast thou to do wi' me?'

---

rumple-fyke anus itch   *doup* backside   *flauchters* flutters
loppert coagulated   *reistit* dried   *crines* shrivels
prick the witch identify the female demon

The tug-o'-war is in me still,
The dog-hank o' the flesh and soul –
Faither in Heaven, what gar'd ye tak'
A village slut to mither me,
Your mongrel o' the fire and clay?
The trollop and the Deity share
My writhen form as tho' I were
A picture o' the time they had
When Licht rejoiced to file itsel'
And Earth upshuddered like a star.

A drucken hizzie gane to bed
Wi' three-in-ane and ane-in-three.

O fain I'd drink until I saw
Scotland a ferlie o' delicht,
1375   And fain bide drunk nor ha'e't recede
Into a shrivelled thistle syne,
As when a sperklin' tide rins oot,
And leaves a wreath o' rubbish there!

Wull a' the seas gang dry at last
(As dry as I am gettin' noo),
Or wull they aye come back again,
Seilfu' as my neist drink to me,
Or as the sunlicht to the mune,
Or as the bonny sangs o' men,
Wha're but puir craturs in themsels,
And save when genius mak's them drunk,
As donnert as their audiences,
– As dreams that mak' a tramp a king,
A madman sane to his ain mind,
Or what a Scotsman thinks himsel',
Tho' naethin' but a thistle kyths.

---

dog-hank dog-knot (during mating)   *gar'd* made   *file* defile
drucken hizzie drunken hussie   *ferlie o' delicht* marvel of delight
nor ha'e't not have it   *seilfu'* blissful   *donnert* stupid   *kyths* appears

The mair I drink the thirstier yet,
And whiles when I'm alowe wi' booze,
I'm like God's sel' and clad in fire,
And ha'e a Pentecost like this.
O wad that I could aye be fou',
And no' come back as aye I maun
To naething but a fule that nane
'Ud credit wi' sic thochts as thae,
A fule that kens they're empty dreams!

Yet but fer drink and drink's effects,
The yeast o' God that barms in us,
We micht as weel no' be alive.
It maitters not what drink is ta'en,
The barley bree, ambition, love,
Or Guid or Evil workin' in's,
Sae lang's we feel like souls set free
Frae mortal coils and speak in tongues
We dinna ken and never wull,
And find a merit in oorsels,
In Cruivies and Gilsanquhars tae,
And see the thistle as ocht but that!

For wha o's ha'e the thistle's poo'er
To see we're worthless and believe 't?

A'thing that ony man can be's
A mockery o' his soul at last.
The mair it shows't the better, and
I'd suner be a tramp than king,
Lest in the pride o' place and poo'er
I e'er forgot my waesomeness.
Sae to debauchery and dirt,
And to disease and daith I turn,
Sin' otherwise my seemin' worth
'Ud block my view o' what is what,
And blin' me to the irony
O' bein' a grocer 'neth the sun,

---

alowe ablaze *barms* ferments *barley bree* whisky
waesomeness woefulness

A lawyer gin Justice ope'd her een,
A pedant like an ant promoted,
A parson buttonholin' God,
Or ony cratur o' the Earth
Sma'-bookt to John Smith, High Street, Perth,
Or sic like vulgar gaffe o' life
Sub specie aeternitatis –
Nae void can fleg me hauf as much
As bein' mysel', whate'er I am,
Or, waur, bein' onybody else.

The nervous thistle's shiverin' like
A horse's skin aneth a cleg,
Or Northern Lichts or lustres o'
A soul that Daith has fastened on,
Or mornin' efter the nicht afore.

Shudderin' thistle, gi'e owre, gi'e owre . . .

Grey sand is churnin' in my lugs
The munelicht flets, and gantin' there
The grave o' a' mankind's laid bare
– On Hell itsel' the drawback rugs!

Nae man can ken his hert until
The tide o' life uncovers it,
And horror-struck he sees a pit
1450   *Returnin' life can never fill! . . .*

Thou art the facts in ilka airt
That breenge into infinity,
Criss-crossed wi' coontless ither facts
Nae man can follow, and o' which
He is himsel' a helpless pairt,
Held in their tangle as he were
A stick-nest in Ygdrasil!

---

sma'-bookt shrunken   *sic like* such similar   *fleg* frighten   *waur* worse
cleg gadfly   *flets* flits   *gantin'* yawning   *drawback rugs* undertow pulls
ilka airt every way   *breenge* spring

The less man sees the mair he is
Content wi't, but the mair he sees
The mair he kens hoo little o'
A' that there is he'll ever see,
And hoo it mak's confusion aye
The waur confoondit till at last
His brain inside his heid is like
Ariadne wi' an empty pirn,
Or like a birlin' reel frae which
A whale has rived the line awa'.

What better's a forhooied nest
Than shasloch scattered owre the grun'?

O hard it is for man to ken
He's no creation's goal nor yet
A benefitter by't at last –
A means to ends he'll never ken,
And as to michtier elements
The slauchtered brutes he eats to him
Or forms o' life owre sma' to see
Wi' which his heedless body swarms,
And a' man's thocht nae mair to them
Than ony moosewob to a man,
His Heaven to them the blinterin' o'
A snail-trail on their closet wa'!

For what's an atom o' a twig
That tak's a billion to an inch
To a' the routh o' shoots that mak'
The bygrowth o' the Earth aboot
The michty trunk o' Space that spreids
Ramel o' licht that ha'e nae end,
– The trunk wi' centuries for rings,
Comets for fruit, November sho'ers
For leafs that in its Autumns fa'
– And Man at maist o' sic a twig
Ane o' the coontless atoms is!

1475

---

pirn bobbin   *birlin'* whirling   *rived* torn   *forhooied* abandoned
shasloch loose straw   *moosewob* spider's web   *blinterin'* glistening
routh plenty   *ramel* branches

My sinnens and my veins are but
As muckle o' a single shoot
Wha's fibre I can ne'er unwaft
O' my wife's flesh and mither's flesh
And a' the flesh o' humankind,
And revelled thrums o' beasts and plants
As gangs to mak' twixt birth and daith
1500   A'e sliver for a microscope;
And a' the life o' Earth to be
Can never lift frae underneath
The shank o' which oor destiny's pairt
As heich's to stand forenenst the trunk
Stupendous as a windlestrae!

I'm under nae delusions, fegs!
The whuppin' sooker at wha's tip
Oor little point o' view appears,
A midget coom o' continents
Wi' blebs o' oceans set, sends up
The braith o' daith as weel as life,
And we maun braird anither tip
Oot owre us ere we wither tae,
And join the sentrice skeleton
As coral insects big their reefs.

What is the tree? As fer as Man's
Concerned it disna maitter
Gin but a giant thistle 'tis
That spreids eternal mischief there,
As I'm inclined to think.
Ruthless it sends its solid growth
Through mair than he can e'er conceive,
And braks his warlds abreid and rives
His Heavens to tatters on its horns.

---

sinnens sinews   *unwaft* unweave   *revelled thrums* ravelled threads
forenenst in relation to   *windlestrae* straw
whuppin' soooker whipping sucker of a tree   *coom* comb   *blebs* drops
braird sprout   *sentrice* scaffold-like   *abreid* asunder   *rives* tears

1525   The nature or the purpose o't
       He needna fash to spier, for he
       Is destined to be sune owre grown
       And hidden wi' the parent wud
       The spreidin' boughs in darkness hap,
       And a' its future life'll be
       Ootwith'm as he's ootwith his banes.

       Juist as man's skeleton has left
       Its ancient ape-like shape ahint,
       Sae states o' mind in turn gi'e way
       To different states, and quickly seem
       Impossible to later men,
       And Man's mind in its final shape
       Or lang'll seem a monkey's spook,
       And, strewth, to me the vera thocht
       O' Thocht already's fell like that!
       Yet still the cracklin' thorns persist
       In fitba' match and peepy show;
       To antic hay a dog-fecht's mair
       Than Jacob *v.* the Angel;
       And through a cylinder o' wombs,
       A star reflected in a dub,
       I see as 'twere my ain wild harns
       The ripple o' Eve's moniplies.

       And faith! yestreen in Cruivie's een
1550   Life rocked at midnicht in a tree,
       And in Gilsanquhar's glower I saw
       The taps o' waves 'neth which the warld
       Ga'ed rowin' like a jeelyfish,
       And whiles I canna look at Jean
       For fear I'd see the sunlicht turn
       Worm-like into the glaur again!

---

fash to spier trouble to ask *wud* wood *hap* cover *or lang* ere long
peepy show cinema *antic hay* grotesque dance *dub* puddle
harns brains *moniplies* intestines *glaur* primal ooze

A black leaf owre a white leaf twirls,
My liver's shadow on my soul,
And clots o' bluid loup oot frae stems
That back into the jungle rin,
Or in the waters underneath
Kelter like seaweed, while I hear
Abune the thunder o' the flood,
The voice that aince commanded licht
Sing 'Scots Wha Ha'e' and hyne awa'
Like Cruivie up a different glen,
And leave me like a mixture o'
A wee Scotch nicht and Judgment Day,
The bile, the Bible, and the *Scotsman*,
Poetry and pigs – Infernal Thistle,
Damnition haggis I've spewed up,
And syne return to like twa dogs!
Blin' Proteus wi' leafs or hands
Or flippers ditherin' in the lift
1575 – Thou Samson in a warld that has
Nae pillars but your cheengin' shapes
That dung doon, rise in ither airts
Like windblawn reek frae smoo'drin' ess!
– Hoo lang maun I gi'e aff your forms
O' plants and beasts and men and Gods
And like a doited Atlas bear
This steeple o' fish, this eemis warld,
Or, maniac heid wi' snakes for hair,
A Maenad, ape Aphrodite,
And scunner the Eternal sea?

Man needna fash and even noo
The cells that mak' a'e sliver wi'm,
The threidy knit he's woven wi',
'Ud fain destroy what sicht he has
O' this puir transitory stage,

---

kelter undulate   *hyne awa'* far away   *dung doon* dashed down
ither airts other ways
windblawn reek frae smoo'drin' ess windblown smoke from smouldering ashes
doited mad   *eemis* ill-poised   *scunner* disgust   *fash* trouble
wi'm with him   *threidy knit* thready knot

Yet tho' he kens the fragment is
O' little worth he e'er can view,
Jalousin' it's a cheatrie weed,
He tyauves wi' a' his micht and main
To keep his sicht despite his kind
Conspirin' as their nature is
'Gainst ocht wi' better sicht than theirs.

What gars him strive? He canna tell –
It may be nocht but cussedness.
1600 – At best he hopes for little mair
Than his suspicions to confirm,
To mock the sicht he hains sae weel
At last wi' a' he sees wi' it,
Yet, thistle or no', whate'er its end,
Aiblins the force that mak's it grow
And lets him see a kennin' mair
Than ither folk and fend his sicht
Agen their jealous plots awhile
'll use the poo'ers it seems to waste,
This purpose ser'd, in ither ways,
That may be better worth the bein'
– Or sae he dreams, syne mocks his dream
Till Life grows sheer awa' frae him,
And bratts o' darkness plug his een.

It may be nocht but cussedness,
But I'm content gin a' my thocht
Can dae nae mair than let me see,
Free frae desire o' happiness,
The foolish faiths o' ither men
In breedin', industry, and War,
Religion, Science, or ocht else
Gang smash – when I ha'e nane mysel',
Or better gin I share them tae,
Or mind at least a time I did!

---

jalousin' suspecting   *cheatrie* fraudulent   *tyauves* struggles
hains preserves   *kennin'* little bit   *fend* defend   *bratts* scum
mind remember

1625   Aye, this is Calvary – to bear
Your Cross wi' in you frae the seed,
And feel it grow by slow degrees
Until it rends your flesh apairt,
And turn, and see your fellow-men
In similar case but sufferin' less
Thro' bein' mair wudden frae the stert! . . .

I'm fu' o' a stickit God.
THAT'S *what's the maitter wi' me.*
Jean has stuck sic a fork in the wa'
That I row in agonie.

Mary never let dab.
SHE *was a canny wumman.*
She hedna a gaw in Joseph at a'
But, wow, this seecund comin'! . . .

Narodbogonosets[1] are my folk tae,
But in a sma' way nooadays –
A faitherly God wi' a lang white beard,
Or painted Jesus in a haze
O' blue and gowd, a gird aboot his heid
Or some sic thing. It's been a sair come-doon,
And the trade's nocht to what it was.
Unnatural practices are the cause.
Baith bairns and God'll be obsolete soon
(The twaesome gang thegither), and forsooth
1650   Scotland turn Eliot's waste – the Land o' Drouth.

But even as the stane the builders rejec'
Becomes the corner-stane, the time may be
When Scotland sall find oot its destiny,
And yield the *vse-chelovek*[2]

---

stickit frustrated
stick a fork in the wa' transfer the pain of childbirth from the woman to the man
row roll   *let dab* let on   *canny* cautious   *gaw* hold   *seecund* second
gird hoop   *Drouth* Drought

[1] God-bearers.
[2] The All-Man or Pan-Human.

– At a' events, owre Europe flaught atween,
My whim (and mair than whim) it pleases
To seek the haund o' Russia as a freen'
In workin' oot mankind's great synthesis . . .

Melville[1] (a Scot) kent weel hoo Christ's
Corrupted into creeds malign,
Begotten strife's pernicious brood
That claims for patron Him Divine.
(The Kirk in Scotland still I cry
Crooks whaur it canna crucify!)

Christ, bleedin' like the thistle's roses,
He saw – as I in similar case –
Maistly, in beauty and in fear,
'Ud 'paralyse the nobler race,
Smite or suspend, perplex, deter,
And, tortured, prove the torturer.'

And never mair a Scot sall tryst,
Abies on Calvary, wi' Christ,
Unless, mebbe, a poem like this'll
Exteriorise things in a thistle,
And gi'e him in this form forlorn
What Melville socht in vain frae Hawthorne[2] . . .

Spirit o' strife, destroy in turn
Syne this fule's Paradise, syne that;
In thee's in Calvaries that owrecome
Daith efter Daith let me be caught,

Or in the human form that hauds
Us in its ignominious thrall,
While on brute needs oor souls attend
Until disease and daith end all,

1675

---

flaught abased, stretched out   *abies* except   *syne . . . syne* now . . . then

[1] Herman Melville.
[2] Nathaniel Hawthorne – Eds.

81

Or in the grey deluded brain,
Reflectin' in anither field
The torments o' its parent flesh
In thocht-preventin' thocht concealed,

Or still in curst impossible mould,
Last thistle-shape men think to tak',
The soul, frae flesh and thocht set free,
On Heaven's strait if unseen rack.

There may be heicher forms in which
We can nae mair oor plicht define,
Because the agonies involved
'll bring us their ain anodyne.

Yet still we suffer and still sall,
Altho', puir fules, we mayna ken 't
As lang as like the thistle we
In coil and in recoil are pent.

1700

And ferrer than mankind can look
Ghast shapes that free but to transfix
Twine rose-crooned in their agonies,
And strive agen the endless pricks.

The dooble play that bigs and braks
In endless victory and defeat
Is in your spikes and roses shown,
And a' my soul is hagger'd wi't . . .

Be like the thistle, O my soul,
Heedless o' praise and quick to tak' affront,
And growin' like a mockery o' a'
Maist life can want or thole,
And manifest forevermair
Contempt o' ilka goal.

O' ilka goal – save ane alane;
To be yoursel', whatever that may be,

---

bigs builds   *hagger'd* hacked apart   *thole* endure

And as contemptuous o' that,
Kennin' nocht's worth the ha'en,
But certainty that nocht can be,
And hoo that certainty to gain.

For this you still maun grow and grope
In the abyss wi' ever-deepenin' roots
That croon your scunner wi' the grue
O' hopeless hope
1725 – And gin the abyss is bottomless,
Your growth'll never stop!...

What earthquake chitters oot
In the Thistle's oorie shape,
What gleids o' central fire
In its reid heids escape,
And whatna coonter forces
In growth and ingrowth graip
In an eternal clinch
In this ootcuissen form
That winna be outcast,
But triumphs at the last
(Owre a' abies itsel'
As fer as we can tell,
Sin' frae the Eden o' the world
Ilka man in turn is hurled,
And ilka gairden rins to waste
That was ever to his taste)?

O keep the Thistle 'yont the wa'
Owre which your skeletons you'll thraw.

I, in the Thistle's land,
As you[1] in Russia where
Struggle in giant form
Proceeds for evermair,

---

scunner disgust   grue revulsion   *chitters* trembles   *oorie* weird
gleids sparks   *whatna* what kind of   *graip* grip   *ootcuissen* rejected
abies except   *'yont the wa'* beyond the wall

[1] Dostoevski.

In my sma' measure bood
Address a similar task,
And for a share o' your
Appallin' genius ask.

Wha built in revelations
What maist men in reserves
(And only men confound!)
A better gift deserves
Frae ane wha like hissel
(As ant-heap unto mountain)
Needs big his life upon
The everloupin' fountain
That frae the Dark ascends
Whaur Life begins, Thocht ends
– A better gift deserves
Than thae wheen yatterin' nerves!

For mine's the clearest insicht
O' man's facility
For constant self-deception,
And hoo his mind can be
But as a floatin' iceberg
That hides aneth the sea
Its bulk: and hoo frae depths
O' an unfaddomed flood
Tensions o' nerves arise
And humours o' the blood
– Keethin's nane can trace
To their original place.

Hoo mony men to mak' a man
It tak's he kens wha kens Life's plan.

But there are flegsome deeps
Whaur the soul o' Scotland sleeps
That I to bottom need
To wauk Guid kens what deid,

1750

1775

---

bood intend to, must   *thae wheen yatterin'* these few chattering
keethin's appearances   *flegsome* frightening   *wauk* waken   *Guid* God
what deid which corpses

84

Play at stertle-a-stobie,
Wi' nation's dust for hobby,
Or wi' God's sel' commerce
For the makin' o' a verse.

'Melville, sea-compelling man,
Before whose wand Leviathan
Rose hoary-white upon the Deep,'[1]
What thou hast sown I fain 'ud reap
O' knowledge 'yont the human mind
In keepin' wi' oor Scottish kind,
And, thanks to thee, may aiblins reach
To what this Russian has to teach,
Closer than ony ither Scot,
Closer to me than my ain thocht,
Closer than my ain braith to me,
As close as to the Deity
Approachable in whom appears

1800   This Christ o' the neist thoosand years.

As frae your baggit wife
You turned whenever able,
And often when you werena,
Unto the gamin' table,
And opened wide to ruin
Your benmaist hert, aye brewin'
A horror o' whatever
Seemed likely to deliver
You frae the senseless strife
In which alane is life,
– As Burns in Edinburgh
Breenged arse-owre-heid thoro'
A' it could be the spur o'
To pleuch his sauted furrow,
And turned frae a' men honour

---

stertle-a-stobie chasing dust puffs baggit big bellied benmaist inmost
breenged arse-owre-heid thoro' burst regardless through pleuch plough
sauted salted

[1] Quoted from Robert Buchanan.

To what could only scunner
Wha thinks that common-sense
Can e'er be but a fence
To keep a soul worth ha'en
Frae what it s'ud be daein'
– Sae I in turn maun gie
My soul to misery,
Daidle disease
Upon my knees,
And welcome madness
Wi' exceedin' gladness
– Aye, open wide my hert
To a' the thistle's smert.

And a' the hopes o' men
Sall be like wiles then
To gar my soul betray
Its only richtfu' way,
Or as a couthie wife
That seeks nae mair frae life
Than domesticity
E'en wi' the likes o' me –
As gin I could be carin'
For her or for her bairn
When on my road I'm farin'
– O I can spend a nicht
In ony man's Delicht
Or wi' ony wumman born
– But aye be aff the morn!

In a' the inklin's cryptic,
Then, o' an epileptic,
I ha'e been stood in you
And droukit in their grue
Till I can see richt through
Ilk weakness o' my frame
And ilka dernin' shame,
And can employ the same

1825

1850

---

daidle dandle   *couthie* cosy and decent   *droukit* drenched
grue revulsion   *dernin'* hiding

To jouk the curse o' fame,
Lowsed frae the dominion
O' popular opinion,
And risen at last abune
The thistle like a mune
That looks serenely doon
On what queer things there are
In an inferior star
That couldna be, or see,
Themsel's, except in me.

Wi' burnt-oot hert and poxy face
I sall illumine a' the place,
And there is ne'er a fount o' grace
That isna in a similar case.

Let a' the thistle's growth
Be as a process, then,
My spirit's gane richt through,
And needna threid again,
Tho' in it sall be haud'n
For aye the feck o' men
Wha's queer contortions there
As memories I ken,
As memories o' my ain
O' mony an ancient pain.
But sin' wha'll e'er wun free
Maun tak' like coorse to me,
A fillip I wad gi'e
Their eccentricity,
And leave the lave to dree
Their weirdless destiny.

It's no' withoot regret
That I maun follow yet
The road that led me past
Humanity sae fast,

1875

---

jouk dodge   *lowsed* freed   *haud'n* held   *the lave* the rest
dree endure   *weirdless* purposeless

Yet scarce can gi'e a fate
That is at last mair fit
To them wha tak' that gait
Than theirs wha winna ha'e't,
Seein' that nae man can get
By ony airt or wile,
A destiny quite worth while
As fer as he can tell
– Or even you yoursel'!

And O! I canna thole
Aye yabblin' o' my soul,
And fain I wad be free
O' my eternal me,
Nor fare mysel' alane
1900   – Withoot that tae be gane,
And this, I ha'e nae doot,
This road'll bring aboot.

The munelicht that owre clear defines
The thistle's shrill cantankerous lines
E'en noo whiles insubstantialises
Its grisly form and 'stead devises
A maze o' licht, a siller-frame,
As 'twere God's dream frae which it came,
Ne'er into bein' coorsened yet,
The essence lowin' pure in it,
As tho' the fire owrecam' the clay,
And left its wraith in endless day.

These are the moments when a' sense
Like mist is vanished and intense
Magic emerges frae the dense
Body o' bein' and beeks immense
As, like a ghinn oot o' a bottle,
Daith rises frae's when oor lives crottle.

---

gait way   *winna ha'e't* will not have it   *airt* way   *thole* endure
yabblin' gabbling   *lowin'* glowing   *owrecam'* overcame   *beeks* shows
crottle crumble

These are the moments when my sang
Clears its white feet frae oot amang
My broken thocht, and moves as free
As souls frae bodies when they dee.
There's naething left o' me ava'
Save a' I'd hoped micht whiles befa'.

1925 Sic sang to men is little worth.
It has nae message for the earth.
Men see their warld turned tapsalteerie,
Drookit in a licht owre eerie,
Or sent birlin' like a peerie –
Syne it turns a' they've kent till then
To shapes they can nae langer ken.

Men canna look on nakit licht.
It flings them back wi' darkened sicht,
And een that canna look at it,
Maun draw earth closer roond them yet
Or, their sicht tint, find nocht insteed
That answers to their waefu' need.

And yet this essence frae the clay
In dooble form aye braks away,
For, in addition to the licht,
There is an e'er-increasin' nicht,
A nicht that is the bigger and
Gangs roond licht like an airn band
That noo and then mair tichtly grips
And snuffs it in a black eclipse,
But rings it maistly as a brough
The mune, till it's juist bricht enough –
O wull I never lowse a licht
I canna dowse again in spite,
1950 Or dull to haud within my sicht?

The thistle canna vanish quite.
Inside a' licht its shape maun glint,
A spirit wi' a skeleton in't.

---

ava' at all	*tapsalteerie* topsy-turvy	*drookit* drenched	*birlin'* spinning
peerie top	*tint* lost	*airn* iron	*brough* halo	*lowse* set free

The world, the flesh, 'll bide in us
As in the fire the unburnt buss,
Or as frae sire to son we gang
And coontless corpses in us thrang.

And e'en the glory that descends
I kenna whence on *me* depends,
And shapes itsel' to what is left
Whaur I o' me ha'e me bereft,
And still the form is mine, altho'
A force to which I ne'er could grow
Is movin' in't as 'twere a sea
That lang syne drooned the last o' me
– That drooned afore the warld began
A' that could ever come frae Man.

And as at sicna times am I,
I wad ha'e Scotland to my eye
Until I saw a timeless flame
Tak' Auchtermuchty for a name,
And kent that Ecclefechan stood
As pairt o' an eternal mood.

1975

Ahint the glory comes the nicht
As Maori to London's ruins,
And I'm amused to see the plicht
O' Licht as't in the black tide droons,
Yet even in the brain o' Chaos
For Scotland I wad hain a place,
And let Tighnabruaich still
Be pairt and paircel o' its will,
And Culloden, black as Hell,
A knowledge it has o' itsel'.

Thou, Dostoevski, understood,
Wha had your ain land in your bluid,
And into it as in a mould

---

buss bush   *thrang* throng   *kenna* don't know   *lang syne* long ago
sicna such   *hain* preserve

The passion o' your bein' rolled,
Inherited in turn frae Heaven
Or sources fer abune it even.

Sae God retracts in endless stage
Through angel, devil, age on age,
Until at last his infinite natur'
Walks on earth a human cratur'
(Or less than human as to my een
The people are in Aiberdeen);
Sae man returns in endless growth
Till God in him again has scouth.

For sic a loup towards wisdom's croon
Hoo fer a man maun base him doon,
Hoo plunge aboot in Chaos ere
He finds his needfu' fittin' there,
The matrix oot o' which sublime
Serenity sall soar in time!

Ha'e I the cruelty I need,
Contempt and syne contempt o' that,
And still contempt in endless meed
That I may never yet be caught
In ony satisfaction, or
Bird-lime that winna let me soar?

Is Scotland big enough to be
A symbol o' that force in me,
In wha's divine inebriety
A sicht abune contempt I'll see?

For a' that's Scottish is in me,
As a' things Russian were in thee,
And I in turn 'ud be an action
To pit in a concrete abstraction
My country's contrair qualities,
And mak' a unity o' these

2000

---

scouth scope   *fittin'* footing

Till my love owre its history dwells,
As owretone to a peal o' bells.

And in this heicher stratosphere
As bairn at giant at thee I peer . . .

O Jean, in whom my spirit sees,
2025 *Clearer than through whisky or disease,*
Its dernin' nature, wad the searchin' licht
Oor union raises poor'd owre me the nicht.

I'm faced wi' aspects o' mysel'
At last wha's portent nocht can tell,
Save that sheer licht o' life that when we're joint
Loups through me like a fire a' else t' aroint.

Clear my lourd flesh, and let me move
In the peculiar licht o' love,
As aiblins in Eternity men may
When their swack souls nae mair are clogged wi' clay.

Be thou the licht in which I stand
Entire, in thistle-shape, as planned,
And no' hauf-hidden and hauf-seen as here
In munelicht, whisky, and in fleshly fear,

In fear to look owre closely at
The grisly form in which I'm caught,
In sic a reelin' and imperfect licht
Sprung frae incongruous elements the nicht!

But were't by thou they were shone on,
Then wad I ha'e nae dreid to con
The ugsome problems shapin' in my soul,
Or gin I hed – certes, nae fear you'd thole!

---

dernin' hidden, lurking   *the nicht* tonight   *t' aroint* to expel
lourd heavy   *swack* supple   *ugsome* horrible   *certes* certainly
thole tolerate

Be in this fibre like an eye,
And ilka turn and twist descry,
2050 Hoo here a leaf, a spine, a rose – or as
The purpose o' the poo'er that brings 't to pass.

Syne liberate me frae this tree,
As wha had there imprisoned me,
The end achieved – or show me at the least
Mair meanin' in't, and hope o' bein' released.

I tae ha'e heard Eternity drip water
(Aye water, water!), drap by drap
On the a'e nerve, like lichtnin', I've become,
And heard God passin' wi' a bobby's feet
Ootby in the lang coffin o' the street
– Seen stang by chitterin' knottit stang loup oot
Uncrushed by th' echoes o' the thunderin' boot,
Till a' the dizzy lint-white lines o' torture made
A monstrous thistle in the space aboot me,
A symbol o' the puzzle o' man's soul
– And in my agony been pridefu' I could still
Tine nae least quiver or twist, watch ilka point
Like a white-het bodkin ripe my inmaist hert,
And aye wi' clearer pain that brocht nae anodyne,
But rose for ever to a fer crescendo
Like eagles that ootsoar wi' skinklan' wings
The thieveless sun they blin'
        – And pridefu' still
That 'yont the sherp wings o' the eagles fleein'
2075 Aboot the dowless pole o' Space,
Like leafs aboot a thistle-shank, my bluid
Could still thraw roses up
        – And up!

O rootless thistle through the warld that's pairt o' you,
Gin you'd withstand the agonies still to come,
You maun send roots doon to the deeps unkent,
Fer deeper than it's possible for ocht to gang,

---

stang paroxysm   *chitterin'* shivering   *tine* lose   *het* hot   *ripe* search
skinklan' shining   *thieveless* dull, powerless   *dowless* imponderable

93

Savin' the human soul,
Deeper than God himsel' has knowledge o',
Whaur lichtnin's canna probe that cleave the warld,
Whaur only in the entire dark there's founts o' strength
Eternity's poisoned draps can never file,
And muckle roots thicken, deef to bobbies' feet.

A mony-brainchin' candelabra fills
The lift and's lowin' wi' the stars;
The Octopus Creation is wallopin'
In coontless faddoms o' a nameless sea.
I am the candelabra, and burn
My endless candles to an Unkent God.
I am the mind and meanin' o' the octopus
That thraws its empty airms through a' th' Inane.

And a' the bizzin' suns ha'e bigged
Their kaims upon the surface o' the sea.
My lips may feast for ever, but my guts
Ken naething o' the Food o' Gods.

'Let there be Licht,' said God, and there was
A little: but He lacked the poo'er
To licht up mair than pairt o' space at aince,
And there is lots o' darkness that's the same
As gin He'd never spoken
        – Mair darkness than there's licht,
And dwarfin't to a candle-flame,
A spalin' candle that'll sune gang oot.
– Darkness comes closer to us than the licht,
And is oor natural element. We peer oot frae't
Like cats' een bleezin' in a goustrous nicht
(Whaur there is nocht to find but stars
That look like ither cats' een),
Like cats' een, and there is nocht to find
Savin' we turn them in upon oorsels;
Cats canna.

2100

---

file defile   deef deaf   bizzin' buzzing   bigged built
kaims honey-combs   spalin' guttering   goustrous frightful, stormy

　　　　　Darkness is wi' us a' the time, and Licht
But veesits pairt o' us, the wee-est pairt
Frae time to time on a short day atween twa nichts.
Nae licht is thrawn on *them* by ony licht.
Licht thraws nae licht upon itsel';
But in the darkness them wha's een
Nae fleetin' lichts ha'e dazzled and deceived
Find qualities o' licht, keener than ony licht,
2125　　Keen and abidin',
That show the nicht unto itsel',
And syne the licht,
That queer extension o' the dark,
That seems a separate and a different thing,
And, seemin' sae, has lang confused the dark,
And set it at cross-purposes wi' itsel'.

　　　　　O little Life
In which Daith guises and deceives itsel',
Joy that mak's Grief a Janus,
Hope that is Despair's fause-face,
And Guid and Ill that are the same,
Save as the chance licht fa's!

And yet the licht is there,
Whether frae within or frae withoot.
The conscious Dark can use it, dazzled nor deceived.
The licht is there, and th' instinct for it,
Pairt o' the Dark and o' the need to guise,
To deceive and be deceived,
But let us then be undeceived;
When we deceive,
When we deceive oorsels.
Let us enjoy deceit, this instinct in us.
Licht cheenges naething,
And gin there is a God wha made the licht
2150　　We are adapted to receive,
He cheenged naething,
And hesna kythed Hissel!

---

kythed Hissel revealed Himself

Save in this licht that fa's whaur the Auld Nicht was,
Showin' naething that the Darkness didna hide,
And gin it shows a pairt o' that
Confoondin' mair than it confides
Ev'n in that.

The epileptic thistle twitches
(A trick o' wund or mune or een – or whisky).
A brain laid bare,
A nervous system,
The skeleton wi' which men labour
And bring to life in Daith
– I, risen frae the deid, ha'e seen
My deid man's eunuch offspring.
– The licht frae bare banes whitening evermair,
Frae twitchin' nerves thrawn aff,
Frae nakit thocht,
Works in the Darkness like a fell disease,
A hungry acid and a cancer,
Disease o' Daith-in-Life and Life-in-Daith.

O for a root in some untroubled soil,
Some cauld soil 'yont this fevered warld,
That 'ud draw darkness frae a virgin source,
2175   And send it slow and easefu' through my veins,
Release the tension o' my grisly leafs,
Withdraw my endless spikes,
Move coonter to the force in me that hauds
Me raxed and rigid and ridiculous
          – And let my roses drap
Like punctured ba's that at a Fair
Fa' frae the loupin' jet!
          – Water again! . . .

Omsk and the Calton turn again to dust,
The suns and stars fizz out with little fuss,
The bobby booms away and seems to bust,
And leaves the world to darkness and to us.

---

raxed stretched   *ba's* balls

The circles of our hungry thought
Swing savagely from pole to pole.
Death and the Raven drift above
The graves of Sweeney's body and soul.

My name is Norval. On the Grampian Hills
It is forgotten, and deserves to be.
So are the Grampian Hills and all the people
Who ever heard of either them or me.

What's in a name? From pole to pole
Our interlinked mentality spins.
I know that you are Deosil, and suppose
That therefore I am Widdershins.

2200   Do you reverse? Shall us? Then let's.
Cyclone and Anti? – how absurd!
She should know better at her age.
Auntie's an ass, upon my word.

This is the sort of thing they teach
The Scottish children in the school.
Poetry, patriotism, manners –
No wonder I am such a fool . . .

Hoo can I graipple wi' the thistle syne,
Be intricate as it and up to a' its moves?
A' airts its sheenin' points are loupin' 'yont me,
Quhile still the firmament it proves.

And syne it's like a wab in which the warld
Squats like a spider, quhile the mune and me
Are taigled in an endless corner o't
Tyauvin' fecklessly . . .

The wan leafs shak' atour us like the snaw.
Here is the cavaburd in which Earth's tint.
There's naebody but Oblivion and us,
Puir gangrel buddies, waunderin' hameless in't.

---

quhile while   *taigled* tangled   *tyauvin' fecklessly* struggling uselessly
atour around   *cavaburd* snowstorm   *tint* lost   *gangrel buddies* vagrants

The stars are larochs o' auld cottages,
And a' Time's glen is fu' o' blinnin' stew.
Nae freen'ly lozen skimmers: and the wund
Rises and separates even me and you.[1]

I ken nae Russian and you ken nae Scots.
2225   We canna tell oor voices frae the wund.
The snaw is seekin' everywhere: oor herts
At last like roofless ingles it has f'und,

And gethers there in drift on endless drift,
Oor broken herts that it can never fill;
And still – its leafs like snaw, its growth like wund –
The thistle rises and forever will! . . .

The thistle rises and forever will,
Getherin' the generations under't.
This is the monument o' a' they were,
And a' they hoped and wondered.

The barren tree, dry leafs and cracklin' thorns,
This is the mind o' a' humanity
– The empty intellect that left to grow
'll let nocht ither be.

Lo! It has choked the sunlicht's gowden grain,
And strangled syne the white hairst o' the mune.
Thocht that mak's a' the food o' nocht but Thocht
Is reishlin' grey abune . . .

O fitly frae oor cancerous soil
May this heraldic horror rise!
The Presbyterian thistle flourishes,
And its ain roses crucifies . . .

---

larochs ruined sites   *blinnin' stew* blinding snowstorm
freen'ly lozen skimmers friendly window glimmers   *ingles* hearths, fireplaces
hairst harvest   *reishlin'* rustling

[1] Dostoevski.

No' Edinburgh Castle or the fields
O' Bannockburn or Flodden
2250   Are dernin' wi' the miskent soul
Scotland sae lang has hod'n.

It hauds nae pew in ony kirk,
The soul Christ cam' to save;
Nae R.S.A.'s ha'e pentit it,
F.S.A.'s fund its grave.

Is it alive or deid? I show
My hert – wha will can see.
The secret clyre in Scotland's life
Has brust and reams through me,

A whummlin' sea in which is heard
The clunk o' nameless banes;
A grisly thistle dirlin' shrill
Abune the broken stanes.

Westminster Abbey nor the Fleet,
Nor England's Constitution, but
In a' the michty city there,
You mind a'e fleggit slut,

As Tolstoi o' Lucerne alane
Minded a'e beggar minstrel seen!
The woundit side draws a' the warld.
Barbarians ha'e lizards' een.

Glesca's a gless whaur Magdalene's
Discovered in a million crimes.
Christ comes again – wheesht, whatna bairn
2275   In backlands cries betimes?

---

dernin' hiding   *hod'n* hidden   *clyre* diseased gland   *brust* burst
reams foams   *whummlin'* overwhelming   *dirlin'* vibrating
mind remember   *a'e fleggit* one frightened   *wheesht* hush
whatna whatever   *backlands* slum tenements

Hard faces prate o' their success,
And pickle-makers awn the hills.[1]
There is nae life in a' the land
But this infernal Thistle kills . . .

Nae mair I see
As aince I saw
Mysel' in the thistle
Harth and haw!

Nel suo profondo vidi che s'interna,
Legato con amore in un volume,
(Or else by Hate, fu' aft the better Love)
Ciò che per l'universo si squaderna;

Sustanze e accidenti e lor costume,
Quasi conflati insieme, per tal modo.
(The michty thistle in wha's boonds I rove)
Che ciò ch' i' dico è un semplice lume.[2]

And kent and was creation
In a' its coontless forms,
Or glitterin' in raw sunlicht,
Or dark wi' hurrying storms.

But what's the voice
That sings in me noo?
– A'e hauf o' me tellin'
The tither it's fou!

2300 It's the voice o' the Sooth
That's held owre lang
My Viking North
Wi' its siren sang . . .

Fier comme un Ecossais.

---

awn own *harth* lean *haw* hollow *fu' aft* very often *a'e hauf* one half

[1] MacDiarmid had in mind Perrins of Ardross Castle – Eds.
[2] Wicksteed's translation of Dante's Italian (*Paradiso*, canto xxxiii, 85-90) is as follows: 'Within its depths I saw ingathered, bound by love in one volume, the scattered leaves of all the universe; substance and accidents and their relations, as though together fused, after such fashion that what I tell of is one simple flame.'

If a' that I can be's nae mair
Than what mankind's been yet, I'll no'
Begink the instincts thistlewise
That dern – and canna show.

Damned threids and thrums and skinny shapes
O' a' that micht, and su'd, ha' been
– Life onyhow at ony price! –
In sic I'll no' be seen!

Fier comme un Ecossais.

The wee reliefs we ha'e in booze,
Or wun at times in carnal states,
May hide frae us but canna cheenge
The silly horrors o' oor fates.

Fier – comme un Ecossais!

There's muckle in the root,
That never can wun oot,
Or't owre what is 'ud sweep
Like a thunderstorm owre sheep.

But shadows whiles upcreep,
And heavy tremors leap. . . .
C'wa', Daith, again, sned Life's vain shoot,
And your ain coonsel keep! . . .

Time like a bien wife,
Truth like a dog's gane –
The bien wife's gane to the aumrie
To get the puir dog a bane.

Opens the aumrie door,
And lo! the skeleton's there,
And the gude dog, Truth, has gotten
Banes for evermair . . .

2325

---

begink cheat   *dern* hide   *thrums* loose ends   *sned* lop off
bien complacent and well-off   *aumrie* cupboard

Maun I tae perish in the keel o' Heaven,
And is this fratt upon the air the ply
O' cross-brath'd cordage that in gloffs and gowls
Brak's up the vision o' the warld's bricht gy?

Ship's tackle and an eemis cairn o' fraucht
Darker than clamourin' veins are roond me yet,
A plait o' shadows thicker than the flesh,
A fank o' tows that binds me hand and fit.

What gin the gorded fullyery on hie
And a' the fanerels o' the michty ship
Gi'e back mair licht than fa's upon them ev'n
Gin sic black ingangs haud us in their grip?

Grugous thistle, to my een
Your widdifow ramel evince
Sibness to snakes wha's coils
2350   Rin coonter airts at yince,
And fain I'd follow each
Gin you the trick'll teach.

Blin' root to bleezin' rose,
Through a' the whirligig
O' shanks and leafs and jags
What sends ye sic a rig?
Bramble yokin' earth and heaven,
Till they're baith stramulyert driven!

Roses to lure the lift
And roots to wile the clay
And wuppit brainches syne
To claught them 'midyards tae
Till you've the precious pair
Like hang'd men dancin' there,

---

fratt fretwork   *cross-brath'd* cross-braided   *gloffs and gowls* dark and light
gy spectacle   *eemis cairn o' fraucht* unsteady stone-pile of cargo   *plait* pleat
fank o' tows coil of rope   *fit* foot   *gorded fullyery on hie* frosted foliage on high
fanerels loose, flapping things   *ingangs haud* deficiencies hold   *grugous* ugly
widdifow ramel perverse branches   *sibness* kinship   *yince* once
stramulyert aghast   *wuppit* binding   *claught* clutch
'midyards together in the middle

102

Wi' mony a seely prickle
You'll fleg a sunburst oot,
Or kittle earthquakes up
Wi' an amusin' root,
While, kilted in your tippet,
They still can mak' their rippit . . .

And let me pit in guid set terms
My quarrel wi' th' owre sonsy rose,
That roond aboot its devotees
A fair fat cast o' aureole throws
2375   That blinds them, in its mirlygoes,
To the necessity o' foes.

Upon their King and System I
Glower as on things that whiles in pairt
I may admire (at least for them),
But wi' nae claim upon my hert,
While a' their pleasure and their pride
Ootside me lies – and there maun bide.

Ootside me lies – and mair than that,
For I stand still for forces which
Were subjugated to mak' way
For England's poo'er, and to enrich
The kinds o' English, and o' Scots,
The least congenial to my thoughts.

Hauf his soul a Scot maun use
Indulgin' in illusions,
And hauf in gettin' rid o' them
And comin' to conclusions
Wi' the demoralisin' dearth
O' onything worth while on Earth . . .

I'm weary o' the rose as o' my brain,
And for a deeper knowledge I am fain
Than frae this noddin' object I can gain.

---

seely happy   *fleg* frighten   *kittle* tickle
kilted in your tippet hanging in your snare   *mak' their rippit* raise a rumpus
th' owre sonsy rose the too contented English rose   *mirlygoes* dazzle
bide remain

Beauty is a'e thing, but it tines anither
(For, fegs, they never can be f'und thegither),
2400   And 'twixt the twa it's no' for me to swither.

As frae the grun' sae thocht frae men springs oot,
A ferlie that tells little o' its source, I doot,
And has nae vera fundamental root.

And cauld agen my hert are laid
The words o' Plato when he said,
'God o' geometry is made.'

Frae my ain mind I fa' away,
That never yet was feared to say
What turned the souls o' men to clay,

Nor cared gin truth frae me ootsprung
In ne'er a leed o' ony tongue
That ever in a heid was hung.

I ken hoo much oor life is fated
Aince its first cell is animated,
The fount frae which the flesh is jetted.

I ken hoo lourd the body lies
Upon the spirit when it flies
And fain abune its stars 'ud rise.

And see I noo a great wheel move,
And a' the notions that I love
Drap into stented groove and groove?

It maitters not my mind the day,
Nocht maitters that I strive to dae,
– For the wheel moves on in its ain way.

2425   I sall be moved as it decides
To look at Life frae ither sides;
Rejoice, rebel, its turn abides.

---

swither hesitate   ferlie marvel   cauld agen cold against
ne'er a leed never a language   lourd heavy   stented appointed

And as I see the great wheel spin
There flees a licht frae't lang and thin
That Earth is like a snaw-ba' in.

(To the uncanny thocht I clutch
– The nature o' man's soul is such
That it can ne'er wi' life tine touch.

Man's mind is in God's image made,
And in its wildest dreams arrayed
In pairt o' Truth is still displayed.)

Then suddenly I see as weel
As me spun roon' within the wheel,
The helpless forms o' God and Deil.

And on a birlin' edge I see
Wee Scotland squattin' like a flea,
And dizzy wi' the speed, and me!

I've often thrawn the warld frae me,
Into the Pool o' Space, to see
The Circles o' Infinity,

Or like a flat stane gar'd it skite,
A Morse code message writ in licht
That yet I couldna read aricht.

The skippin' sparks, the ripples, rit
Like skritches o' a grain o' grit
'Neth Juggernaut in which I sit.

Twenty-six thoosand years it tak's
Afore a'e single roond it mak's,
And syne it melts as it were wax.

The Phœnix guise 't'll rise in syne
Is mair than Euclid or Einstein
Can dream o' or's in dreams o' mine.

---

snaw-ba' snowball   *tine* lose   *birlin'* spinning   *skite* skip   *rit* scrape
skritches scratches

Upon the huge circumference are
As neebor points the Heavenly War
That dung doun Lucifer sae far,

And that upheaval in which I
Sodgered 'neth the Grecian sky
And in Italy and Marseilles,

And there isna room for men
Wha the haill o' history ken
To pit a pin twixt then and then.

Whaur are Bannockburn and Flodden?
– O' a'e grain like facets hod'n,
Little wars (twixt that which God in

Focht and won, and that which He
Took baith sides in hopelessly),
Less than God or I can see.

By whatna cry o' mine oot-topped
Sall be a' men ha'e sung and hoped
2475   When to a'e note they're telescoped?

And Jesus and a nameless ape
Collide and share the selfsame shape
That nocht terrestrial can escape?

But less than this nae man need try.
He'd better be content to eye
The wheel in silence whirlin' by.

Nae verse is worth a ha'et until
It can join issue wi' the Will
That raised the Wheel and spins it still,

But a' the music that mankind
'S made yet is to the Earth confined,
Poo'erless to reach the general mind,

---

dung doun dashed down   *sodgered* soldiered   *o' a'e* of one single
hod'n held   *focht* fought   *ha'et* whit

106

Poo'erless to reach the neist star e'en,
That as a pairt o'ts sel' is seen,
And only men can tell between.

Yet I exult oor sang has yet
To grow wings that'll cairry it
Ayont its native speck o' grit,

And I exult to find in me
The thocht that this can ever be,
A hope still for humanity.

For gin the sun and mune at last
Are as a neebor's lintel passed,
The wheel'll tine its stature fast,

2500   And birl in time inside oor heids
Till we can thraw oot conscious gleids
That draw an answer to oor needs,

Or if nae answer still we find
Brichten till a' thing is defined
In the huge licht-beams o' oor kind,

And if we still can find nae trace
Ahint the Wheel o' ony Face,
There'll be a glory in the place,

And we may aiblins swing content
Upon the wheel in which we're pent
In adequate enlightenment.

Nae ither thocht can mitigate
The horror o' the endless Fate
A'thing's whirled in predestinate.

O whiles I'd fain be blin' to it,
As men wha through the ages sit,
And never move frae aff the bit,

---

e'en even   *gleids* sparks   *a'thing* everything   *the bit* the same place

Wha hear a Burns or Shakespeare sing,
Yet still their ain bit jingles string,
As they were worth the fashioning.

Whatever Scotland is to me,
Be it aye pairt o' a' men see
O' Earth and o' Eternity

Wha winna hide their heids in't till
It seems the haill o' Space to fill,
As 'twere an unsurmounted hill.

He canna Scotland see wha yet
Canna see the Infinite,
And Scotland in true scale to it.

Nor blame I muckle, wham atour
Earth's countries blaw, a pickle stour,
To sort wha's grains they ha'e nae poo'er.

E'en stars are seen thegither in
A'e skime o' licht as grey as tin
Flyin' on the wheel as 'twere a pin.

Syne ither systems ray on ray
Skinkle past in quick array
While it is still the self-same day,

A'e day o' a' the million days
Through which the soul o' man can gaze
Upon the wheel's incessant blaze,

Upon the wheel's incessant blaze
As it were on a single place
That twinklin' filled the howe o' space.

A'e point is a' that it can be,
I wis nae man 'll ever see
The rest o' the rotundity.

2525

---

ain bit own pathetic   *wham atour* them who around
pickle stour a dust of small particles   *a'e skime* a single glimmer
skinkle twinkle   *howe* void   *wis* know

Impersonality sall blaw
Through me as 'twere a bluffert o' snaw
To scour me o' my sense o' awe,

A bluffert o' snaw, the licht that flees
Within the Wheel, and Freedom gi'es
Frae Dust and Daith and a' Disease,

– The drumlie doom that only weighs
On them wha ha'ena seen their place
Yet in creation's lichtnin' race,

In the movement that includes
As a tide's resistless floods
A' their movements and their moods –

Until disinterested we,
O' a' oor auld delusions free,
Lowe in the wheel's serenity

As conscious items in the licht,
And keen to keep it clear and bricht
In which the haill machine is dight,

The licht nae man has ever seen
Till he has felt that he's been gi'en
The stars themsels insteed o' een,

And often wi' the sun has glowered
At the white mune until it cowered,
As when by new thocht auld's o'erpowered.

Oor universe is like an e'e
Turned in, man's benmaist hert to see,
And swamped in subjectivity.

But whether it can use its sicht
To bring what lies withoot to licht
To answer's still ayont my micht.

2550

2575

---

bluffert blast   *drumlie* troubled   *lowe* flame   *dight* arrayed
benmaist inmost   *withoot* outside

But when that inturned look has brocht
To licht what still in vain it's socht
Ootward maun be the bent o' thocht.

And organs may develop syne
Responsive to the need divine
O' single-minded humankin'.

The function, as it seems to me,
O' Poetry is to bring to be
At lang, lang last that unity . . .

But wae's me on the weary wheel!
Higgledy-piggledy in't we reel,
And little it cares hoo we may feel.

Twenty-six thoosand years 't'll tak'
For it to threid the Zodiac
– A single roond o' the wheel to mak'!

Lately it turned – I saw mysel'
In sic a company doomed to mell,
I micht ha'e been in Dante's Hell.

It shows hoo little the best o' men
E'en o' themsels at times can ken
– I sune saw *that* when I gaed ben.

2600   The lesser wheel within the big
That moves as merry as a grig,
Wi' mankind in its whirligig,

And hasna turned a'e circle yet
Tho' as it turns we slide in it,
And needs maun tak' the place we get.

I felt it turn, and syne I saw
John Knox and Clavers in my raw,
And Mary Queen o' Scots ana',

---

mell mix   *gaed ben* entered   *grig* lively child   *raw* row, tier

And Rabbie Burns and Weelum Wallace,
And Carlyle lookin' unco gallus,
And Harry Lauder (to enthrall us).

And as I looked I saw them a',
A' the Scots baith big and sma',
That e'er the braith o' life did draw.

'Mercy o' Gode, I canna thole
Wi' sic an orra mob to roll.'
– 'Wheesht! It's for the guid o' your soul.'

'But what's the meanin', what's the sense?'
   – 'Men shift but by experience.
'Twixt Scots there is nae difference.

They canna learn, sae canna move,
But stick for aye to their auld groove
– The only race in History who've

Bidden in the same category
Frae stert to present o' their story,
And deem their ignorance their glory.

The mair they differ, mair the same.
The wheel can whummle a' but them,
– They ca' their obstinacy "Hame,"

And "Puir Auld Scotland" bleat wi' pride,
And wi' their minds made up to bide
A thorn in a' the wide world's side.

There ha'e been Scots wha ha'e ha'en thochts,
They're strewn through maist o' the various lots
– Sic traitors are nae langer Scots!'

'But in this huge ineducable
Heterogeneous hotch and rabble,
Why am I condemned to squabble?'

2625

---

unco gallus extremely wild, unmanageable   *thole* stand
whummle overturn   *hotch* swarm

'A Scottish poet maun assume
The burden o' his people's doom,
And dee to brak' their livin' tomb.

Mony ha'e tried, but a' ha'e failed.
Their sacrifice has nocht availed.
Upon the thistle they're impaled.

You maun choose but gin ye'd see
Anither category ye
Maun tine your nationality.'

And I look at a' the random
Band the wheel leaves whaur it fand 'em
      'Auch, to Hell,
I'll tak' it to avizandum.' . . .

O wae's me on the weary wheel,
And fain I'd understand them!

And blessin' on the weary wheel
Whaurever it may land them! . . .

But aince Jean kens what I've been through
The nicht, I dinna doot it,
She'll ope her airms in welcome true,
And clack nae mair aboot it . . .

   * * * * *

The stars like thistle's roses floo'er
The sterile growth o' Space ootour,
That clad in bitter blasts spreids oot
Frae me, the sustenance o' its root.

O fain I'd keep my hert entire,
Fain hain the licht o' my desire,
But ech! the shinin' streams ascend,
And leave me empty at the end.

2650

---

dee die *fand* found
tak' it to avizandum take under judicial advisement, to defer any decision
clack talk *ootour* out over *hain* preserve

For aince it's toomed my hert and brain,
The thistle needs maun fa' again.
– But a' its growth 'll never fill
The hole it's turned my life intill! . . .

Yet ha'e I Silence left, the croon o' a'.

No' her, wha on the hills langsyne I saw
Liftin' a foreheid o' perpetual snaw.

No' her, wha in the how-dumb-deid o' nicht
Kyths, like Eternity in Time's despite.

No' her, withooten shape, wha's name is Daith,
No' Him, unkennable abies to faith

– God whom, gin e'er He saw a man, 'ud be
E'en mair dumfooner'd at the sicht than he

– But Him, whom nocht in man or Deity,
Or Daith or Dreid or Laneliness can touch,
Wha's deed owre often and has seen owre much.

O I ha'e Silence left

                    – 'And weel ye micht,'
Sae Jean'll say, 'efter sic a nicht!'

2675

---

toomed emptied   *langsyne* long ago
how-dumb-deid uttermost depths of midnight   *kyths* appears   *abies* except
dumfooner'd dumbfoundered

113

Lourd on My Hert

Lourd on my hert as winter lies
The state that Scotland's in the day.
Spring to the North has aye come slow
But noo dour winter's like to stay
      For guid,
      And no' for guid!

O wae's me on the weary days
When it is scarce grey licht at noon;
It maun be a' the stupid folk
Diffusin' their dullness roon and roon
      Like soot
      That keeps the sunlicht oot.

Nae wonder if I think I see
A lichter shadow than the neist
I'm fain to cry: 'The dawn, the dawn!
I see it brakin' in the East.'
      But ah
      – It's juist mair snaw!

from *Frae Anither Window in Thrums*

Here in the hauf licht waitin' till the clock
Chops: while the winnock
Hauds me as a serpent hauds a rabbit
Afore it's time to grab it
– A serpent faded to a shadow
In the stelled een its een ha'e haud o'

---

lourd heavy   *dour* hard, grim   *guid* good   *neist* next

hauf licht half-light   *chops* strikes   *winnock* window   *stelled* fixed
ha'e haud o' have hold of

Here in the daurk, while like a frozen
Scurl on Life's plumm the lozen
Skimmers – or goams in upon me
Wan as Dostoevski
Glowered through a wudden dream to find
Stavrogin in the corners o' his mind,

– Or I haud it, a 'prentice snake, and gar
Heaven dwine to a haunfu' haar
Or am like cheengeless deeps aneth
Tho' ice or sunshine, life or death,
Chequer the tap; or like Stavrogin
Joukin' his author wi' a still subtler grin...

And yet I canna for the life o' me see
That I'd write better poetry
If like the feck o' Scots insteed
I read the books they read
And drew my thochts o' God and Man
Frae Neil Munro and Annie Swan!

Fu' weel I ken I would mak' verses which
'Ud notably enrich
'Oor Scots tradition' – in the minds
O' ministers and hinds;
And fain I'd keep as faur frae that
As Proust frae Johnnie Gibb – that's flat!

– Can I get faurer frae't than here
Whaur a' life's fictions disappear
And I'm left face to face wi' nocht
But sicna drab splash as brocht
My like to be, to mak' wi't what I can,
Back at the stert whaur a' began?

---

scurl scab   *plumm* deep pool in a river   *lozen* window-pane
skimmers shimmers   *goams* gazes stupidly   *wudden dream* nightmare
gar make   *dwine* dwindle   *a haunfu' haar* a handful of mist
joukin' dodging   *feck* majority

115

Seed in my womb, I ken nae mair
Than ony wife what bairn I'll bear
– Christ or a village idiot there
A thronèd king, or corpse i' the air? . . .

Nature to Art is still a witch
Confinin't by waefu' metamorphosis
To Life, a memory mindin' which
It bairnlies itsel' again like this . . .

For if it's no' by thocht that Poetry's wrocht
It's no' by want o' thocht
The verse that flatters ignorance maun seem
To ignorant folk supreme
Sin' nane can read the verse that disna
The damned thing bides as if it isna!

*   *   *

That's the condition o't or near
Grey glumshin' o' the winda here,
– As fit a subject for immortal sang
As ocht wi' which men's minds are thrang . . .

*   *   *

Here in the hauf licht hoo I've grown!
Seconds but centuries hae flown
Sin I was a reporter here
Chroniclin' the toon's sma' beer
Tinin' the maist o' life to get
The means to hain the least wee bit.

I wha aince in Heaven's height
Gethered to me a' the licht
Can nae mair reply to fire,
'Neth deid leafs buriet in the mire.

---

waefu' woeful   *bairnlies itsel'* makes a child of itself   *wrocht* wrought
disna does not   *glumshin'* sulky appearance

116

Sib to dewdrop, rainbow, ocean,
No' for me their hues and motion.
This foul clay has filed me till
It's no' to ken I'm water still.

Pars aboot meetins, weddins, sermons, a'
The crude events o' life-in-the-raw
Vanish like snowflakes on this river...
Dans le flot sans honneur de quelque noir mélange...
On wha's black bank I stand and shiver;
Nakit! – What gin the boss, as weel he micht,
Comes in and switches on the licht?

The Twentieth Century at Eternity
Gapes – and the clock strikes: Tea!
And sombrous I arise
Under his silly eyes
And doon the stairs, the devil at my back.
I doot the morn I'll get the sack!

'What was I dae'n sittin' in the dark?'
'Huntin' like Moses for the vital spark,
– A human mole
Wi' a hole for a soul?'
'I sud think o' my wife and faimly'
I listen to him tamely.

'Cut oot this poetry stuff, my lad. Get on
Wi' advts. and puffs, and eident con
The proofs; it's in you gin you care
To dae't and earn (your maister) mair.
    Furth Fortune fill the fetters!
Apply yersel' to what's worth while
And I'll reward ye: that's my style.'

---

sib related   *filed* defiled

'Yessir, I'm sorry. It'll no'
Heppen again. The clock was slow
And I was slower still, I'm sorry
In gettin' back again afore ye
To sicna state as fits the job
O' ane wha's brains you lout to rob.'

Curse on the system that can gie
A coof like this control o' me
– No' that he's in the least bit waur
Or better, than ither bosses are –
And on the fate that gars a poet
Toady to find a way to show it!

Curse his new hoose, his business, his cigar,
His wireless set, and motor car
Alsatian, gauntlet gloves, plus fours and wife,
– A'thing included in his life;
And, abune a', his herty laughter,
And – if he has yin – his hereafter.

Owre savage? Deil the bit! That's nocht
To what men like the Boss deserve;
Maist men that is – anon I'll gie
Them a' their paiks, wi' muckle verve.

He has an angry birthmark on his cheek,
   ...*Le roy Scotiste*
   Qui demy face ot, ce dit-on,
   Vermeille comme une amatiste
   Depuys le front jusqu'au menton...
A purple pig's fit – a' his skin
Sud lowe forever in black burnin' shame
To mak' his ootside like his in.

I'd send it owre him like a flypin knife
Till like a carcase in a butcher's shop
He fronts the world – affrontin' it;
A rinnin' wound that nocht'll stop.

---

lout stoop	*coof* fool	*waur* worse	*paiks* deserved punishment
lowe blaze	*flypin knife* skinning knife	*fit* foot	

For sae the will to ignorance o' his kind,
Their line o' least resistance ruins life
As wha maun tine through foul disease
The heich ideas wi' which he's rife...

Curse a'thing that gars me pretend or feel
That life as maist folk hae't is real
Or waste my time on their ideas
Or silly sociabilities,
Service, meanin' or ocht that'll tak'
My mind off ony verse it'll mak.

> I'm no' the kind o' poet
> That opens sales o' work...

Curse on my dooble life and dooble tongue,
– Guid Scots wi' English a' hamstrung –

> Speakin' o' Scotland in English words
> As it were Beethoven chirpt by birds;
> Or as if a Board school teacher
> Tried to teach Rimbaud and Nietzsche.

And on this curst infirmity o' will
That hauds me bletherin' this way still
On things that like a midge-swarm pass
Sub specie aeternitatis.

*   *   *

Gin but the oor 'ud chop and set me free
Frae this accursed drudgery
Aiblins – aince I had had my tea –
I could address mysel' to poetry,
Sufferin' nae mair th'embarrassment o' riches
Wi' which desire brute circumstance bewitches
Till my brain reels and canna faddom which is,
'Mid endless cues, the ane for which it itches.

---

maun tine must lose   *heich* high   *hae't* have it   *aiblins* perhaps

Thrang o' ideas that like fairy gowd
'll leave me the 'Review' reporter still
Waukenin' to my clung-kite faimly on a hill
O' useless croftin' whaur naething's growed
But Daith, sin Christ for an idea died
On a gey similar but less heich hillside.
Ech, weel for Christ: for he was never wed
And had nae weans clamourin' to be fed!

As 'tis I ken that ilka instant gies,
If I could haud it lang eneuch to seize
Them, coontless opportunities
For reams o' verse in as mony different keys,
– And that's damned nonsense for they canna a'
Lead t'owt worth while – gin owt's worth while ava'.

> (Hell tak this improvisin'
> That leads a' airts and nane;
> A kind o' anti-poetry
> That is true poetry's bane!)

* * *

I'm weary o' the shapes mere chance can thraw
In this technique and that; and seek that law
To pit the maitter on a proper basis
My faith in which a feature o' the case is
I canna deal wi' here, but efter tea
Will – if the wife and bairns – we'll wait and see...
A' this is juist provisional and 'll hae
A tea-change into something rich and Scots
When I wha needs use English a' the day
Win back to the true language o' my thochts.

* * *

---

clung-kite faimly shrunken-bellied family   *weans* little ones   *ava'* at all
thraw cast   *pit the maitter* put the matter

Hokum

It isna fair to my wife and weans
It isna fair to mysel',
To persist in poverty-stricken courses
And never ring Fortune's bell.
Thoosands o' writers wi' nae mair brains
In their heids than I've in my pinkie
Are rowin' in wealth while I toil for a dole,
– Hoo's that accoontit for, thinkee?

Oh, it's easy, easy accoontit for, fegs.
I canna gie the folk hokum.
I can poke 'em and shock 'em and mock 'em,
But the a'e thing needfu' is hokum!
It pits a'thing else on its legs.

Losh! They'd ha' put me a brass plate up
In Langholm Academy,
And asked me to tak' the chair
At mony a London Scots spree.
They'd a' gien me my portrait in oils
By Henry Kerr, and the LL.D.,
And my wife and weans 'ud been as weel aff
As gin I'd been a dominie,

    If I'd only had hokum, hokum,
    Juist a wee thing common hokum!

A seat on the Bank o' Scotland buird,
And a public for my poetry...

    If I'd only had hokum, hokum,
    A modicum o' hokum!

---

pinkie little finger   *dominie* schoolmaster

It maitters little what line ye tak'
If you hae hokum wi't;
Butter or snash, it's a' alike,
Gar them laugh or greet.
There's naething the public winna stand
And pay for through the nose,
Barrin' the medicine that's ser'd up neat,
Whether it's bitter or whether it's sweet,
Wi' nae hokum to the dose.

But what I canna accoont for's no'
Bein' able to gie folk hokum.
I can joke 'em and sock 'em and choke 'em
But the a'e thing needfu' is hokum.
– I wish I was Neil Munro.

It isna fair to my wife and weans,
It isna fair to mysel'.
The day's lang by when Gaels gaed oot
To battle and aye fell.
I wish I was Harry Lauder,
Will Fyffe or J.J. Bell,
– Or Lauchlan Maclean Watt
For the maitter o' that!
– Dae I Hell!

Oh, it's hokum, hokum, hokum,
And this is as near't as I'll get.
The nearest I've got yet,
Losh, but it's unco like *it*,
– That sine-qua-non,
A soupçon
O' precious hokum-pokum!

*   *   *

---

butter or snash flattery or sneers   *greet* weep

The Weapon

Scots steel tempered wi' Irish fire
Is the weapon that I desire.

*   *   *

To hell wi' happiness!

To hell wi' happiness!
I sing the terrifying discipline
O' the free mind that gars a man
Mak' his joys kill his joys,
The weakest by the strongest,
The temporal by the fundamental
(Or hope o' the fundamental)
And prolong wi'in himself
Threids o' thocht sae fragile
It needs the help and contrivance
O' a' his vital poo'er
To haud them frae brakin'
As he pu's them owre the gulfs.
Oor humanity canna follow us
To lichts sae faur removed.
A man ceases to be himsel'
Under sicna constraint.
Will he find life or daith
At the end o' his will,
At Thocht's deepest depth,
Or some frichtfu' sensation o' seein'
Nocht but the ghastly glimmer
O' his ain puir maitter?
                What does it maitter?
                It's the only road.
The beaten track is *beaten* frae the stert.

*   *   *

My love is to the light of lights

My love is to the light of lights
As a gold fawn to the sun
And men, wha love ocht else, to her
Their ways ha' scarce begun.

For God their God's a jealous God
And keeps her frae their sight
He hasna had her lang eneuch
Himsel' to share his delight

And kens gin he'd been worth his saut
He'd ha' made her first, no' last,
Since but a'e glimpse, a'e thocht, o' her
Discredits a' the Past.

(A'e glimpse, a'e thocht, and men might cease
To honour his tardy pooers;
And he's no' shair she winna prove
To be no' his – but oors!)

Yet praise the Past sin' but for it
We never might ha' seen her
– And still to oor een maun temper wi't
The glory that's been gi'en her.

My love she is the hardest thocht
That ony brain can ha'e,
And there is nocht worth ha'en in life
That doesna lead her way.

My love is to a' else that is
As meaning's meaning, or the sun
Men see ahint the sunlight whiles
Like lint-white water run. . . .

At My Father's Grave

The sunlicht still on me, you row'd in clood,
We look upon each ither noo like hills
Across a valley. I'm nae mair your son.
It is my mind, nae son o' yours, that looks,
And the great darkness o' your death comes up
And equals it across the way.
A livin' man upon a deid man thinks
And ony sma'er thocht's impossible.

The Seamless Garment

Whene'er the mist which stands 'twixt God and thee
Defecates to a pure transparency
                              Coleridge

You are a cousin of mine
    Here in the mill.
It's queer that born in the Langholm
    It's no' until
Juist noo I see what it means
To work in the mill like my freen's.

I was tryin' to say something
    In a recent poem
Aboot Lenin. You've read a guid lot
    In the news – but ken the less o'm?
Look, Wullie, here is his secret noo
In a way I can share it wi' you.

His secret and the secret o' a'
    That's worth ocht.
The shuttles fleein' owre quick for my een
    Prompt the thocht,
And the coordination atween
    Weaver and machine.

---

row'd wrapped

The haill shop's dumfoonderin'
  To a stranger like me.
Second nature to you; you're perfectly able
  To think, speak and see
Apairt frae the looms, tho' to some
That doesna sae easily come.

Lenin was like that wi' workin' class life,
  At hame wi't a'.
His fause movements couldna been fewer,
  The best weaver Earth ever saw.
A' *he'd* to dae wi' moved intact
    Clean, clear, and exact.

A poet like Rilke did the same
  In a different sphere,
Made a single reality – a' a'e 'oo' –
  O' his love and pity and fear;
A seamless garment o' music and thought
But you're owre thrang wi' puirer to tak' tent o't.

What's life or God or what you may ca't
  But something at ane like this?
Can you divide yoursel' frae your breath
  Or – if you say yes –
Frae your mind that as in the case
O' the loom keeps that in its place?

Empty vessels mak' the maist noise
  As weel you ken.
Still waters rin deep, owre fu' for soond.
  It's the same wi' men.
Belts fleein', wheels birlin' – a river in flood,
Fu' flow and tension o' poo'er and blood.

---

fause false *a' a'e 'oo'* all one thing *thrang* busy
tak' tent o't take notice of it *ca't* call it *birlin'* whirling

126

Are you equal to life as to the loom?
　　Turnin' oot shoddy or what?
Claith better than man? D'ye live to the full,
　　Your poo'ers a' deliverly taught?
Or scamp a'thing else? Border claith's famous.
Shall things o' mair consequence shame us?

Lenin and Rilke baith gied still mair skill,
　　Coopers o' Stobo, to a greater concern
Than you devote to claith in the mill.
　　Wad it be ill to learn
To keep a bit eye on *their* looms as weel
And no' be hailly ta'en up wi' your 'tweel'?

The womenfolk ken what I mean.
　　Things maun fit like a glove,
Come clean off the spoon – and syne
　　There's time for life and love.
The mair we mak' natural as breathin' the mair
Energy for ither things we'll can spare,
　　But as lang as we bide like this
Neist to naething we ha'e, or miss.

Want to gang back to the handloom days?
　　Nae fear!
Or paintin' oor hides? Hoo d'ye think we've got
　　Frae there to here?
We'd get a million times faurer still
If maist folk change profits didna leav't till
A wheen here and there to bring it aboot
– Aye, and hindered no' helped to boot.

Are you helpin'? Machinery's improved, but folk?
　　Is't no' high time
We were tryin' to come into line a' roon?
　　(I canna think o' a rhyme.)
Machinery in a week mak's greater advances
Than Man's nature twixt Adam and this.

---

claith cloth　　　*deliverly* continually　　　*wheen* little

Hundreds to the inch the threids lie in,
   Like the men in a communist cell.
There's a play o' licht frae the factory windas.
   Could you no' mak' mair yoursel'?
Mony a loom mair alive than the weaver seems
For the sun's still nearer than Rilke's dreams.

Ailie Bally's tongue's keepin' time
   To the vibration a' richt.
Clear through the maze your een signal to Jean
   What's for naebody else's sicht
Short skirts, silk stockin's – fegs, hoo the auld
Emmle-deugs o' the past are curjute and devauld!

And as for me in my fricative work
   I ken fu' weel
Sic an integrity's what I maun ha'e,
   Indivisible, real,
Woven owre close for the point o' a pin
   Onywhere to win in.

Water of Life

Wha looks on water and's no' affected yet
By memories o' the Flood, and, faurer back,
O' that first flux in which a' life began,
And won sae slowly oot that ony lack
O' poo'er's a shrewd reminder o' the time
   We ploutered in the slime?

It's seldom in my active senses tho'
That water brings sic auld sensations as that
(Gin it's no' mixed wi' something even yet
A wee taet stronger); but in lookin' at
A woman at ony time I mind oor source
   And possible return of course.

---

emmle-deugs tatters of clothes   *curjute* overthrown   *devauld* relinquished

ploutered floundered   *taet* bit

Happy wha feels there's solid ground beneath
His feet at ony time – if ony does.
Happy? That's aiblins ga'en a bit owre faur.
I only mean he differs frae me thus
Tho' I'm whiles glad when a less shoogly sea
      Than ithers cradles me.

And if I'm no' aye glad o't it's because
I was sae used to waters as a loon
That I'm amphibious still. A perfect maze
O' waters is aboot the Muckle Toon,
Apairt frae't often seemin' through the weather
      That sea and sky swap places a'thegither.

Ah, vivid recollection o' trudgin' that
Crab-like again upon the ocean-flair! –
Juist as in lyin' wi' a woman still
I feel a sudden cant and sweesh aince mair
Frae Sodom or Gomorrah wi' yon Eastern whore
      T'oor watery grave o' yore.

She clung to me mair tightly at the end
Than ane expects or wants in sic a case,
Whether frae love or no' I needna say,
A waste o' guid material – her face
Fastened on mine as on a flag a sooker
      And naething shook her.

Although my passion was sair diluted then
I mind the cratur' still frae tip to tae
Better than ony that I've troked si' syne
– The gowden pendants frae her lugs, her skin
Sae clear that in her cheeks the glints 'ud play
As whiles wi' bits o' looking-glass as loons
      We'd gar the sun loup roon's.

---

aiblins perhaps   *shoogly* insecure   *loon* boy   *swap* exchange
flair floor   *sweesh* swish   *sooker* sucker   *cratur'* creature
troked had to do with   *si' syne* since then   *lugs* ears
loup roon's jump around us

Nae doot the sudden predicament we shared
Has fixed her in my mind abune the lave,
A kind o' compensation for the way
She was sae tashed and lightlied by the wave
Oot o' my recognition and slarried by
    The infernal sly.

A man never faced wi' death kens nocht o' life.
But a' men are? But micht as weel no' be!
The ancient memory is alive to few
And fewer when it is ken what they see,
But them that dae fear neither life nor death,
    Mindin' them baith.

Nae man can jouk and let the jaw gang by.
To seem to's often to dodge a silly squirt
While bein' whummled in an unseen spate
Lodgin' us securely in faur deeper dirt
Or carryin' us to heichts we canna see
    For th' earth in oor e'e.

Nae gulfs that open 'neath oor feet'll find
Us hailly at a loss if we juist keep
The perspective the deluge should ha' gien's
And if we dinna, or if they're mair deep
Than even that is muckle guidance in,
    It's there altho' we're blin'.

Whatever is to be, what's been has been;
Even if it's hailly undune that deed'll bear
A sense o' sequence forever in itsel',
Implyin', and dependent on, what erst was there.
Tho' it's no' conscious o't – less conscious o't
    Than men o' their historic lot.

---

lave remainder   *tashed* ruined   *lightlied* slighted   *slarried* stained
sly green slime on stagnant water   *jouk* duck   *jaw* wave
whummled overturned   *gien's* given us   *hailly* wholly

130

Hoo I got oot o' yon I dinna ken,
But I am ready noo at ony time
To be hurled back or forrit to ony stage
O' ocht we've ever been twixt sun and slime
Or can become, trustin' what's brocht aboot
　　A' th' ither sequels to the water-shute.

Shall wellspring and shower, ebb-tide and neap,
Refuse their separate pairts cryin' let's be ane,
In function as natur', appearance as fact?
Foul here, fair there, to sea and sky again
The river keeps its course and ranges
　　Unchanged through a' its changes.

Wha speak o' vice and innocence, peace and war,
Culture and ignorance, humility and pride,
Describe the Fairy Loup, the thunder-plump,
The moss-boil on the moor, the white-topped tide;
And the ane as sune as the tither 'll be
　　Brocht doon to uniformity.

Ah, weel I ken that ony ane o' them,
Nae maitter hoo vividly I ca't to mind,
Kennin' the world to men's as light to water,
Has endless beauties to which my een are blind,
My ears deaf – aye, and ilka drap a world
　　Bigger than a' Mankind has yet unfurled.

　　　　　　　　Excelsior
　　　　Sae worked the instinct in the seas
　　　　And jungles we were born in
　　　　But sicna cares are useless noo
　　　　Tho' aiblins no' for scornin'.

---

forrit forward　　　*ocht* ought　　　*thunder-plump* thunder-shower
moss-boil a spring in a mossy place　　　*tither* other

sicna such　　　*aiblins* perhaps

Sae worked the kindnesses we got
Frae shadows gane ayont recall.
Sae work whatever relationships
May haud us still in thrall.

Still on we fare and tine oor need
O' modern mither's as monkey's care,
Syne wives, bairns, freens, and in the end
Oorsels we weel can spare.

And aye the force that's brocht life up
Frae chaos to the present stage
Creates new states as ill for us
As oors for eels to gauge.

The promise that there'll be nae second Flood
I tak' wi' a' the salt I've saved since then.
Extinction? What's that but to return
To juist anither Muckle Toon again?
– A salutary process bringin' values oot
    Ocht less 'ud leave in doot.

It teach't me mony lessons I've ne'er forgot –
That it's no' easy to thraw cauld water on life;
The changes a man can safely undergang
And bide essentially unchanged; the strife
To tak' new forms and in it no' forget
    We've never managed yet.

The Factory Gullets and the Skipper's Pool
Are different as Dr Jekyll and Mr Hyde
But the quick changes o' the Esk that joins
These twa afore it meets the Solway Tide
'Ud faur ootrin the divers thochts o' Man
    Sin' Time began.

---

tine lose   *ocht* ought   *teach't* taught

And yet, tho' hospitable to them a',
The Esk is drawn on like a knotless threid
Juist owre lang for's to see the end o't yet,
Tho' noo and then I tak' it in my heid
That the pirn in the hills it's birlin' frae
   Maun near ha' ser'd its day.

Or else I feel like payin' oot line
Forever to an unimaginable take,
And ken that in the Buck and Croon Hotels
They'd lauch my tale to scorn, altho' gudesake,
They credit mony hardly less faur-fetched.
   Heaven kens if mine is stretched!

The Buck and Croon Hotels – guid judges baith
O' credibility I've cause to ken;
A wee hauf wi' the emphasis on the wee,
And day and daily d'they no' see again
A miracle clean-flypit, in the maitter
   O' wine turn't back to water?

Weel the Waterside folk kent what I mean;
They were like figures seen on fountains whiles.
The river made sae free wi' them – poored in and oot
O' their een and ears (no' mooths) in a' its styles,
Till it clean scooped the insides o' their skulls
   O' a' but a wheen thochts like gulls.

Their queer stane faces and hoo green they got!
Juist like Rebecca in her shawl o' sly.
I'd never faur to gang to see doon there
A wreathèd Triton blaw his horn or try,
While at his feet a clump o' mimulus shone
   Like a dog's een wi' a' the world a bone.

---

pirn reel   *birlin'* whirling   *flypit* turned inside out   *wheen* few
sly green slime on water

from *Second Hymn to Lenin*

Are my poems spoken in the factories and fields,
    In the streets o' the toon?
Gin they're no', then I'm failin' to dae
    What I ocht to ha' dune.

Gin I canna win through to the man in the street,
    The wife by the hearth,
A' the cleverness on earth 'll no' mak' up
    For the damnable dearth.

'Haud on, haud on; what poet's dune that?
    Is Shakespeare read,
Or Dante or Milton or Goethe or Burns?'
    – You heard what I said.

Milk-Wort and Bog-Cotton

(To Seumas O'Sullivan)

Cwa' een like milk-wort and bog-cotton hair!
I love you, earth, in this mood best o' a'
When the shy spirit like a laich wind moves
And frae the lift nae shadow can fa'
Since there's nocht left to thraw a shadow there
Owre een like milk-wort and milk-white cotton hair.

Wad that nae leaf upon anither wheeled
A shadow either and nae root need dern
In sacrifice to let sic beauty be!
But deep surroondin' darkness I discern
Is aye the price o' licht. Wad licht revealed
Naething but you, and nicht nocht else concealed.

from *Water Music*

(To William and Flora Johnstone)

Wheesht, wheesht, Joyce, and let me hear
    Nae Anna Livvy's lilt,
But Wauchope, Esk, and Ewes again,
    Each wi' its ain rhythms till't.

I

Archin' here and arrachin there,
    Allevolie or allemand,
Whiles appliable, whiles areird,
    The polysemous poem's planned.

---

cwa' come away   *een* eyes   *laich* low   *lift* sky   *dern* hide

wheesht hush   *till't* to it   *arrachin* tumultuous   *allevolie* at random
allemand to conduct in a formal and courtly style   *appliable* compliant
areird stubborn

135

Lively, louch, atweesh, atween,
   Auchimuty or aspate,
Threidin' through the averins
   Or bightsom in the aftergait.

Or barmybrained or barritchfu',
   Or rinnin' like an attercap,
Or shinin' like an Atchison,
   Wi' a blare or wi' a blawp.

They ken a' that opens and steeks,
   Frae Fiddleton Bar to Callister Ha',
And roon aboot for twenty miles,
   They bead and bell and swaw.

Brent on or boutgate or beshacht,
   Bellwaverin' or borne-heid,
They mimp and primp, or bick and birr,
   Dilly-dally or show speed.

Brade-up or sclafferin', rouchled, sleek,
   Abstraklous or austerne,
In belths below the brae-hags
   And bebbles in the fern.

Bracken, blaeberries, and heather
   Ken their amplefeysts and toves,
Here gangs ane wi' aiglets jinglin',
   Through a gowl anither goves.

---

louch downcast   *atweesh* between   *atween* between   *auchimuty* paltry
averins heather stems   *bightsom* ample   *aftergait* outcome
barmybrained wanton, giddy   *barritchfu'* troublesome   *attercap* spider
Atchison a copper coin washed with silver   *blawp* belch   *steeks* shuts
bead gather   *bell* bubble up   *swaw* ripple   *brent on* straight ahead
boutgate roundabout   *beshacht* crooked   *bellwaverin'* undecided
borne-heid headlong   *mimp* act affectedly
bick and birr make a cry like a grouse   *brade-up* with address or propriety
sclafferin' slovenly   *rouchled* ruffled   *abstraklous* outrageous
austerne austere   *belths* sudden swirls   *brae-hags* overhanging banks
bebbles droplets   *amplefeysts* fits of sulks   *toves* moods
aiglets tipped boot-laces   *gowl* glen   *goves* comes angrily

Lint in the bell whiles hardly vies
   Wi' ane the wind amows,
While blithely doon abradit linns
   Wi' gowd begane anither jows.

Cougher, blocher, boich and croichle,
   Fraise in ane anither's witters,
Wi' backthraws, births, by-rinnin's,
   Beggar's broon or blae – the critters!

Or burnet, holine, watchet, chauve,
   Or wi' a' the colours dyed
O' the lift abune and plants and trees
   That grow on either side.

Or coinyelled wi' the midges,
   Or swallows a' aboot,
The shadow o' an eagle,
   The aiker o' a troot.

Toukin' ootrageous face
   The turn-gree o' your mood,
I've climmed until I'm lost
   Like the sun ahint a clood.

But a tow-gun frae the boon tree,
A whistle frae the elm,
A spout-gun frae the hemlock,
And, back in this auld realm,
Dry leafs o' dishielogie
To smoke in a 'partan's tae'!

---

lint in the bell flax in flower   *whiles* sometimes   *amows* vexes
abradit linns worn rocky stairways   *gowd* gold   *begane* decorated
jows rocks along   *cougher* onomatopoetic sound
blocher to cough noisily because of phlegm   *boich* to cough
croichle onomatopoetic sound
fraise in ane anither's witters to run through each other   *backthraws* recoilings
by-rinnin's side-runs   *beggar's broon* snuff   *blae* blue   *critters* creatures
burnet brown   *holine* holly green   *watchet* dark green
chauve black and white   *coinyelled* pitted   *aiker* motion
toukin' distorted   *turn-gree* winding stair   *climmed* climbed
tow-gun pop gun   *boon-tree* elder tree   *spout-gun* hollow stem (blow-pipe)
dishielogie colt's foot   *partan's tue* clay pipe

And you've me in your creel again,
   Brim or shallow, bauch or bricht,
Singin' in the mornin',
   Corrieneuchin' a' the nicht.

Cheville

(For Kaikhosru Sorabji)

Who remembers the Great Flood? The scope
Of the waters and their deafening din
Towering like God over the spirits of men,
Flocks, forests, and villages cast to the deep,
Who can sustain the menace of Nature
And praise forces to which life is straw
– Or glimpse them without seeming to outgrow
His mortality in huge recognition?
Tiger-cub torrent, shall I watch you and try
To think of all water is to the world? –
Seeing, and sorry for, all drowned things, sorry
Yet with, *cheville*, a sense of God's glory.

Dytiscus

The problem in the pool is plain.
Must men to higher things ascend
For air like the Dytiscus there,
Breathe through their spiracles, and turn
To diving bells and seek their share
Of sustenance in the slime again
Till they clear life, as he his pool

---

bauch dull   *corrieneuchin'* murmuring

To starve in purity, the fool,
Their finished faculties mirrored, fegs,
Foiled-fierce as his three pairs of legs?
Praise be Dytiscus-men are rare.
Life's pool still foul and full of fare.
Long till to suicidal success attain
We water-beetles of the brain!

Of John Davidson

I remember one death in my boyhood
That next to my father's, and darker, endures;
Not Queen Victoria's, but Davidson, yours,
And something in me has always stood
Since then looking down the sandslope
On your small black shape by the edge of the sea,
– A bullet-hole through a great scene's beauty,
God through the wrong end of a telescope.

Bracken Hills in Autumn[1]

These beds of bracken, climax of the summer's growth,
Are elemental as the sky or sea.
In still and sunny weather they give back
The sun's glare with a fixed intensity
      As of steel or glass
      No other foliage has.

There is a menace in their indifference to man
As in tropical abundance. On gloomy days
They redouble the sombre heaviness of the sky
And nurse the thunder. Their dense growth shuts the narrow ways
      Between the hills and draws
      Closer the wide valleys' jaws.

This flinty verdure's vast effusion is the more
Remarkable for the shortness of its stay.
From November to May a brown stain on the slopes
Downbeaten by frost and rain, then in quick array
      The silvery crooks appear
      And the whole host is here.

Useless they may seem to men and go unused, but cast
Cartloads of them into a pool where the trout are few
And soon the swarming animalcula upon them
Will proportionately increase the fishes too.
      Miracles are never far away
      Save bringing new thought to play.

In summer islanded in these grey-green seas where the wind plucks
The pale underside of the fronds on gusty days
As a land breeze stirs the white caps in a roadstead
Glimpses of shy bog gardens surprise the gaze
      Or rough stuff keeping a ring
      Round a struggling water-spring.

---

[1] This poem was first published in the journal *New Saltire* (no.5, August 1962), from a holograph manuscript discovered in an antiquarian bookshop in 1961, after a collector had recognized MacDiarmid's handwriting. Previous to this it had been lost for thirty years. – Eds.

Look closely. Even now bog asphodel spikes, still alight at the tips,
Sundew lifting white buds like those of the whitlow grass
On walls in spring over its little round leaves
Sparkling with gummy red hairs, and many a soft mass
      Of the curious moss that can clean
      A wound or poison a river, are seen.

Ah! well I know my tumultuous days now at their prime
Will be brief as the bracken too in their stay
Yet in them as the flowers of the hills 'mid the bracken
All that I treasure is needs hidden away
      And will also be dead
      When its rude cover is shed.

Conception

I have reached the stage when questioning myself
Concerning the love of Scotland and turning inward
Upon my own spirit, there comes to me
The suggestion of something utterly unlike
All that is commonly meant by loving
One's country, one's brother man, not altruism,
Not kindly feeling, not outward-looking sympathy,
But something different from all these,
Something almost awful in its range,
Its rage and fire, its scope and height and depth,
Something growing up, within my own
Separate and isolated lonely being,
Within the deep dark of my own consciousness,
Flowering in my own heart, my own self
(Not the Will to Power, but the Will to Flower!)
So that indeed I could not be myself
Without this strange, mysterious, awful finding
Of my people's very life within my own
– This terrible blinding discovery
Of Scotland in me, and I in Scotland,
Even as a man, loyal to a man's code and outlook,
Discovers within himself woman alive and eloquent,
Pulsing with her own emotion,
Looking out on the world with her own vision.

The Skeleton of the Future

(At Lenin's Tomb)

Red granite and black diorite, with the blue
Of the labradorite crystals gleaming like precious stones
In the light reflected from the snow; and behind them
The eternal lightning of Lenin's bones.

Stony Limits

(In Memoriam: Charles Doughty, 1843-1926)

Under no hanging heaven-rooted tree,
Though full of mammuks' nests,
Bone of old Britain we bury thee
But heeding your unspoken hests
Naught not coeval with the Earth
And indispensable till its end
With what whom you despised may deem the dearth
Of your last resting-place dare blend.
Where nature is content with little so are you
So be it the little to which all else is due.

Nor in vain mimicry of the powers
That lifted up the mountains shall we raise
A stone less of nature's shaping than of ours
    To mark the unfrequented place.
You were not filial to all else
Save to the Dust, the mother of all men,
And where you lie no other sign needs tells
(Unless a gaunt shape resembles you again
In some momentary effect of light on rock)
But your family likeness to all her stock.

Flowers may be strewn upon the grave
    Of easy come easy go.
Fitly only some earthquake or tidal wave
O'er you its red rose or its white may throw

But naught else smaller than darkness and light
– Both here, though of no man's bringing! –
And as any past time had been in your sight
Were you now from your bed upspringing,
Now or a billion years hence, you would see
Scant difference, eyed like eternity.

How should we have anything to give you
        In death who had nothing in life,
Attempting in our sand-riddles to sieve you
Who were with nothing, but the sheer elements rife?
Anchor of truth, facile as granite you lie,
A plug suspended in England's false dreams.
Your worth will be seen by and by,
Like God's purpose in what men deem their schemes,
Nothing ephemeral can seek what lies in this ground
Since nothing can be sought but the found.

The poem that would praise you must be
Like the glass of some rock, sleek brown, crowded
With dark incipient crystal growths, we see;
Or a glimpse of Petavius may have endowed it
With the tubular and dumb-bell-shaped inclusions surrounded
        By the broad reaction rims it needs.
I have seen it in dreams and know how it abounded
– Ah! would I could find in me like seeds! –
As the north-easterly garden in the lunation grows,
A spectacle not one man in ten millions knows.

I belong to a different country than yours
And none of my travels have been in the same lands
Save where Arzachel or Langrenus allures
Such spirits as ours, and the Straight Wall stands,
But crossing shear planes extruded in long lines of ridges,
Torsion cylinders, crater rings, and circular seas
And ultra-basic xenoliths that make men look midges
Belong to my quarter as well, and with ease
I too can work in bright green and all the curious interference
Colours that under crossed nicols have a mottled appearance.

Let my first offering be these few pyroxenes twinned
On the orthopinacoid and hour-glass scheme,
Fine striae, microline cross-hatchings, and this wind
Blowing plumes of vapour forever it would seem
From cone after cone diminishing sterile and grey
In the distance; dun sands in ever-changing squalls;
Crush breccias and overthrusts; and such little array
Of Geology's favourite fal-de-lals
And demolitions and entrenchments of weather
As any turn of my eyes brings together.

I know how on turning to noble hills
And stark deserts happily still preserved
For men whom no gregariousness fills
With the loneliness for which they are nerved
– The lonely at-one-ment with all worth while –
I can feel as if the landscape and I
Became each other and see my smile
In the corners of the vastest contours lie
And share the gladness and peace you knew,
– The supreme human serenity that was you!

I have seen Silence lift his head
And Song, like his double, lift yours,
And know, while nearly all that seems living is dead,
You were always consubstantial with all that endures.
Would it were on Earth! Not since Ezekiel has that faw sun ringed
A worthier head; red as Adam you stood
In the desert, the horizon with vultures black-winged,
And sang and died in this still greater solitude
Where I sit by your skull whose emptiness is worth
The sum of almost all the full heads now on Earth
– By your roomy skull where most men might well spend
Longer than you did in Arabia, friend!

On a Raised Beach

(To James H. Whyte)

All is lithogenesis – or lochia,
Carpolite fruit of the forbidden tree,
Stones blacker than any in the Caaba,
Cream-coloured caen-stone, chatoyant pieces,
Celadon and corbeau, bistre and beige,
Glaucous, hoar, enfouldered, cyathiform,
Making mere faculae of the sun and moon,
I study you glout and gloss, but have
No cadrans to adjust you with, and turn again
From optik to haptik and like a blind man run
My fingers over you, arris by arris, burr by burr,
Slickensides, truité, rugas, foveoles,
Bringing my aesthesis in vain to bear,
An angle-titch to all your corrugations and coigns,
Hatched foraminous cavo-rilievo of the world,
Deictic, fiducial stones. Chiliad by chiliad
What bricole piled you here, stupendous cairn?
What artist poses the Earth écorché thus,
Pillar of creation engouled in me?
What eburnation augments you with men's bones,
Every energumen an Endymion yet?
All the other stones are in this haecceity it seems,
But where is the Christophanic rock that moved?
What Cabirian song from this catasta comes?

Deep conviction or preference can seldom
Find direct terms in which to express itself.
Today on this shingle shelf
I understand this pensive reluctance so well,
This not discommendable obstinacy,
These contrivances of an inexpressive critical feeling,
These stones with their resolve that Creation shall not be
Injured by iconoclasts and quacks. Nothing has stirred
Since I lay down this morning an eternity ago
But one bird. The widest open door is the least liable to intrusion,
Ubiquitous as the sunlight, unfrequented as the sun.
The inward gates of a bird are always open.
It does not know how to shut them.
That is the secret of its song,
[ll.1-38]

146

But whether any man's are ajar is doubtful.
I look at these stones and know little about them,
But I know their gates are open too,
Always open, far longer open, than any bird's can be,
That every one of them has had its gates wide open far longer
Than all birds put together, let alone humanity,
Though through them no man can see,
No man nor anything more recently born than themselves
And that is everything else on the Earth.
I too lying here have dismissed all else.
Bread from stones is my sole and desperate dearth,
From stones, which are to the Earth as to the sunlight
Is the naked sun which is for no man's sight.
I would scorn to cry to any easier audience
Or, having cried, to lack patience to await the response.
I am no more indifferent or ill-disposed to life than death is;
I would fain accept it all completely as the soil does;
Already I feel all that can perish perishing in me
As so much has perished and all will yet perish in these stones.
I must begin with these stones as the world began.

Shall I come to a bird quicker than the world's course ran?
        To a bird, and to myself, a man?
        And what if I do, and further?
I shall only have gone a little way to go back again
And be like a fleeting deceit of development,
Iconoclasts, quacks. So these stones have dismissed
All but all of evolution, unmoved by it,
(Is there anything to come they will not likewise dismiss?)
As the essential life of mankind in the mass
Is the same as their earliest ancestors yet.

Actual physical conflict or psychological warfare
        Incidental to love or food
Brings out animal life's bolder and more brilliant patterns
        Concealed as a rule in habitude.
        There is a sudden revelation of colour,
        The protrusion of a crest,
        The expansion of an ornament,
– But no general principle can be guessed
From these flashing fragments we are seeing,
These foam-bells on the hidden currents of being.

                                             [ll.39-78]

The bodies of animals are visible substances
And must therefore have colour and shape, in the first place
Depending on chemical composition, physical structure, mode of
        growth,
Physiological rhythms and other factors in the case,
But their purposive function is another question.
Brilliant-hued animals hide away in the ocean deeps;
The mole has a rich sexual colouring in due season
Under the ground; nearly every beast keeps
Brighter colours inside it than outside.
What the seen shows is never anything to what it's designed to hide,
The red blood which makes the beauty of a maiden's cheek
Is as red under a gorilla's pigmented and hairy face.
Varied forms and functions though life may seem to have shown
They all come back to the likeness of stone,
So to the intervening stages we can best find a clue
In what we all came from and return to.
There are no twirly bits in this ground bass.

We must be humble. We are so easily baffled by appearances
And do not realise that these stones are one with the stars.
It makes no difference to them whether they are high or low,
Mountain peak or ocean floor, palace, or pigsty.
There are plenty of ruined buildings in the world but no ruined
        stones.
No visitor comes from the stars
But is the same as they are.
– Nay, it is easy to find a spontaneity here,
An adjustment to life, an ability
To ride it easily, akin to 'the buoyant
Prelapsarian naturalness of a country girl
Laughing in the sun, not passion-rent,
But sensing in the bound of her breasts vigours to come
Powered to make her one with the stream of earthlife round her,'
But not yet as my Muse is, with this ampler scope,
This more divine rhythm, wholly at one
With the earth, riding the Heavens with it, as the stones do
And all soon must.
But it is wrong to indulge in these illustrations
Instead of just accepting the stones.
It is a paltry business to try to drag down
The arduous furor of the stones to the futile imaginings of men,
[ll.79-117]

148

To all that fears to grow roots into the common earth,
As it soon must, lest it be chilled to the core,
As it will be – and none the worse for that.
Impatience is a poor qualification for immortality.
Hot blood is of no use in dealing with eternity.
It is seldom that promises or even realisations
Can sustain a clear and searching gaze.
But an emotion chilled is an emotion controlled;
This is the road leading to certainty,
Reasoned planning for the time when reason can no longer avail.
It is essential to know the chill of all the objections
That come creeping into the mind, the battle between opposing
        ideas
Which gives the victory to the strongest and most universal
Over all others, and to wage it to the end
With increasing freedom, precision, and detachment
A detachment that shocks our instincts and ridicules our desires.
All else in the world cancels out, equal, capable
Of being replaced by other things (even as all the ideas
That madden men now must lose their potency in a few years
And be replaced by others – even as all the religions,
All the material sacrifices and moral restraints,
That in twenty thousand years have brought us no nearer to God
Are irrelevant to the ordered adjustments
Out of reach of perceptive understanding
Forever taking place on the Earth and in the unthinkable regions
        around it;
This cat's cradle of life; this reality volatile yet determined;
This intense vibration in the stones
That makes them seem immobile to us)
But the world cannot dispense with the stones.
They alone are not redundant. Nothing can replace them
Except a new creation of God.

I must get into this stone world now.
Ratchel, striae, relationships of tesserae,
        Innumerable shades of grey,
        Innumerable shapes,
And beneath them all a stupendous unity,
Infinite movement visibly defending itself
Against all the assaults of weather and water,
Simultaneously mobilised at full strength

                                        [ll.118-156]

149

At every point of the universal front,
　　Always at the pitch of its powers,
　　The foundation and end of all life.
I try them with the old Norn words – hraun
Duss, rønis, queedaruns, kollyarun;
They hvarf from me in all directions
Over the hurdifell – klett, millya hellya, hellyina bretta,
Hellyina wheeda, hellyina grø, bakka, ayre, –
　　And lay my world in kolgref.

This is no heap of broken images.
Let men find the faith that builds mountains
Before they seek the faith that moves them. Men cannot hope
To survive the fall of the mountains
Which they will no more see than they saw their rise
Unless they are more concentrated and determined,
Truer to themselves and with more to be true to,
Than these stones, and as inerrable as they are.
Their sole concern is that what can be shaken
Shall be shaken and disappear
And only the unshakeable be left.
What hardihood in any man has part or parcel in the latter?
It is necessary to make a stand and maintain it forever.
These stones go through Man, straight to God, if there is one.
What have they not gone through already?
Empires, civilisations, aeons. Only in them
If in anything, can His creation confront Him.
They came so far out of the water and halted forever.
That larking dallier, the sun, has only been able to play
With superficial by-products since;
The moon moves the waters backwards and forwards,
But the stones cannot be lured an inch farther
Either on this side of eternity or the other.
Who thinks God is easier to know than they are?
Trying to reach men any more, any otherwise, than they are?
These stones will reach us long before we reach them.
Cold, undistracted, eternal and sublime.
They will stem all the torrents of vicissitude forever
With a more than Roman peace.

Death is a physical horror to me no more.
I am prepared with everything else to share
[ll.157-196]

Sunshine and darkness and wind and rain
And life and death bare as these rocks though it be
In whatever order nature may decree,
But, not indifferent to the struggle yet
Nor to the ataraxia I might get
By fatalism, a deeper issue see
Than these, or suicide, here confronting me.
It is reality that is at stake.
Being and non-being with equal weapons here
Confront each other for it, non-being unseen
But always on the point, it seems, of showing clear,
Though its reserved contagion may breed
This fancy too in my still susceptible head
And then by its own hidden movement lead
Me as by aesthetic vision to the supposed
Point where by death's logic everything is recomposed,
Object and image one, from their severance freed,
As I sometimes, still wrongly, feel 'twixt this storm beach and me.
What happens to us
Is irrelevant to the world's geology
But what happens to the world's geology
Is not irrelevant to us.
We must reconcile ourselves to the stones,
Not the stones to us.
Here a man must shed the encumbrances that muffle
Contact with elemental things, the subtleties
That seem inseparable from a humane life, and go apart
Into a simple and sterner, more beautiful and more oppressive
          world,
Austerely intoxicating; the first draught is overpowering;
Few survive it. It fills me with a sense of perfect form,
The end seen from the beginning, as in a song.
It is no song that conveys the feeling
That there is no reason why it should ever stop,
But the kindred form I am conscious of here
Is the beginning and end of the world,
The unsearchable masterpiece, the music of the spheres,
Alpha and Omega, the Omnific Word.
These stones have the silence of supreme creative power,
The direct and undisturbed way of working
Which alone leads to greatness.
What experience has any man crystallised,

[ll.197-237]

151

What weight of conviction accumulated,
What depth of life suddenly seen entire
In some nigh supernatural moment
And made a symbol and lived up to
With such resolution, such Spartan impassivity?
It is a frenzied and chaotic age,
Like a growth of weeds on the site of a demolished building.
How shall we set ourselves against it,
Imperturbable, inscrutable, in the world and yet not in it,
    Silent under the torments it inflicts upon us,
        With a constant centre,
With a single inspiration, foundations firm and invariable;
        By what immense exercise of will,
Inconceivable discipline, courage, and endurance,
        Self-purification and anti-humanity,
            Be ourselves without interruption,
                Adamantine and inexorable?
It will be ever increasingly necessary to find
In the interests of all mankind
Men capable of rejecting all that all other men
        Think, as a stone remains
Essential to the world, inseparable from it,
        And rejects all other life yet.
Great work cannot be combined with surrender to the crowd.
        – Nay, the truth we seek is as free
From all yet thought as a stone from humanity.
Here where there is neither haze nor hesitation
Something at least of the necessary power has entered into me.
I have still to see any manifestation of the human spirit
That is worthy of a moment's longer exemption than it gets
From petrifaction again – to get out if it can.
All is lithogenesis – or lochia;
And I can desire nothing better,
An immense familiarity with other men's imaginings
Convinces me that they cannot either
(If they could, it would instantly be granted
– The present order must continue till then)
Though, of course, I still keep an open mind,
A mind as open as the grave.
You may say that the truth cannot be crushed out,
That the weight of the whole world may be tumbled on it,
And yet, in puny, distorted, phantasmal shapes albeit,
[ll.238-279]

It will braird again; it will force its way up
Through unexpectable fissures? look over this beach.
What ruderal and rupestrine growth is here?
What crop confirming any credulities?
Conjure a fescue to teach me with from this
And I will listen to you, but until then
Listen to me – Truth is not crushed;
It crushes, gorgonises all else into itself.
The trouble is to know it when you see it?
You will have no trouble with it when you do.
Do not argue with me. Argue with these stones.
Truth has no trouble in knowing itself.
This is it. The hard fact. The inoppugnable reality,
Here is something for you to digest.
Eat this and we'll see what appetite you have left
For a world hereafter.
I pledge you in the first and last crusta,
The rocks rattling in the bead-proof seas.

O we of little faith,
As romanticists viewed the philistinism of their days
As final and were prone to set over against it
Infinite longing rather than manly will –
Nay, as all thinkers and writers find
The indifference of the masses of mankind, –
So are most men with any stone yet,
Even those who juggle with lapidary's, mason's, geologist's words
    And all their knowledge of stones in vain,
Tho' these stones have far more differences in colour, shape and size
    Than most men to my eyes –
Even those who develop precise conceptions to immense distances
    Out of these bleak surfaces.
All human culture is a Goliath to fall
To the least of these pebbles withal.
A certain weight will be added yet
To the arguments of even the most foolish
And all who speak glibly may rest assured
That to better their oratory they will have the whole earth
For a Demosthenean pebble to roll in their mouths.

I am enamoured of the desert at last,
The abode of supreme serenity is necessarily a desert.

                                        [ll.280-319]

My disposition is towards spiritual issues
Made inhumanly clear; I will have nothing interposed
Between my sensitiveness and the barren but beautiful reality;
The deadly clarity of this 'seeing of a hungry man'
Only traces of a fever passing over my vision
Will vary, troubling it indeed, but troubling it only
In such a way that it becomes for a moment
Superhumanly, menacingly clear – the reflection
Of a brightness through a burning crystal.
A culture demands leisure and leisure presupposes
A self-determined rhythm of life; the capacity for solitude
Is its test; by that the desert knows us.
It is not a question of escaping from life
But the reverse – a question of acquiring the power
To exercise the loneliness, the independence, of stones,
And that only comes from knowing that our function remains
However isolated we seem fundamental to life as theirs.
    We have lost the grounds of our being,
    We have not built on rock.
Thinking of all the higher zones
Confronting the spirit of man I know they are bare
Of all so-called culture as any stone here;
Not so much of all literature survives
As any wisp of scriota that thrives
On a rock – (interesting though it may seem to be
As de Bary's and Schwendener's discovery
Of the dual nature of lichens, the partnership,
Symbiosis, of a particular fungus and particular alga).
These bare stones bring me straight back to reality.
    I grasp one of them and I have in my grip
The beginning and the end of the world,
My own self, and as before I never saw
The empty hand of my brother man,
The humanity no culture has reached, the mob.
Intelligentsia, our impossible and imperative job!

'Ah!' you say, 'if only one of these stones would move
– Were it only an inch – of its own accord.
    This is the resurrection we await,
– The stone rolled away from the tomb of the Lord.
    I know there is no weight in infinite space,
      No impermeability in infinite time,
[ll.320-360]

But it is as difficult to understand and have patience here
        As to know that the sublime
Is theirs no less than ours, no less confined
To men than men's to a few men, the stars of their kind.'
        (The masses too have begged bread from stones,
            From human stones, including themselves,
        And only got it, not from their fellow-men,
        But from stones such as these here – if then.)
Detached intellectuals, not one stone will move,
Not the least of them, not a fraction of an inch. It is not
        The reality of life that is hard to know.
It is nearest of all and easiest to grasp,
But you must participate in it to proclaim it.
– I lift a stone; it is the meaning of life I clasp
Which is death, for that is the meaning of death;
How else does any man yet participate
        In the life of a stone,
How else can any man yet become
Sufficiently at one with creation, sufficiently alone,
Till as the stone that covers him he lies dumb
And the stone at the mouth of his grave is not overthrown?
– Each of these stones on this raised beach,
        Every stone in the world,
Covers infinite death, beyond the reach
Of the dead it hides; and cannot be hurled
Aside yet to let any of them come forth, as love
        Once made a stone move
    (Though I do not depend on that
        My case to prove).
So let us beware of death; the stones will have
Their revenge; we have lost all approach to them,
But soon we shall become as those we have betrayed,
And they will seal us fast in our graves
As our indifference and ignorance seals them;
        But let us not be afraid to die.
No heavier and colder and quieter then,
No more motionless, do stones lie
        In death than in life to all men.
It is not more difficult in death than here
– Though slow as the stones the powers develop
To rise from the grave – to get a life worth having;
And in death – unlike life – we lose nothing that is truly ours.
                                                [ll.361-402]

Diallage of the world's debate, end of the long auxesis,
Although no ébrillade of Pegasus can here avail,
I prefer your enchorial characters – the futhorc of the future –
To the hieroglyphics of all the other forms of Nature.
Song, your apprentice encrinite, seems to sweep
The Heavens with a last entrochal movement;
And, with the same word that began it, closes
Earth's vast epanadiplosis.
[ll.403-410]

First Love

    I have been in this garden of unripe fruit
        All the long day,
    Where cold and clear from the hard green apples
        The light fell away.

    I was wandering here with my own true love,
        But as I bent o'er,
    She dwindled back to her childhood again
        And I saw her no more.

    A wind sprang up and a hail of buds
        About me rolled,
    Then this fog I knew before I was born
        But now – cold, cold!

With the Herring Fishers

(To 'A.T. Cunninghame')

'I see herrin'.' – I hear the glad cry
And 'gainst the moon see ilka blue jowl
In turn as the fishermen haul on the nets
And sing: 'Come, shove in your heids and growl.'

---

ilka every

'Soom on, bonnie herrin', soom on,' they shout,
Or 'Come in, O come in, and see me,'
'Come gie the auld man something to dae.
It'll be a braw change frae the sea.'

O it's ane o' the bonniest sichts in the warld
To watch the herrin' come walkin' on board
In the wee sma' 'oors o' a simmer's mornin'
As if o' their ain accord.

For this is the way that God sees life,
The haill jing-bang o's appearin'
Up owre frae the edge o' naethingness
– It's his happy cries I'm hearin'.

'Left, right – O come in and see me,'
Reid and yellow and black and white
Toddlin' up into Heaven thegither
At peep o' day frae the endless night.

'I see herrin',' I hear his glad cry,
And 'gainst the moon see his muckle blue jowl,
As he handles buoy-tow and bush-raip
Singin': 'Come, shove in your heids and growl!'

from *The War with England*

I was better with the sounds of the sea
    Than with the voices of men
And in desolate and desert places
    I found myself again.
For the whole of the world came from these
And he who returns to the source
May gauge the worth of the outcome
And approve and perhaps reinforce
Or disapprove and perhaps change its course.

---

soom swim   *dae* do   *braw* fine   *wee sma' 'oors* the early hours
simmer summer   *haill jing-bang o's* the whole collection of us
thegither together   *buoy-tow* buoy rope   *bush-raip* rope attached to net

Now I deal with the hills at their roots
    And the streams at their springs
And am to the land that I love
    As he who brings
His bride home, and they know each other
Not as erst, like their friends, they have done,
But carnally, causally, knowing that only
By life nigh undone can life be begun,
    And accept and are one.

The Little White Rose

(To John Gawsworth)

The rose of all the world is not for me.
I want for my part
Only the little white rose of Scotland
That smells sharp and sweet – and breaks the heart.

Skald's Death

I have known all the storms that roll.
I have been a singer after the fashion
Of my people – a poet of passion.
    All that is past.
Quiet has come into my soul.
    Life's tempest is done.
    I lie at last
A bird cliff under the midnight sun.

Harry Semen

I ken these islands each inhabited
Forever by a single man
Livin' in his separate world as only
In dreams yet maist folk can.

Mine's like the moonwhite belly o' a hoo
Seen in the water as a fisher draws in his line.
I canna land it nor can it ever brak awa'.
It never moves, yet seems a' movement in the brine;
A movin' picture o' the spasm frae which I was born,
It writhes again, and back to it I'm willy-nilly torn.
A' men are similarly fixt; and the difference 'twixt
    The sae-ca'd sane and insane
Is that the latter whiles ha'e glimpses o't
    And the former nane.

Particle frae particle'll brak asunder,
Ilk ane o' them mair livid than the neist.
A separate life? – incredible war o' equal lichts,
Nane o' them wi' ocht in common in the least.
Nae threid o' a' the fabric o' my thocht
Is left alangside anither; a pack
O' leprous scuts o' weasels riddlin' a plaid
    Sic thrums could never mak'.
Hoo mony shades o' white gaed curvin' owre
To yon blae centre o' her belly's flower?
Milk-white, and dove-grey, wi' harebell veins.
Ae scar in fair hair like the sun in sunlicht lay,
And pelvic experience in a thin shadow line;
Thocht canna mairry thocht as sic saft shadows dae.

Grey ghastly commentaries on my puir life,
A' the sperm that's gane for naething rises up to damn
In sick-white onanism the single seed
Frae which in sheer irrelevance I cam.
What were the odds against me? Let me coont.

---

hoo dogfish   *sae-ca'd* so-called   *whiles* sometimes   *ilk ane* each one
ocht anything   *sic thrums* ravelled loose threads   *blae* ghastly

What worth am I to a' that micht ha'e been?
To a' the wasted slime I'm capable o'
Appeals this lurid emission, whirlin' lint-white and green.
Am I alane richt, solidified to life,
Disjoined frae a' this searin' like a white-het knife,
And vauntin' my alien accretions here,
Boastin' sanctions, purpose, sense the endless tide
I cam frae lacks – the tide I still sae often feed?
O bitter glitter; wet sheet and flowin' sea – and what beside?

Sae the bealin' continents lie upon the seas,
   Sprawlin' in shapeless shapes a' airts,
Like ony splash that ony man can mak'
   Frae his nose or throat or ither pairts,
Fantastic as ink through blottin'-paper rins.
But this is white, white like a flooerin' gean
Passin' frae white to purer shades o' white,
Ivory, crystal, diamond, till nae difference is seen
Between its fairest blossoms and the stars
Or the clear sun they melt into,
And the wind mixes them amang each ither
Forever, hue upon still mair dazzlin' hue.

Sae Joseph may ha'e pondered; sae a snawstorm
Comes whirlin' in grey sheets frae the shadowy sky
And only in a sma' circle are the separate flakes seen.
White, whiter, they cross and recross as capricious they fly,
Mak' patterns on the grund and weave into wreaths,
Load the bare boughs, and find lodgements in corners frae
The scourin' wind that sends a snawstorm up frae the earth
To meet that frae the sky, till which is which nae man can say.
They melt in the waters. They fill the valleys. They scale the peaks.
There's a tinkle o' icicles. The topmaist summit shines oot.
Sae Joseph may ha'e pondered on the coiled fire in his seed,
The transformation in Mary, and seen Jesus tak' root.

---

bealin' festering   *a' airts* all directions   *flooerin' gean* flowering cherry-tree

John Maclean (1879-1923)

All the buildings in Glasgow are grey
With cruelty and meanness of spirit,
But once in a while one greyer than the rest
    A song shall merit
Since a miracle of true courage is seen
For a moment its walls between.

Look at it, you fools, with unseeing eyes
And deny it with lying lips!
But your craven bowels well know what it is
    And hasten to eclipse
In a cell, as black as the shut boards of the Book
You lie by, the light no coward can brook.

It is not the blue of heaven that colours
The blue jowls of your thugs of police,
And 'justice' may well do its filthy work
    Behind walls as filthy as these
And congratulate itself blindly and never know
The prisoner takes the light with him as he goes below.

Stand close, stand close, and block out the light
As long as you can, you ministers and lawyers,
Hulking brutes of police, fat bourgeoisie,
Sleek derma for congested guts – its fires
Will leap through yet; already it is clear
Of all Maclean's foes not one was his peer.

As Pilate and the Roman soldiers to Christ
Were Law and Order to the finest Scot of his day,
One of the few true men in our sordid breed,
A flash of sun in a country all prison-grey.
Speak to others of Christian charity; I cry again
For vengeance on the murderers of John Maclean.
Let the light of truth in on the base pretence
Of Justice that sentenced him behind these grey walls.
All law is the contemptible fraud he declared it.
Like a lightning-bolt at last the workers' wrath falls
On all such castles of cowards whether they be
Uniformed in ermine, or blue, or khaki.

Royal honours for murderers and fools! The 'fount of honour'
Is poisoned and spreads its corruption all through,
But Scotland will think yet of the broken body
And unbreakable spirit, Maclean, of you,
And know you were indeed the true tower of its strength,
As your prison of its foul stupidity, at length.

from *Ode to All Rebels*

*In his appearance not overdazzling; so that you might without difficulty
recognise him as belonging to that class of men of letters who are continuously
hated by the Rich.*

PETRONIUS, *Satiricon* lxxxiii.

Wherefore are all they happy that deal very treacherously?

JEREMIAH, XII. I (Vulgate).

I mind when my first wife died.
    I was a young fella then,
Strang, and ta'en up wi' life, and she'd come
    By a sudden and terrible en',
My haill warld gane – but I was livin' on
    Tho' hoo I could hardly ken.
Yet even in the middle o' kistin' her
In the hour o' my grief I felt the stir
    O' auld feelin's again.
Feelin's I had when I courted her first,
No' syne, and hated noo and cursed.
Hoo could I trust love again if a'
The tender ties twixt us twa
Like this could be wantonly snapt,
While afore her corpse was decently hapt
I was kindlin' aince mair in a different airt,
My rude bluid warnin' my woe for its pairt
It bood ha'e anither wife, and sune?

---

kistin' burying (lit. placing the corpse in the coffin)

Nay, I felt the cratur juist hoverin' roon.
At ony meenut her face 'ud kyth.
– Ahint my dule and self-scunner already,
    My Second, you were skinklan' blithe.
Or I kent gin you'd be virgin or widdy,
    A thocht I mind ha'en
Even as frae lowerin' the coffin I raze
Conscious o' my nature in a wud amaze
And strauchtened up my muckle animal frame
That kent what it wanted and kent nae shame
    And stood in a burst o' sun
    Glowerin' at the bit broken grun'.

*   *   *

Think not that I forget a single pang
    O' a' that folk ha'e tholed,
Agonies and abominations 'yont a' tellin'
    Sights to daunt the maist bold.

There are buildings in ilka toon where daily
    Unthinkable horrors tak' place.
I am the woman in cancer's toils,
    The man withoot a face.

I am a' cruelty and lust and filth,
    Corruption and law-made crime,
– The helpless prisoners badgered in their cells
    In every land and clime.

A' 'gallant sodgers' murderin' for pay,
    (Plus 'little Belgium' or like affairs)
– And heroic airmen prood to gi'e
    Puir tribes hell frae the air.

And a' the hidden but nae less hideous deeds
    Soond citizens are aye privily at
– Only the mean natures and vicious looks
    O' their bairns, themsel's, or their underlings caught.

---

kyth appear   wud amaze crazed astonishment

O there's as muckle o't in Britain here
  As in Sing-Sing or in Cayenne
– Differently disguised, of course, and dernin'
  In the maist 'decent and God-fearin'' men.

There is nae horror history's ever kent
  Mob passion or greedy fear wadna soon
Mak' them dae owre again – slovens and cowards
  Movin' pig-eened in their daily roon'.

They face nocht – their haill lives depend
  On ignorance and base contempt
For a' that's worth-while in the poo'ers o' Man
  – Frae ony share in't exempt.

In the midst o' plenty in poverty,
  To Art nae better than apes
– Thinkna that I'm unaware
  O' ane o' their ugsome shapes....

You may thank God for good health
  And be proud to be pure
In body and mind – unlike some.
  I am not so sure.

You may feel certain that God
  Is on the side of the sane
And prefers your condition to syphilis.
  I am not so sure.

Congratulate yourselves you're spared
  The ghastly ills others endure.
God's with the majority surely.
  I am not so sure....

On the Ocean Floor

Now more and more on my concern with the lifted waves of
    genius gaining
I am aware of the lightless depths that beneath them lie;
And as one who hears their tiny shells incessantly raining
On the ocean floor as the foraminifera die.

At the Cenotaph

Are the living so much use
That we need to mourn the dead?
Or would it yield better results
To reverse their roles instead?
The millions slain in the War –
Untimely, the best of our seed? –
Would the world be any the better
If they were still living indeed?
The achievements of such as are
To the notion lend no support;
The whole history of life and death
Yields no scrap of evidence for't. –
Keep going to your wars, you fools, as of yore;
I'm the civilisation you're fighting for.

One of the Principal Causes of War

O she was full of loving fuss
When I cut my hand and the blood gushed out
And cleverly she dressed the wound
And wrapt it in a clout.

O tenderly she tended me
Though deep in her eyes I could tell
The secret joy that men are whiles
Obliged to bleed as well.

I thanked her kindly and never let on,
Seeing she could not understand,
That she wished me a wound far worse to staunch –
And not in the hand!

O Ease My Spirit

*And as for their appearances, they four had one likeness, as if a wheel had been
in the midst of a wheel.*

EZEKIEL

O ease my spirit increasingly of the load
Of my personal limitations and the riddling differences
Between man and man with a more constant insight
Into the fundamental similarity of all activities.

And quicken me to the gloriously and terribly illuminating
Integration of the physical and the spiritual till I feel how easily
I could put my hand gently on the whole round world
As on my sweetheart's head and draw it to me.

As Lovers Do

Here at the height of passion
        As lovers do
I can only speak brokenly
        Of trifles too.

Idiot incoherence
        I know full well
Is the only language
        That with God can deal.

Light and Shadow

Like memories of what cannot be
Within the reign of memory...
That shake our mortal frames to dust.
                                    SHELLEY

On every thought I have the countless shadows fall
Of other thoughts as valid that I cannot have;
Cross-lights of errors, too, impossible to me,
Yet somehow truer than all these thoughts, being with more
    power aglow.

May I never lose these shadowy glimpses of unknown thoughts
That modify and minify my own, and never fail
To keep some shining sense of the way all thoughts at last
Before life's dawning meaning like the stars at sunrise pale.

In the Children's Hospital

Does it matter – losing your legs?...
                    SIEGFRIED SASSOON

Now let the legless boy show the great lady
How well he can manage his crutches.
It doesn't matter though the Sister objects,
'He's not used to them yet,' when such is
The will of the Princess. Come, Tommy,
Try a few desperate steps through the ward.
Then the hand of Royalty will pat your head
And life suddenly cease to be hard.
For a couple of legs are surely no miss
When the loss leads to such an honour as this!
One knows, when one sees how jealous the rest
Of the children are, it's been all for the best! –
But would the sound of your sticks on the floor
Thundered in her skull for evermore!

Lo! A Child is Born

I thought of a house where the stones seemed suddenly changed
And became instinct with hope, hope as solid as themselves,
And the atmosphere warm with that lovely heat,
The warmth of tenderness and longing souls, the smiling anxiety
That rules a home where a child is about to be born.
The walls were full of ears. All voices were lowered.
Only the mother had the right to groan or complain.
Then I thought of the whole world. Who cares for its travail
And seeks to encompass it in like lovingkindness and peace?
There is a monstrous din of the sterile who contribute nothing
To the great end in view, and the future fumbles,
A bad birth, not like the child in that gracious home
Heard in the quietness turning in its mother's womb,
A strategic mind already, seeking the best way
To present himself to life, and at last, resolved,
Springing into history quivering like a fish,
Dropping into the world like a ripe fruit in due time. –
But where is the Past to which Time, smiling through her tears
At her new-born son, can turn crying: 'I love you'?

The Covenanters

The waves of their purposefulness go flooding through me.
This religion is simple, naked. Its values stand out
In black and white. It is the wind of God;
Like standing on a mountain top in a gale
Binding, compelling, yet gloriously freeing.
It contains nothing tawdry or trivial.
Its very ugliness is compelling,
Its bleakness uplifting.
It holds me in a fastness of security.

Another Epitaph on an Army of Mercenaries[1]

It is a God-damned lie to say that these
Saved, or knew, anything worth any man's pride.
They were professional murderers and they took
Their blood money and impious risks and died.
In spite of all their kind some elements of worth
With difficulty persist here and there on earth.

The Two Parents

I love my little son, and yet when he was ill
I could not confine myself to his bedside.
I was impatient of his squalid little needs,
His laboured breathing and the fretful way he cried
And longed for my wide range of interests again,
Whereas his mother sank without another care
To that dread level of nothing but life itself
And stayed day and night, till he was better, there.

Women may pretend, yet they always dismiss
Everything but mere being just like this.

In the Slums of Glasgow

I have caught a glimpse of the seamless garment
And am blind to all else for evermore.
The immaculate vesture, the innermost shift,
    Of high and low, of rich and poor,
The glorious raiment of bridegroom and bride,
    Whoremonger and whore,
I have caught a glimpse of the seamless garment
And have eyes for aught else no more.

---

[1] In reply to A.E. Housman's.

Deep under the γνῶθι σεαυτόν of Thales I've seen
The Hindu Atmānam ātmanā pāsya, and far deeper still
In every man, woman, and child in Scotland even
The inseparable inherent cause, the inalienable thrill,
The subtle movement, the gleam, the hidden well-water,
All the lin-gāni of their souls, God's holy will.
As a shining light needs no other light to be seen
The soul is only known by the soul or knows anything still.

It was easier to do this in the slums, as who prefers
A white-faced lass – because the eyes show better, so.
Life is more naked there, more distinct from mind,
Material goods and all the other extraneous things that grow
Hardening over and hiding the sheer life. Behind speech, mind
    and will
Behind sensation, reflection, knowledge, and power – lo!
Life, to which all these are attached as the spokes of a wheel to
    the nave;
The immensity abiding in its own glory of which I have caught
    the glow.

The same earth produces diamonds, rock-crystal, and vermilion,
The same sun produces all sorts of plants, the same food
Is converted into hair, nails and many other forms.
These dogmas are not as I once thought true nor as afterwards
    false
But each the empty shadow of an intimate personal mood.
I am indifferent to shadows, possessing the substance now.
I too look on the world and behold it is good.

I am deluded by appearances no more – I have seen
The goodness, passion, and darkness from which all things spring,
Identical and abundant in the slums as everywhere else
Taking other forms – to which changing and meaningless names
    cling, –
But cancelling out at last, dissolving, vanishing,
  Like the stars before the rising sun.
Foam, waves, billows and bubbles are not different from the sea,
But riding the bright heavens or to the dark roots of earth sinking
Water is multiform, indivisible and one,
Not to be confused with any of the shapes it is taking.

170

I have not gained a single definite belief that can be put
In a scientific formula or hardened into a religious creed.
A conversion is not, as mostly thought, a turning towards a belief,
It is rather a turning round, a revolution indeed.
It has no primary reference to any external object.
It took place in me at last with lightning speed.
I suddenly walk in light, my feet are barely touching the ground,
I am free of a million words and forms I no longer need.

In becoming one with itself my spirit is one with the world.
The dull, aching tension is gone, all hostility and dread.
All opposing psychic tendencies are resolved in sweet song
My eyes discard all idle shows and dwell instead
In my intercourse with every man and woman I know
On the openings and shuttings of eyes, the motions of mind,
    and, especially, life, and are led
Beyond colour, savour, odour, tangibility, numbers, extensions,
Individuality, conjunction, disjunction, priority, posteriority –
    like an arrow sped,
And sheer through intellection, volition, desire, aversion,
Pleasure, pain, merit and demerit – to the fountain-head,
To the unproduced, unproducing, solitary, motionless soul
By which alone they can be known, by which alone we are not
    misled.

I have seen this abhyasa most clearly in the folk of these slums,
Even as I have known the selfless indefatigable love of a mother
Concerned only for the highest possible vitality of her children,
Leaving their lives free to them, not seeking to smother
Any jet of their spirits in her own preconceptions or wishes. –
Would such were the love of every one of us for each other!

I have seen this abhyasa most clearly in the folk of these slums
Even as I know how every one of the women there,
Irrespective of all questions of intelligence, good looks, fortune's
    favour,
Can give some buck-navvy or sneak-thief the joy beyond compare –
Naked, open as to destitution and death, to the unprudential
Guideless life-in-death of the ecstasy they share –
Eternity, as Boethius defined it, – though few lovers give it his
    terms –
'To hold and possess the whole fulness of life anywhere

In a moment; here and now, past, present and to come.' –
The bliss of God glorifying every squalid lair.

The sin against the Holy Ghost is to fetter or clog
The free impulse of life – to weaken or cloud
The glad wells of being – to apply other tests,
To say that these pure founts must be hampered, controlled,
Denied, adulterated, diluted, cowed,
The wave of omnipotence made recede, and all these lives, these
    lovers,
Lapse into cannon-fodder, sub-humanity, the despised slum-
    crowd.

I am filled forever with a glorious awareness
Of the inner radiance, the mystery of the hidden light in these
    dens,
I see it glimmering like a great white-sailed ship
Bearing into Scotland from Eternity's immense,
Or like a wild swan resting a moment in mid-flood.
It has the air of a winged victory, in suspense
By its own volition in its imperious way.
As if the heavens opened I gather its stupendous sense.

For here too, Philosophy has a royal and ancient seat,
And, holding an eternal citadel of light and immortality,
With Study her only comrade, sets her victorious foot
On the withering flower of the fast-ageing world. – Let all men see.
Now the babel of Glasgow dies away in our ears,
The great heart of Glasgow is sinking to rest,
Na nonanunno nunnono nana nananana nanu,
Nunno nunnonanunneno nanena nunnanunnanut.
We lie cheek to cheek in a quiet trance, the moon itself no more
    still.
There is no movement but your eyelashes fluttering against me,
And the fading sound of the work-a-day world,
Dadadoduddadaddadi dadadodudadidadoh,
Duddadam dadade dudde dadadadadadodadah.

Glasgow, 1960[1]

Returning to Glasgow after long exile
Nothing seemed to me to have changed its style.
Buses and trams all labelled 'To Ibrox'
Swung past packed tight as they'd hold with folks.
Football match, I concluded, but just to make sure
I asked; and the man looked at me fell dour,
Then said, 'Where in God's name are *you* frae, sir?
It'll be a record gate, but the cause o' the stir
Is a debate on "la loi de l'effort converti"
Between Professor MacFadyen and a Spainish pairty.'
I gasped. The newsboys came running along,
'Special! Turkish Poet's Abstruse New Song.
Scottish Authors' Opinions' – and, holy snakes,
I saw the edition sell like hot cakes!

---

[1] First printed in the *London Mercury* in 1935 – Eds.

The Glass of Pure Water

Hold a glass of pure water to the eye of the sun!
It is difficult to tell the one from the other
Save by the tiny hardly visible trembling of the water.
This is the nearest analogy to the essence of human life
Which is even more difficult to see.
Dismiss anything you can see more easily;
It is not alive – it is not worth seeing.
There is a minute indescribable difference
Between one glass of pure water and another
With slightly different chemical constituents.
The difference between one human life and another
Is no greater; colour does not colour the water;
You cannot tell a white man's life from a black man's.
But the lives of these particular slum people
I am chiefly concerned with, like the lives of all
The world's poorest, remind me less
Of a glass of water held between my eyes and the sun
– They remind me of the feeling they had
Who saw Sacco and Vanzetti in the death cell
On the eve of their execution.
– One is talking to God.

I dreamt last night that I saw one of His angels
Making his centennial report to the Recording Angel
On the condition of human life.
Look at the ridge of skin between your thumb and forefinger.
Look at the delicate lines on it and how they change
– How many different things they can express –

174

As you move out or close in your forefinger and thumb.
And look at the changing shapes – the countless
Little gestures, little miracles of line –
Of your forefinger and thumb as you move them.
And remember how much a hand can express,
How a single slight movement of it can say more
Than millions of words – dropped hand, clenched fist,
Snapping fingers, thumb up, thumb down,
Raised in blessing, clutched in passion, begging,
Welcome, dismissal, prayer, applause,
And a million other signs, too slight, too subtle,
Too packed with meaning for words to describe,
A universal language understood by all.
And the angel's report on human life
Was the subtlest movement – just like that – and no more;
A hundred years of life on the Earth
Summed up, not a detail missed or wrongly assessed,
In that little inconceivably intricate movement.

The only communication between man and man
That says anything worth hearing
– The hidden well-water; the finger of destiny –
Moves as that water, that angel, moved.
Truth is the rarest thing and life
The gentlest, most unobtrusive movement in the world.
I cannot speak to you of the poor people of all the world
But among the people in these nearest slums I know
This infinitesimal twinkling, this delicate play
Of tiny signs that not only say more
Than all speech, but all there is to say,
All there is to say and to know and to be.
There alone I seldom find anything else,
Each in himself or herself a dramatic whole,
An 'agon' whose validity is timeless.

Our duty is to free that water, to make these gestures,
To help humanity to shed all else,
All that stands between any life and the sun,
The quintessence of any life and the sun;
To still all sound save that talking to God;
To end all movements save movements like these.
India had that great opportunity centuries ago

And India lost it – and became a vast morass,
Where no water wins free; a monstrous jungle
Of useless movement; a babel
Of stupid voices, drowning the still small voice.
It is our turn now; the call is to the Celt.

This little country can overcome the whole world of wrong
As the Lacedaemonians the armies of Persia.
Cornwall – Gaeldom – must stand for the ending
Of the essential immorality of any man controlling
Any other – for the ending of all Government
Since all Government is a monopoly of violence;
For the striking of this water out of the rock of Capitalism;
For the complete emergence from the pollution and fog
With which the hellish interests of private property
In land, machinery, and credit
Have corrupted and concealed from the sun,
From the gestures of truth, from the voice of God,
Hundreds upon hundreds of millions of men,
Denied the life and liberty to which they were born
And fobbed off with a horrible travesty instead
– Self-righteous, sunk in the belief that they are human,
When not a tenth of one per cent show a single gleam
Of the life that is in them under their accretions of filth.

And until that day comes every true man's place
Is to reject all else and be with the lowest,
The poorest – in the bottom of that deepest of wells
In which alone is truth; in which
Is truth only – truth that should shine like the sun,
With a monopoly of movement, and a sound like talking to
    God . . .

The Glen of Silence

πέφϱιϰα τὰν ὠλεσίοιϰον
θεόν οὐ θεοῖς ὁμοίαν
      AESCHYLUS: *The Seven Against Thebes*

By this cold shuddering fit of fear
My heart divines a presence here,
Goddess or ghost yclept;
Wrecker of homes....
      G.M. Cookson's translation, *vide*
      Four Plays of Aeschylus, p.142

Where have I 'heard' a silence before
Like this that only a lone bird's cries
And the sound of a brawling burn today
Serve in this desolate glen but to emphasize?

Every doctor knows it – the stillness of foetal death,
The indescribable silence over the abdomen then!
A silence literally 'heard' because of the way
It stands out in the auscultation of the abdomen.

Here is an identical silence picked out
By a bickering burn and a lone bird's wheeple
– The foetal death in this great 'cleared' glen
Where the *fear-tholladh nan tighean*[1] has done its foul work
– The tragedy of an unevolved people!

---

[1] The Destroyer of Homes.

177

Perfect

On the Western Seaboard of South Uist
(Los muertos abren los ojos a los que viven)

I found a pigeon's skull on the machair,
All the bones pure white and dry, and chalky,
But perfect,
Without a crack or a flaw anywhere.

At the back, rising out of the beak,
Were twin domes like bubbles of thin bone,
Almost transparent, where the brain had been
That fixed the tilt of the wings.

Island Funeral

The procession winds like a little snake
Between the walls of irregular grey stones
Piled carelessly on one another.
Sometimes, on this winding track,
The leaders are doubled back
Quite near to us.

It is a grey world, sea and sky
Are colourless as the grey stones,
And the small fields are hidden by the walls
That fence them on every side.

Seen in perspective, the walls
Overlap each other
As far as the skyline on the hill,
Hiding every blade of grass between them,
So that all the island appears
One jumble of grey boulders.
The last grey wall outlined on the sky
Has the traceried effect
Of a hedge of thorns in winter.

The men in the stiff material
Of their homespun clothes
Look like figures cut from cardboard,
But shod in their rawhide rivelins
They walk with the springing step of mountaineers.
The women wear black shawls,
And black or crimson skirts.

A line of tawny seaweed fringes the bay
Between high-water mark and low.
It is luminous between the grey of rocky shore
And the grey of sullen water.

We can now and then look over a wall
Into some tiny field. Many of these
Are nothing but grey slabs of limestone,
Smooth as any pavement,
With a few blades of grass
Struggling up through the fissures,
And the grey surface of that rock
Catches and holds the light
As if it was water lying there.

At last the long line halts and breaks up,
And, like a stream flowing into a loch,
The crowd pours from the narrow lane
Into the cemetery where on an unfenced sandhill
The grey memorial stones of the island
Have no distinction from the country.
The coffin lies tilted a little sideways
On the dark grey sand flung up from the grave.

A little priest arrives; he has a long body and short legs
And wears bicycle clips on his trousers.
He stands at the head of the grave
And casts a narrow purple ribbon round his neck
And begins without delay to read the Latin prayers
As if they were a string of beads.
Twice the dead woman's son hands him a bottle
And twice he sprinkles the coffin and the grave
With holy water. In all the faces gathered round
There is a strange remoteness.

They are weather-beaten people with eyes grown clear,
Like the eyes of travellers and seamen,
From always watching far horizons.
But there is another legend written on these faces,
A shadow – or a light – of spiritual vision
That will seldom find full play
On the features of country folk
Or men of strenuous action.
Among these mourners are believers and unbelievers,
And many of them steer a middle course,
Being now priest-ridden by convention
And pagan by conviction,
But not one of them betrays a sign
Of facile and self-lulling piety,
Nor can one see on any face
'A sure and certain hope
Of the Resurrection to eternal life.'
This burial is just an act of nature,
A reassertion of the islanders' inborn certainty
That 'in the midst of life we are in death.'
It is unlike the appointed funerals of the mainland
With their bitter pageantry
And the ramp of undertakers and insurance companies
That makes death seem incredible and cruel.
There are no loafing onlookers.
Everyone is immediately concerned
In what is taking place.
All through their lives death has been very close to them,
And this funeral of one who had been 'a grand woman'
Seems to be but a reminder
Of the close comradeship between living and dying.

Down in the bay there is a row of curraghs
Drawn up on the sand. They lie keel upwards,
Each one shining black and smooth
Like some great monster of the sea,
Symbols to the island folk of their age-long
Battle with the waves, a battle where in daily life
The men face death and the women widowhood.

Four men fill in the grave with dark grey sand,
Then they cover the sand
With green sods and rough-hewn boulders,
And finally an old man with a yellow beard
Helps the four young gravediggers
In levering a great slab of stone
Until it lies flat upon the grave,
And the people watch all this in silence.
Then the crowd scatters east and west
And, last, the four gravediggers,
All of them laughing now
With the merriment of clowns.

There are few and fewer people
On the island nowadays,
And there are more ruins of old cottages
Than occupied homes.
I love to go into these little houses
And see and touch the pieces of furniture.
I know all there is to know
About their traditional plenishing
And native arts and crafts,
And can speak with authority
About tongue-and-groove cleats,
The lipped drawer, and the diameters of finials.
But I know them also in their origin
Which is the Gaelic way of life
And can speak with equal authority
About a people one of whose proverbs
Is the remarkable sentence:
'Every force evolves a form.'
While this thing lasted
It was pure and very strong.
In an old island room the sense is still strong
Of being above and beyond the familiar,
The world as we know it,
In an atmosphere purified,
As it were, from the non-essentials of living
– An intangible feeling,
Difficult to describe,
But easy to recall to anyone

Who has stood in such a room
And been disturbed by the certainty
That those who once inhabited it
Were sure of every thought they had.

To enter almost any of the island rooms even today
Is to be profoundly conscious of this emanation,
At once so soothing and so strangely agitating.
Fifty years ago a visitor wrote: 'They are there to stay,
And that fact accounts for a great deal.
It is partial explanation of the contentment
On the faces of the island women.
It is a reason for the repose and settledness
Which pervade an island village
– That indefinable something,
So altogether unlike the life of ordinary villages,
And which you feel in the air,
And are conscious of by some instinct, as men claim
To be aware of the presence of spirits.
There is no restlessness,
Or fret of business,
Or anxiety about anything.
It is as if the work was done,
And it was one eternal afternoon.'
But they have not, in fact, stayed,
Foully forced out by their inferiors –
Red-faced, merely physical people
Whose only thought looking over
These incomparable landscapes
Is what sport they will yield
– How many deer and grouse.
The old stock are few and fewer now.
But they expected to stay,
And they deserved to stay,
Just as they expected there would always be
Thousands of them to work incessantly and serenely
At the making of objects which said:
'There is great beauty in harmony.'
They lived as much like one another as possible,
And they kept as free as they could of the world at large.
It is not their creed as such, however,
That explains them and the beauty of their work.

It is rather the happiness with which they held it,
The light-heartedness with which they enslaved themselves
To the various rituals it demanded,
And also the circumstance that they were all
Poor people – whose notions of form
Were both ancient and basic.
They began with the barest patterns, the purest beginnings
Of design, in their minds, and then
Something converted them into artists
With an exalted lyric gift.
What that something was
No one can claim perfectly to know.
Some of them were reported as believing
In assistance from the angels.
Whatever the source, the result was some
Of the most beautiful work the world has ever seen.

And even now, in Edinburgh or Glasgow or London,
I often move my ear up close
The better to distinguish in the raucous mixture
The sound of the cornet I want to hear,
And you may see my face light up
With recognition and appreciation at various points,
And hear me comment, 'The greatest of them all.'
The term is justified   this island note,
This clear old Gaelic sound,
In the chaos of the modern world,
Is like a phrase from Beiderbecke's cornet,
As beautiful as any phrase can be.
It is, in its loveliness and perfection,
Unique, as a phrase should be;
And it is ultimately indescribable.
Panassié speaks of it as 'full and powerful,'
But also as 'so fine
As to be almost transparent,'
And there is in fact
This extraordinary delicacy in strength.
He speaks of phrases that soar;
And this, too, is in fact
A remarkable and distinguishing quality.
Otis Ferguson speaks of 'the clear line
Of that music,' of 'every phrase

As fresh and glistening as creation itself,'
And there is in fact
This radiance, and simple joyousness.
These terms tell a great deal, but there remains
Much that eludes words completely
And can only be heard.
And though one can account for the music
Up to a certain point by the quality of the person
– The 'candour, force, personal soundness, good humour' –
There have been other people – and still are, no doubt –
With candour, force, personal soundness and good humour
And one has still to explain, as always,
How these qualities translated themselves
In this instance into such musical phrases.
In the din of our modern world
The Gaelic spirit plays merely
As an unfeatured member of well-known bands
– Which means that one hears it sometimes – very rarely! –
For a full chorus, sometimes merely for a phrase,
Sometimes only in the background with the rest of the brass.
But even the phrase detaches itself from its surroundings
As something exquisite and perfect; and even playing
Along with others in the background
It stands out from them,
Not through any aggressiveness but solely
Through the distinctive quality of its style.
'The greatest of them all' – but
There is little left on the island now,
And soon the last funeral
Will take place there,
And in the rowdy chaos of the world
The sound of this cornet will be heard no more
– One will listen, and one's face will never
Light up with recognition and appreciation again.

Yet if the nature of the mind is determined
By that of the body, as I believe,
It follows that every type of human mind
Has existed an infinite number of times
And will do so. Materialism promises something
Hardly to be distinguished from eternal life.
Minds or souls with the properties I love

184

– The minds or souls of these old islanders –
Have existed during an eternal time in the past
And will exist for an eternal time in the future.
A time broken up of course
By enormous intervals of non-existence,
But an infinite time.
If one regards these personalities
As possessing some value
There is a certain satisfaction
In the thought that in eternity
They will be able to develop
In all possible environments
And to express themselves
In all the ways possible to them
– A logical deduction from thoroughgoing Materialism
And independent of the precise type
Of materialism developed.
It is quite unimportant whether we call
Our ultimate reality matter, electric charge,
Ψ-waves, mind-stuff, neural stuff, or what not,
Provided it obeys laws which can, in principle,
Be formulated mathematically.

The cornet solo of our Gaelic islands
Will sound out every now and again
Through all eternity.

I have heard it and am content for ever.

from *Cornish Heroic Song for Valda Trevlyn*

I sing of Cornwall.

Chip of Atlantis, that clings to England still,
Alien in its traditions, utterly different,
This granite-bound corner, storm-washed,
With the smell of seaspray in its fields,
This boon to man, with its gentle air,
Its entrancing colours – Cornwall!
– Cha! I am no good at *natures-mortes!*

Cornwall, epic *intime!*

Cornwall and England, David and Goliath!

Not the ideal but the actual Cornwall
Full of the wandering abscess of the English influence!

*   *   *

(The Celtic genius – Cornwall, Scotland, Ireland, Wales –
Is to the English Ascendancy, the hideous khaki Empire,
As the white whale is to the killer whale,
The white whale displaying in its buccal cavity
The heavy oily blood-rich tongue which is the killer's especial
    delight.
The killer slips his head into the behemoth's mouth
And rives away part after part of the tongue until
Nothing remains in the white whale's mouth but a cicatrised
    stump.
Yet to-day we laugh gaily and show our healthy red tongues,
Red rags to John Bull – the Celtic colour flaunting again
In a world where the ravening sub-fusc more and more
Prevails. We young Celts arise with quick tongues intact
Though our elders lie tongueless under the ocean of history.
We show ourselves as ever and again through great grey volumes
    of smoke
Red blasts of the fire come quivering – yea, we dare
To shoot out our tongues under the very noses of the English.
The fate of our forefathers has not made us afraid
To open our mouths and show our red glory of health,

Nay, we sail again, laughing, on the crown of the sea,
'Not so much bound to any haven ahead
As rushing from all havens astern,'
The deepest blood-being of the white race crying to England
'Consummatum est! Your Imperial *Pequod* is sunk.'
We young Celts disport ourselves fearlessly
Knowing that we are the units
Of a far greater cycle than Melville's great Northern cycle
And that in us it completes its round.)

*   *   *

His attitude towards woman is the basic point
A man must have thought out to know
Where he honestly stands.
Since praise is well, and compliment is well,
But affection – that is the last and final
And most precious reward any man can win.

I remember when you were like that shrub
Which is smothered with carillons of little brick-red bells
Finely striped with yellow lines;
That, when the sun shines through them,
Glow like hot blown glass.
But ah! now, beloved, it is as when on the Carmine Cherry,
A hundred feet high and with a spread
Coinciding with the circumference of the earth,
The ruby-red flowerbuds open, and the whole tree
Bursts into carmine flame, a mass of blossom, stark crimson.
To see the sun through its branches
When the tree is in full bloom
Is a thing that can never be forgotten.
Nor the sight of your eyes now, Valda,
Through the toppling wave of love.
Love's scarlet banner is over us.
We conquer Chaos, a new Creation.

Happy on Heimaey

Meanwhile, the last of the human faculties
To be touched by the finger of science,
Still unanalysed, still immeasurable,
The sense of smell is the one little refuge
In the human mind still inviolate and unshareable
Because communicable in no known language,
But some day this the most delicate of perceptions
Will be laid bare too – there will be
Chairs of osmology in our universities,
Ardent investigators searching out, recording, measuring,
Preserving in card indexes
The departing smells of the countryside.
Hayfields will be explained in terms of Coumarin,
Beanfields in Ionone, hedge-roses in Phenyl-Ethyl-Propionate,
Hawthorn as Di-Methyl-Hydroquinone.
(But will they ever capture the scent of violets
Among the smoke of the shoeing-forge, or explain
The clean smell of a road wet with summer rain?)
Until that day, on Heimaey, 400 miles due North-West
Of Rona in the Hebrides, I am content to walk out
Into an unreal country of yellow fields
Lying at the foot of black volcanic cliffs
In the shadow of dead Helgafell,
And watch a few farmers scything
(Careful of the little birds' nests,
Iceland wheatear, snow bunting, white wagtail, meadow pipit,
And leaving clumps of grass to protect them)
A sweet but slender hay-crop
And tell its various constituents to myself
– White clover, chickenweed, dandelion,
A very large buttercup, silverweed, horsetail,
Thrift, sorrel, yellow bedstraw,
Poa, carex, and rushes –
Or look out of my bedroom window
In the farmhouse near Kaupstadur
On a garden planted with angelica,
Red current, rhubarb, and the flower of Venus,
Or at midnight watch the sun
Roll slowly along the northern horizon
To dip behind the great ice-caps

And jokulls of distant Iceland.
'Mellach lem bhith ind ucht ailiuin
    for beind cairrge,
Conacind and ar a mheinci
    feth na fairrci.'[1]
Ah me! It is a far better thing to be sitting
Alive on Heimaey, bare as an egg though it were,
Than rolled round willy-nilly with yonder sun.

---

[1] From an ancient poem ascribed to Colum Cille, meaning: 'Pleasant, methinks,
to be on an isle's breast, on a pinnacle of rock, that I might see there in its
frequency the ocean's aspect.'

from *The Battle Continues*[1]

One loves the temporal, some unique manifestation,
Something irreplaceable that dies.

But one is loyal to an ideal limit
Involved in all specific objects of love
And in all cooperating wills.

Shall the lonely griefs and joys of men
Forever remain a pluralistic universe?
Need they, if thought and will are bent in common interest
In making this universe *one*?

*   *   *

Major Road Ahead

The workers of Spain have themselves become the Cid Campeador.
A name whose original meaning is 'to be in the field,
The pasture.'
It has the further meanings of
'To frisk in the field,'
And so 'to be in the field of battle,'
And, especially, 'to be prominent in the field of battle,'
And so it came to mean 'surpassing in bravery'
And, in the mouths of their detractors,
'Men of the field, yokels.'
The word went from mouth to mouth among the timorous
Who had no better defence than their irony;
It slipped glibly from lips unctuous with envy.
'We are men of the field,' they cried,
Catching the jesting word like a ball hard driven,

---

[1] Although *The Battle Continues* was not published until 1957, it was written as a direct, almost instantaneous reply to the publication of Roy Campbell's *The Flowering Rifle: a Poem from the Battlefield of Spain* (London, 1939). MacDiarmid may have read extracts of Campbell's pro-Franco poem in magazines. The passage from 'England's Double Knavery' (published in *A Clyack-Sheaf* in 1969) also belongs to this period. MacDiarmid supplied a footnote to a part of the poem not reprinted here referring to a letter from Roy Campbell to the *TLS*, published on 25 February 1939, which effectively dates the composition of his poem at around that time. – Eds.

Accepting the nickname with pride,
And launching it into the firmament,
And on their lips
The jesting word assumed a dignity
And sparkled and shone and flashed
And became a blazon and a star

Who was the first to say it?
No man can tell. None of them knew.
It found itself suddenly upon all lips.
Was it born from the earth?
Did it fall from the sky,
From stones and trees,
From the dust and the air,
It was born from everywhere
At the same time.
It filled all space like light.

The heart of Spain expanded at the name
And embraced the world.
The name rose up,
Rose up into space,
Was charged and condensed
And fell again in a heroic rain.
A flight of swallows flying overhead
Caught up the name on the wing
And carried it to all the corners of the world.
The swallows sang it as they flew
And Spain grew by leagues
As it heard the name.

So their name issued suddenly
From all the pores of the earth,
And found itself upon all tongues,
Singing like a tree in the sun.
It was born and grew and ascended into Heaven,
Multiplied and was one with the forests,
Invaded the plains, crossed the mountains,
Covered Spain, leapt the frontiers and seas,
Filled all Europe,
Burst the boundaries of the world,

And grew and ascended,
And stayed only at Hope's zenith.

History and geography
Were obsessed with the name.
To the north, to the south,
To the east, to the west,
It was borne by the wind like a rose.
It passed above all banners and all birds
With a noise like a thousand banners,
A thousand birds,
While, beneath, a multitude
Weeping for joy,
Followed its passage on their knees
– Millions of heads
Raised in a branch of offering.
That heroic name is an eagle's nest
On the highest peak of History,
Sending through History a surge of song.
And there it remains through all eternity
Nestling on the strings of a lute

You come to me shining from beyond the bourne of death,
You come to me across life,
Over a wide sea beneath a sky of doves.
The tide of the battle surges upon the gleaming shore of your eyes.

Your eyes are two bas-reliefs of your glory.
Your hands are folded to offer up your heart.
Clothed in a comet,
You soar above Spain,
Above human history,
Into the infinite.

Your fury of love and faith
Planted four crosses to the wind
The garland of the four corners of the compass.
The hurricanes of God conjured you above your battles.
I saw you dedicate yourself
And arise out of your flesh
In a divine frenzy
Drawn up towards the infinite

In a mystic ecstasy,
A celestial drunkenness.

You are a tree which climbs and climbs
To bear up once more the Christ
Who came down to visit souls.

Bent over a flight of thunderbolts,
With your eyes fixed upon a journey,
Whither are you going?
In an immense sweep you soar resplendent
Up to the kingdom that is within yourself.
He who would now seek to follow the march of your thoughts
Would lose his reason in dismay,
Would go astray in abysses of vertigo.
There are no limits to your soul.
Whither are you going?
How can I follow you?

The courses of the seven planets
Are reflected in the mirror of your shield.
Go your ways, go your ways,
Leave your flesh behind and go your ways
Clad in Epic.
I will watch beside you
As you roam the spaces of the stars
Without form and void,
As you circle the ellipse of God
I will keep vigil at the foot of your memory.
Your heart leaves a wake of spreading deeds
And perhaps I can follow you with my eyes.

They are gone.
Before my eyes
Their sword gleams and twists in a sudden blaze
And sprouts wings – two great wings of fire and flaming feather.

The sword moves, it is lifted up,
It soars, soars above my head, above the world.
I hear a hecatomb of planets falling into chaos.
I hear windows opening in space.
I hear eternity rushing in my ears.

Where am I? What is happening to me?
A whirlpool of light sucks me into its centre
And I fall down, down, down. . . .

I have returned to earth,
To Spain.
I have come back to myself.

from *England's Double Knavery*

Left-wing poetry represents a rise in the price of bread,
And starving workless peasants, a bread queue, a stricken field.
Represents is right, i.e. *Protests against!* – not *causes*.
That is the proud prerogative of Right-wing poetry
And since in Britain and America at least
The latter outbulks the former by ninety-nine to one,
Surely it could nullify the one per cent,
If there were any truth in the ludicrous charge?
How does Campbell explain its impotence?
His logic is as rotten as his poetry
And all his precious harvest can possibly produce
Is an epidemic of pellagra – the true
Harvest of the Right in very fact. Poor opisthocoelian Campbell,
The hollowest of all the hollow men, and so
Fit champion of his wholly indefensible cause,
Which, if it had been good, his bonehead gaucherie
Would have let down and ruined in any case!
Not that his typical reader would have known!
– A stout man, walking with a waddle, with a face
Creased and puffed into a score
Of unhealthy rolls and crevices
And a red and bulbous nose;
A rich man who fawns his way through life,
With a thick husky voice, naturally coarse,
Through which with grotesque insistence runs a tone
Of mock culture – a man whose fat finger
Ticks off the feet in Campbell's lines
'Left, right! Left, right!' and whose aesthetic sense
Delights to hear the recurrent crack

194

Of the hippopotamus hide whip or to note
The sibilance as of rubber truncheons every here and there.
So you went for a soldier, did you,
Campbell? – a soldier in Spain?
The hero of a penny novelette
With the brain of a boy scout!
All soldiers are fools.
That's why they kill each other.
The deterioration of life under the régime
Of the soldier is a commonplace; physical power
Is a rough substitute for patience and intelligence
And co-operative effort in the governance of man;
Used as a normal accompaniment of action
Instead of a last resort it is a sign
Of extreme social weakness. Killing
Is the ultimate simplification of life. And while
The effort of culture is towards greater differentiation
Of perceptions and desires and values and ends,
Holding them from moment to moment
In a perpetually changing but stable equilibrium
The animus of war is to enforce uniformity
– To extirpate whatever the soldier
Can neither understand nor utilise...

Poetry and Science

Science is the Differential Calculus of the mind,
Art is the Integral Calculus; they may be
Beautiful apart, but are great only when combined.
SIR RONALD ROSS

The rarity and value of scientific knowledge
Is little understood – even as people
Who are not botanists find it hard to believe
Special knowledge of the subject can add
Enormously to the aesthetic appreciation of flowers!
Partly because in order to identify a plant
You must study it very much more closely
Than you would otherwise have done, and in the process
Exquisite colours, proportions, and minute shapes spring to
      light
Too small to be ordinarily noted.
And more than this – it seems the botanist's knowledge
Of the complete structure of the plant
(Like a sculptor's of bone and muscle)
– Of the configuration of its roots stretching under the earth,
The branching of stems,
Enfolding of buds by bracts,
Spreading of veins on a leaf –
Enriches and makes three-dimensional
His awareness of its complex beauty.

Wherefore I seek a poetry of facts. Even as
The profound kinship of all living substance
Is made clear by the chemical route.
Without some chemistry one is bound to remain
Forever a dumbfounded savage
In the face of vital reactions.
The beautiful relations
Shown only by biochemistry
Replace a stupefied sense of wonder
With something more wonderful
Because natural and understandable.
Nature is more wonderful
When it is at least partly understood.
Such an understanding dawns

On the lay reader when he becomes
Acquainted with the biochemistry of the glands
In their relation to diseases such as goitre
And their effects on growth, sex, and reproduction.
He will begin to comprehend a little
The subtlety and beauty of the action
Of enzymes, viruses, and bacteriophages,
These substances which are on the borderland
Between the living and the non-living.

He will understand why the biochemist
Can speculate on the possibility
Of the synthesis of life without feeling
That thereby he is shallow or blasphemous.
He will understand that, on the contrary,
He finds all the more
Because he seeks for the endless
– 'Even our deepest emotions
May be conditioned by traces
Of a derivative of phenanthrene!'

Scotland

It requires great love of it deeply to read
The configuration of a land,
Gradually grow conscious of fine shadings,
Of great meanings in slight symbols,
Hear at last the great voice that speaks softly,
See the swell and fall upon the flank
Of a statue carved out in a whole country's marble,
Be like Spring, like a hand in a window
Moving New and Old things carefully to and fro,
Moving a fraction of flower here,
Placing an inch of air there,
And without breaking anything.

So I have gathered unto myself
All the loose ends of Scotland,
And by naming them and accepting them,
Loving them and identifying myself with them,
Attempt to express the whole.

Scotland Small?

Scotland small? Our multiform, our infinite Scotland *small*?
Only as a patch of hillside may be a cliché corner
To a fool who cries 'Nothing but heather!' where in
   September another
Sitting there and resting and gazing round
Sees not only the heather but blaeberries
With bright green leaves and leaves already turned scarlet,
Hiding ripe blue berries; and amongst the sage-green leaves
Of the bog-myrtle the golden flowers of the tormentil shining;
And on the small bare places, where the little Blackface sheep
Found grazing, milkworts blue as summer skies;
And down in neglected peat-hags, not worked
Within living memory, sphagnum moss in pastel shades
Of yellow, green, and pink; sundew and butterwort
Waiting with wide-open sticky leaves for their tiny winged prey;
And nodding harebells vying in their colour
With the blue butterflies that poise themselves delicately
   upon them,
And stunted rowans with harsh dry leaves of glorious colour.
'Nothing but heather!' – How marvellously descriptive! And
   incomplete!

Bagpipe Music

Let me play to you tunes without measure or end,
Tunes that are born to die without a herald,
As a flight of storks rises from a marsh, circles,
And alights on the spot from which it rose.

Flowers. A flower-bed like hearing the bagpipes.
The fine black earth has clotted into sharp masses
As if the frost and not the sun had come.
It holds many lines of flowers.
First faint rose peonies, then peonies blushing,
Then again red peonies, and behind them,
Massive, apoplectic peonies, some of which are so red
And so violent as to seem almost black; behind these
Stands a low hedge of larkspur, whose tender apologetic blossoms
Appear by contrast pale, though some, vivid as the sky above
    them,
Stand out from their fellows, iridescent and slaty as a pigeon's
    breast.
The bagpipes – they are screaming and they are sorrowful.
There is a wail in their merriment, and cruelty in their triumph.
They rise and they fall like a weight swung in the air at the end of
    a string.
They are like the red blood of those peonies.
And like the melancholy of those blue flowers.
They are like a human voice – no! for the human voice lies!
They are like human life that flows under the words.
That flower-bed is like the true life that wants to express itself
And does... while we human beings lie cramped and fearful.

Dìreadh III

*So, in the sudden sight of the sun, has man stopped, blinded,
paralysed and afraid?*

I am reft to the innermost heart
Of my country now,
History's final verdict upon it,
The changeless element in all its change,
Reified like the woman I love.

Here in this simple place of clean rock and crystal water,
With something of the cold purity of ice in its appearance,
Inhuman and yet friendly,
Undecorated by nature or by man
And yet with a subtle and unchanging beauty
Which seems the antithesis of every form of art.

Here near the summit of Sgurr Alasdair
The air is very still and warm,
The Outer Isles look as though
They were cut out of black paper
And stuck on a brilliant silver background,
(Even as I have seen the snow-capped ridges of Hayes Peninsula
Stand out stark and clear in the pellucid Arctic atmosphere
Or, after a wild and foggy night, in the dawn
Seen the jagged line of the Tierra del Fuego cliffs
Looking for all the world as if they were cut out of tin,
Extending gaunt and desolate),
The western sea and sky undivided by horizon,
So dazzling is the sun
And its glass image in the sea.
The Cuillin peaks seem miniature
And nearer than is natural
And they move like liquid ripples
In the molten breath
Of the corries which divide them.
I light my pipe and the match burns steadily
Without the shielding of my hands,
The flame hardly visible in the intensity of light
Which drenches the mountain top.

I lie here like the cool and gracious greenery
Of the water-crowfoot leafage, streaming
In the roping crystalline currents,
And set all about on its upper surface
With flecks of snow blossom that, on closer looking,
Show a dust of gold.
The blossoms are fragile to the touch
And yet possess such strength and elasticity
That they issue from the submergence of a long spate
Without appreciable hurt – indeed, the whole plant
Displays marvellous endurance in maintaining
A rooting during the raging winter torrents.
Our rivers would lose much if the snowy blossom
And green waving leafage of the water-crowfoot
Were absent – aye, and be barer of trout too!
And so it is with the treasures of the Gaelic genius
So little regarded in Scotland to-day.

Yet emerging unscathed from their long submergence,
Impregnably rooted in the monstrous torrents[1]
– The cataracting centuries cannot rive them away –
And productive of endless practical good,
Even to people unaware of their existence,
In the most seemingly-unlikely connections.

I am possessed by this purity here
As in a welling of stainless water
Trembling and pure like a body of light
Are the webs of feathery weeds all waving,
Which it traverses with its deep threads of clearness
Like the chalcedony in moss agate
Starred here and there with grenouillette.

It is easy here to accept the fact
That that which the 'wisdom' of the past
And the standards of the complacent elderly rulers
Of most of the world to-day regard
As the most fixed and eternal verities –
The class state, the church,
The old-fashioned family and home,
Private property, rich and poor,
'Human nature' (to-day meaning mainly
The private-profit motive), their own race,
Their Heaven and their 'immortal soul' –
Is all patently evanescent,
Even as we know our fossil chemical accumulations
Of energy in coal, peat, oil, lignite and the rest
Are but ephemeral, a transitory blaze
Even on the small time-scale of civilized man,
And that running water, though eminently convenient and
        practicable
For the present, will give us a mere trickle
Of the energy we shall demand in the future.

And suddenly the flight of a bird reminds me
Of how I once went out towards sunset in a boat
Off the rocky coast of Wigtownshire
And of my glimpse of the first rock-pigeon I saw.

---

[1] See John Ruskin's description of the spring at Carshalton.

It darted across one of the steep gullies
At the bottom of which our boat lay rocking
On the dark green water – and vanished into safety
In a coign of the opposite wall
Before a shot could be fired.
It swerved in the air,
As though doubtful of its way,
Then with a glad swoop of certainty
It sped forward, turned upward,
And disappeared into some invisible cranny
Below the overhanging brow of the cliff.

There was such speed, such grace, such happy confidence of
    refuge in that swoop
That it struck me with the vividness of a personal experience.
For an instant I seemed to see into the bird's mind
And to thrill with its own exhilaration of assured safety.
Why should this be? It was as though
I had seen the same occurrence,
Or some part of it, before.

Then I knew. Into the back of my mind had come
The first line of the loveliest chorus in *Hippolytus*,
That in which the Troezenian women,
Sympathizing with the unhappy Phaedra,
Who is soon to die by her own hand,
Sing of their yearning to fly away from the palace
Whose sunny terraces are haunted by misery and impending
    doom.
They long to escape with the flight of the sea-birds
To the distant Adriatic and the cypress-fringed waters of Eridanus
Or to the fabulous Hesperides,
Where beside the dark-blue ocean
Grow the celestial apple-trees.
It is the same emotion as filled the Hebrew poet
Who cried: 'O for the wings of a dove,
That I might flee away and be at rest.'
'ἠλιβάτοις ὑπὸ κευθμῶσι γενοίμαν.'
The untranslatable word in that line
Is the ὑπὸ. It includes more
Than a single word of English can contain.
Up-in-under: so had the pigeon

202

Flown to its refuge in 'the steep hiding-places,'
So must Euripides have seen a sea-bird
Dart to its nest in the cliffs of Attica.
For an instant, sitting in that swaying boat
Under the red rocks, while the sunset ebbed down the sky
And the water lapped quietly at my side,
I again felt the mind of the poet reaching out
Across the centuries to touch mine.
Scotland and China and Greece!
Here where the colours –
Red standing for heat,
Solar, sensual, spiritual;
Blue for cold – polar, bodily, intellectual;
Yellow luminous and embodied
In the most enduring and the brightest form in gold –
Remind me how about this
Pindar and Confucius agreed.
Confucius who was Pindar's contemporary
For nearly half a century!
And it was Pindar's 'golden snow'
My love and I climbed in that day.
I in Scotland as Pindar in Greece
Have stood and marvelled at the trees
And been seized with honey-sweet yearning for them;
And seen too mist condensing on an eagle,
His wings 'streamlined' for a swoop on a leveret,
As he ruffled up the brown feathers on his neck
In a quiver of excitement;
Pindar, greatest master of metaphor the world has seen,
His spirit so deeply in tune
With the many-sidedness of both Man and Nature
That he could see automatically all the basal resemblances
His metaphors imply and suggest.
Scotland and China and Greece!

So every loveliness Scotland has ever known,
Or will know, flies into me now,
Out of the perilous night of English stupidity,
As I lie brooding on the fact
That 'perchance the best chance
Of reproducing the ancient Greek temperament

Would be to "cross" the Scots with the Chinese.'[1]
The glory of Greece is imminent again to me here
With the complete justification his sense of it
In Germany – his participation in that great awakening
Taking the form of an imaginative reliving,
On behalf of his people, of the glory of Athens –
Lacked in Hölderlin. I see all things
In a cosmic or historical perspective too.
Love of country, in me, is love of a new order.
In Greece I also find the clue
To the mission of the poet
Who reveals to the people
The nature of their gods,
The instrument whereby his countrymen
Become conscious of the powers on whom they depend
And of whom they are the children,
Knowing, in himself, the urgency of the divine creativeness of
    Nature
And most responsive to its workings in the general world.
'Wer das Tiefste gedacht, liebt das Lebendigste.'

And remembering my earlier poems in Scots
Full of my awareness 'that language is one
Of the most cohesive or insulating of world forces
And that dialect is always a bond of union,'[2]
I covet the mystery of our Gaelic speech
In which *rughadh* was at once a blush,
A promontory, a headland, a cape,
Leadan, musical notes, litany, hair of the head,
And *fonn*, land, earth, delight, and a tune in music,[3]
And think of the Oriental provenance of the Scottish Gael,
The Eastern affiliations of his poetry and his music,
'...the subtler music, the clear light
Where time burns back about th' eternal embers,'
And the fact that he initiated the idea of civilization
That to-day needs renewal at its native source

Wer das Tiefste... He who has thought most deeply, loves those things which
are most alive.

[1] Sir Richard Livingstone.
[2] Sir James Crichton-Browne.
[3] Macfarlane's *English and Gaelic Vocabulary* (Constable, Edinburgh, 1815).

Where, indeed, it is finding it, since Georgia,
Stalin's native country, was also the first home of the Scots.

The Gaelic genius that is in this modern world
As sprays of quake grass are in a meadow,
Or light in the world, which notwithstanding
The *Fiat Lux* scores of thousands of years ago,
Is always scanty and dubious enough
And at best never shares the empery of the skies
On more than equal terms with the dark,
Or like sensitive spirits among the hordes of men,
Or seldom and shining as poetry itself.
Quake grass, the 'silver shakers', with their glumes shaped and
    corded
Like miniature cowrie shells, and wrapped
In bands of soft green and purple, and strung
(Now glittering like diamonds,
Now chocolate brown like partridge plumage)
On slender stems and branchlets, quick
To the slightest touch of air!

So Scotland darts into the towering wall of my heart
And finds refuge now. I give
My beloved peace, and her swoop has recalled
That first day when my human love and I,
Warmed and exhilarated by the sunny air,
Put on our skis and began
A zigzag track up the steep ascent.
There was no sound but the faint hiss and crush
Of the close-packed snow, shifting under our weight.
The cloudless bowl of the sky
Burned a deep gentian. In the hushed, empty world,
Where nothing moved but ourselves,
Our bodies grew more consciously alive.
I felt each steady beat of my heart.
The drawing and holding of my breath
Took on a strange significance.
Nor was I merely conscious of myself.
I began to be equally aware of my love;
Her little physical habits
Sinking into my mind
Held the same importance as my own.

How fragrant, how infinitely refreshing and recreating
Is the mere thought of Deirdre!
How much more exhilarating to see her, as now!

'She said that she at eve for me would wait;
Yet here I see bright sunrise in the sky.'[1]

Farewell all else! I may not look upon the dead,
Nor with the breath of dying be defiled,
And thou, I see, art close upon that end.

I am with Alba – with Deirdre – now
As a lover is with his sweetheart when they know
That personal love has never been a willing and efficient slave
To the needs of reproduction, that to make
Considerations of reproduction dictate the expression of personal
    love
Not infrequently destroys the individual at his spiritual core,
Thus 'eugenic marriages' cannot as a whole
Be successful so far as the parents are concerned,
While to make personal love master over reproduction
Under conditions of civilization is to degrade
The germ plasm of the future generations,
And to compromise between these two policies
Is to cripple both spirit and germ,
And accept the only solution – unyoke the two,
Sunder the fetters that from time immemorial
Have made them so nearly inseparable,
And let each go its own best way,
Fulfilling its already distinct function,
An emancipation the physical means for which
Are now known for the first time in history!

Let what can be shaken, be shaken,
And the unshakeable remain.
The Inaccessible Pinnacle[2] is not inaccessible.
So does Alba surpass the warriors

---

[1] From a Chinese eight-line lyric, twenty-seven centuries old.
[2] Of Sgurr Dearg, in Skye.

As a graceful ash surpasses a thorn,
Or the deer who moves sprinkled with the dewfall
Is far above all other beasts
– Its horns glittering to Heaven itself.[1]

---

[1] See *Volsungakvida en forna*, 41 (*Saemundar Edda*, Jónsson).

from *The Kind of Poetry I Want*

A poetry that never for a moment forgets
That if we study the position of the foetus
As it appears in about the ninth month
Of its development, we see the tiny body
Curled up with its head bowed over,
The hands crossed, and the knees drawn up
To permit the whole structure
Of bones, muscles, nerves,
And arteries to fit comfortably
Into the cage or matrix.
As it was in the beginning
So it is again at the end of life.
Think of the decrepit old human being,
Bent over, head bowed,
Seated in a weary, curled-up position
Exactly similar to the unborn babe's.
The cycle of life begins and ends
In the same design. Only the proportion,
Size, and shape of the human being
Change as he passes through the stages
Of babyhood, youth, maturity, and old age.
The eternal oval, the egg itself.
A poetry therefore to approach with two instruments
– Which, being mutually destructive,
Like fire and water, one can use
Only one at a time
– Even as one may attempt to describe
The relative positions of the Imperial Palace,
Hagia Sophia, and the Circus, in Constantinople.
On the one side the Palace was connected,
By open arcades and paradoxical gardens,
With the Golden Egg of Hagia Sophia;
On the other side an intestinal system
Of passages and winding stairs
Led to the Circus. But as regards
Byzantium in especial, these things are merely
The elements which combine to form
A stupendous life pregnant with symbolism.
Because the theme of that life
Was the world-embracing mystery

Of God and man
It stands supreme
Above its ingredients.
The ingredients resemble the things
For which a woman with child longs.
Like the juice of the oyster,
The aroma of the wild strawberry,
The most subtle and diversified elements
Are here intermingled to form
A higher organism.

A poetry concerned with all that is needed
Of the sum of human knowledge and expression,
The sustaining consciousness,
The reasonable will of our race,
To produce this super-individuality, Man,
In whom we all even now participate
Is the immediate purpose of the human race.

The only alternatives we can envisage
Are intolerable prospects of biological disaster,
Chronic war, social deterioration, diseases,
Specific differentiation generation after generation
Of distressed existences with extinction looming at the end.

Either we take hold of our destiny, or, failing that,
We are driven towards our fate.

Cyclopean prejudices, innate misconceptions,
Oceans, mountain barriers, limitless space,
The protean blind obstructions of nature
Within us and without, will not prevail
Against the crystallizing will; the ordered solvent knowledge,
The achieved clear-headedness of an illuminated race.

*   *   *

I dream of poems like the bread-knife
Which cuts three slices at once . . .

*   *   *

...Or like Fred Astaire, who has combined
All forms of dancing into one perfect whole
– Endowed his work with all the intricacies,
Incorporated all the things that make dancing difficult,
But developed them to such a point that they seem simple
– So great an artist that he makes you feel
You could do the dance yourself – Is not that great art?
A poetry in which the disorder and irrelevancies
Of the real world are seen
As evidence of the order, relevance, and authority
Of the law behind, so that what
Is misleading (private or untidy) becomes
By its very irrelevance significant of a reality
Beyond the bewilderment of external reality;
And a brain and an imagination that takes
Every grade without changing gears.
Like glancing at the rev-counter, partially closing the throttle,
And gliding down to make a fine
Three-point landing into the wind.

*   *   *

Ah, sweetheart, what a pool! Broad, deep, strong, silent, and
    sedate!
The foam-patches spinning round in the eddies and then
Hurrying onwards betray the speed of the current.
A sturdy Norsk-Murdoch spinning-rod, a 4-inch Silex reel,
A steel trace, and a box of artificial minnows
– A selection essentially for a big water.
(Very unlike the dainty but deadly outfit
Used when the streams are at summer level.)
Indeed, the river is a gorgeous colour,
Golden in the shallows, black in the depths,
Foam-flecked over all the pools.
For the initial attempt I choose a 3-inch anti-kink minnow, brown
    and gold.
– First, one or two casts downstream, to make sure
The tension of the reel is correctly adjusted to the weight of the
    bait,
That the line is well and truly wound,
Then out goes the minnow at the correct angle,
To drop on a circle of foam possibly 50 yards away.

Minnow, line, and rod are in one straight line.
The rod-point, dipping low almost to the surface,
Is slowly moved around, the minnow is bravely spinning its way
    across,
When a vicious tug sets the reel screaming.
A salmon is on; it makes no attempt
To increase the distance between us.
After I persuade it out of the full strength of the current
And get on terms with it
I keep it moving to a speedy end,
A perfect picture of a fish of 17 lb.
With the silver of the sea undimmed.

*   *   *

A poetry like the hope of achieving ere very long
A tolerable idea of what happens from first to last
If we bend a piece of wire
Backwards and forwards until it breaks.

*   *   *

A poetry that goes all the way
From Brahma to a stock,
A poetry like pronouncing the Shemhameporesh,
Unremitting, relentless,
Organised to the last degree.
Ah, Lenin, politics is child's play
To what this must be.

*   *   *

A poetry like the character of Indian culture
Which is and always has been its universal contacts.
Motifs flood in from Iran and Persia,
Nestorian monks colour the practice
Of Tibetan devotees, and in the Court
Of the rude Mahmud of Ghazni is a Moslem scholar
Acquainted with Plato. A wonderful panorama
In which, though its strength is rather
In arts and thought and race
Than in social structure and growth,

Innumerable reflections and parallels
For European culture strike us,
In the types of wergeld and feudal fief,
Land custom, paternal justice, and the bards;
A vast picture in which we see
The furious passage of Tamerlane or Zinghis Khan,
Or the great conquerors who have left hardly a wrack behind,
Taxila, with its memories of Alexander,
The Greek king who reigned in Sialkot,
And thousands more – with everywhere
The impression of universality,
Of the million grains of sand and gold
Which have rolled to the delta.

*   *   *

A poetry the quality of which
Is a stand made against intellectual apathy,
Its material founded, like Gray's, on difficult knowledge
And its metres those of a poet
Who has studied Pindar and Welsh poetry,
But, more than that, its words coming from a mind
Which has experienced the sifted layers on layers
Of human lives – aware of the innumerable dead
And the innumerable to-be-born,
The voice of the centuries, of Shakespeare's history plays
Concentrated and deepened,
'The breath and finer spirit of all knowledge,
The impassioned expression
Which is in the countenance of all science.'

*   *   *

A poetry full of *cynghanedd*,[1] and hair-trigger relationships,
With something about it that is plasmic,
Resilient, and in a way alarming – to make cry
'I touched something – and it was *alive*.'
There is no such shock in touching what
Has never lived; the mineral world is vast.

---

[1] A complicated device in Welsh poetry.

It is mighty, rigid, and brittle. But the hand
That touches vital matter – though the man were blind –
Infallibly recognizes the feel of life, and recoils in excitement.

*　　*　　*

And a poetry in which as in a film
Pure setting – the physical conditions
Under which action takes place – is extremely important,
So important, in fact, as to make us sometimes impatient
With a tale that is but crudely attached to it.
A poetry, in short, like that great Sheep Dog Film[1]
Whose setting is in my own native countryside;
The landscape and the people match perfectly.
The slow roll of the Border valleys,
The timeless fells and the ledges of rough rock,
The low dark sky and the hard going of the ground
Are an environment for no other human beings
Than those seen in this film. The first sequence
Brings men and stones together in one meaning.
After that we would watch with fascination
Anything whatever that happened, and believe it.
Then, of course, there are the dogs which introduce
The ripple of movement into an otherwise rock world.
They are the spirit of the place, not only
When they streak after their sheep at the trial
– The high moment, naturally, of the film –
But at all times.
They have the freedom of the mountains,
And it is their movements,
Even when they are miles away,
That the minds of the people follow.
It is through the dogs that the men become alive,
And again it might not matter too much what the dogs did,
Or whether what they did was intrinsically interesting.
We are committed to them from the moment
We see them as part of this world
And understand their rôle in it.
The film has won us long before

---

[1] *To the Victor* (Gaumont British).

We know it has a story to develop.
This is something that can only happen
In the movie art. I want a poetry
In which this happens too,
In a poetry that stands for production, use, and life,
As opposed to property, profits and death.

A poetry throwing light on the problems of value
– Deriving its stimulating quality, its seminal efficacy,
Not from the discovery, as old as the Greeks,
That moral codes are relative to social factors,
But from the nice and detailed study of the mechanisms
Through which society
Determines attitudes in its members
By opening to them certain possibilities
By induction into objectively recognised statuses
While closing quite effectively other possibilities
– A poetry, not offering a compromise between naïve atomism
Giving an utterly unrelated picture of social phenomena,
And the unrealistic conception of a mystical social *Gestalt*,
The defining quality of which is intuited by transcendental means
(That growing danger, as a reaction from the bankruptcy
Of the atomistic approach, of a mystical
Organismic approach instinct with anti-rationalistic obscurantism),
But seeking to do justice to the discrete
As well as to the organically integrated aspects of society,
To the disruptive as well as to the cohesive forces.
– A poetry that men weary of the unscientific wrangling
Of contemporary social and political dogmatists
Will find a liberating experience
– Rich in its discoveries of new problems,
Important questions so far unsuspected,
For which field research does not yet supply
The data necessary to answer them.

A poetry that is – to use the terms of Red Dog[1] –
High, low, jack, and the goddamn game.

---

[1] Red Dog – American pastime.

Or like riding a squealing *oscuro*
Whose back has never held a saddle before

Or a *grulla* with a coat
Like a lady's blue-grey suede glove

Or a bayo coyote in the red morning sun,
His coat shining like something alive,

A poetry wilder than a heifer
You have to milk into a gourd.

*   *   *

Poetry of such an integration as cannot be effected
Until a new and conscious organisation of society
Generates a new view
Of the world as a whole
As the integration of all the rich parts
Uncovered by the separate disciplines.
That is the poetry that I want.

A poetry abstruse as hedge-laying
And full as the countryside in which
I have watched the practice of that great old art,
– Full of the stumbling boom of bees,
Cuckoos contradicting nightingales all through a summer day,
Twilight deepening with a savage orange light,
Pheasants travelling on fast, dark wings,
– Or like a village garden I know well
Where the pear-trees bloom with a bravery of buds,
The cydonia blossoms gloriously against its wall,
And roses abound through April, May, and June,
– And always with a surprising self-sufficiency
Like that of almost any descriptive passage of Mary Webb's[1]
– The fact that she was wholly herself in all she wrote
Creating a sort of finality and completeness
In each part of any given whole,

---

[1] Several of the verses given here are inspired by the fact that Mary Webb, author
of *Precious Bane* and other novels, was a personal friend of the poet's.

The integrity of her experience revealing itself in many ways,
In the fulfilment of rare powers of observation,
In the kind of inward perception which recognised
'The story of any flower' is 'not one of stillness,
But of faint gradations of movement that we cannot see,'
The outer magic and the inward mystery imaginatively
    reconciled,
Her deep kinship, her intuitive sympathy with leaf and flower
Extending without a break into the human kingdom,
And flowering there in an exquisite appreciation
Of the humours of single characters,
And a rare power to make them live and speak
In their own right and idiom.

There are few writers who can so capture
The elusive spirit of a countryside.
Alive and deeply felt in the mind
It dies on the pen,
Slain by the cold winds of propaganda,
The mists of exaggeration,
The warm fog of sentimentality.
The very desire to pin it down is in itself
Almost sufficient to ensure its doom.
It dies, and its corpse,
Pinned to each page by the unwitting writer,
Becomes overwhelmingly offensive to the sensitive reader.
To capture it alive and undamaged,
To display it with unfaded colours,
Is a miracle – only to be achieved
By humility, simplicity,
A sharp sense of humour,
And a practical working knowledge,
Subtly concealed, of country matters,
With decoration that clarifies,
And raises to heights of imagination,
The bare facts – literary graces concealing
No poverty of context, lack of virility, emptiness of thought,
But, held in perfect control,
Contributing the substance of poetry
To subjects 'with quietness on them like a veil',
A manifold of fast-vanishing speech,
Customs and delights,

– Cussomes, wivetts, short and long bachelors,
Short and long hag-hatters,
Rogue-why-winkest-thou,
And Jenny-why-gettest-thou....[1]

*   *   *

A poetry which in all connections will constantly render such
    services
As the protest of the nature poetry of the English poets
Of the Romantic Reaction on behalf of value,
On behalf of the organic view of nature,
A protest, invaluable to science itself,
Against the exclusion of value
From the essence of matter of fact.[2]

*   *   *

And thus a poetry which fully understands
That the era of technology is a necessary fact,
An inescapable phase in social activity,
Within which men are to rise
To ever greater mental and emotional heights,
And that only artists who build on all that men have created,
Who are infused with a sympathy and sensitive appreciation
Of the new technological order
And all it may mean for their art,
Can play their role with any certainty
That their work will survive historically
And in so doing they will also make
Their contribution to the New Order.

---

[1] These unfamiliar terms are references to old English rural customs and expressions.
[2] *Vide* A.N. Whitehead's *Science and the Modern World*.

from *Further Passages from* The Kind of Poetry I Want[1]

A poetry like a lance at rest,
Motionless but vibrant with hidden power.

*   *   *

The greatest poets undergo a kind of crisis in their art,
A change proportionate to their previous achievement.
Others approach it and fail to fulfil it – like Wordsworth.
Some, like Keats, the crisis helps to kill.
Rimbaud underwent a normal, not an abnormal, poetic crisis.
What was abnormal was his extreme youth, his circumstances,
      his peasant stock.
It killed Keats, but Keats was not born of French peasants.
It kept Milton practically silent for twenty years.
Rimbaud died at the end of nineteen. Yet he explored it seems
After his own manner an even more hidden way.
Claudel said that, after reading him, he felt
'L'impression vivante et presque physique de surnaturel...
Il n'était pas de ce monde.' The priest who confessed him
Said to his sister: 'I have rarely met a faith
Of the quality of his.' That was not to be taken
(As his sister took it) in any easy pious sense;
He remained very much *de ce monde*.
But it seems that through these years
He walked in granite within and without,
And perhaps only his poetry had not found
– And he but thirty-seven –
A method of being which was, for him,
What he desired, perdurable as the granite.
– I am forty-six; of tenacious, long-lived country folk.
Fools regret my poetic change – from my 'enchanting early lyrics' –
But I have found in Marxism all that I need –
(I on my mother's side of long-lived Scottish peasant stock
And on my father's of hardy keen-brained Border mill-workers).
It only remains to perfect myself in this new mode.

*   *   *

---

[1] Although *The Kind of Poetry I Want* was not published as a book until 1961, these extracts appeared in *Lucky Poet* in 1943. It is therefore appropriate to group all the extracts here. – Eds.

A poetry like the barrel of a gun
Weaving like a snake's head.

A poetry that can put all its chips on the table
And back it to the limit.

* * *

Great art has inspired action.
Even poor Essex
Before his futile rising tried to give
Drive and tone to his endeavour
By having performed before him
And his fellow protestors *Richard II*.
When Liberty once again
Becomes a faith and enthusiasm,
When the books are opened
And tyranny's claim
That it might do any violence
Because it alone
Could be 'efficient'
Is disproved – then
It is not improbable
That we shall see the new rally
Express itself in a culmination
Of the present dance-form,
As Aeschylus in his new drama
Gave form and voice
To the Greek liberation from Persia.
This is the poetry that I want.

Two Memories

Religion? Huh! Whenever I hear the word
It brings two memories back to my mind.
Choose between them, and tell me which
You think the better model for mankind.

Fresh blood scares sleeping cows worse than anything on earth.
An unseen rider leans far out from his horse with a freshly-skinned
Weaner's hide in his hands, turning and twisting the hairy slimy
    thing
And throwing the blood abroad on the wind.

A brilliant flash of lightning crashes into the heavens.
It reveals the earth in a strange yellow-green light,
Alluring yet repelling, that distorts the immediate foreground
And makes the gray and remote distance odious to the sight.

And a great mass of wraithlike objects on the bed ground
Seems to upheave, to move, to rise, to fold and undulate
In a wavelike mobility that extends to an alarming distance.
The cows have ceased to rest; they are getting to their feet.

Another flash of lightning shows a fantastic and fearsome vision.
Like the branches of some enormous grotesque sprawling plant
A forest of long horns waves, and countless faces
Turn into the air, unspeakably weird and gaunt.

The stroke of white fire from the sky is reflected back
To the heavens from thousands of bulging eyeballs,
And into the heart of any man who sees
This diabolical mirroring of the lightning numbing fear falls.

Is such a stampede your ideal for the human race?
Haven't we milled in it long enough? My second memory
Is of a flight of wild swans. Glorious white birds in the blue
    October heights
Over the surly unrest of the ocean! Their passing is more than
    music to me
And from their wings descends, and in my heart triumphantly
    peals,
The old loveliness of Earth that both affirms and heals.

from *Good-bye Twilight*

(For Neil M. Gunn)

Back to the great music, Scottish Gaels. Too long
You have wallowed as in the music of Delius.
Make a heroic effort now to swing yourselves round
To the opposite pole – the genius of Sibelius.
(Out of the West Highlands and Islands of Scotland now
What a symphony should come, more ghastly and appalling
Than Sibelius's gaunt El-Greco-emaciated ecstatic Fourth!
Far beyond *Squinting Peter's Flame of Wrath*
Or *Too Long in This Condition*[1]
But like the great jigs, whirling electrons of musical energy,
Like *The Shaggy Great Buck* or *The Baldooser*,
Fantastic, incredible, all but impossible to human fingers.)

It is impossible perhaps to imagine two men
More utterly unlike in temperament than these.
Sibelius lacks wholly the rather morbid preoccupation
With what is vaguely termed 'Nature' Delius possesses,
An obsession that does not allow of any very clear
Spiritual vision or insight into the true inwardness of the thing
That is the obsession. Delius looks upon 'Nature' and promptly
     becomes
Doped, drugged, besotted – my countrymen, even as you.

Sibelius, on the other hand, keeps all his very fine
Acute Northern wits – not a commodity to be found
Growing on blackberry bushes here in the North, you know –
Very well on the alert; he knows
That that aspect of the matter is an aspect only,
That there's much more to it than only that,
And the magic of his Finland is in his very nerves and bones
As the magic of our Scotland should be in ours.

If and when he does indulge in a specific piece
Of 'nature' writing, as in the *Oceanides*, one has the feeling
That in those parts at least it is felt and he too feels

---

[1] Titles of two of the great *piobaireachd*.

That the outward aspect of the thing vaguely called 'nature'
Is itself a magical manifestation as much as
Any transportation, materialisation, or like phenomenon might
    be.

Delius merely exclaims, with a catch of his breath,
'Oh, how lovely! – and how sad it must all come to an end!'
And promptly dissolves into tears. Sibelius
Does not think or feel it sad at all for he knows
That one piece of magic is as good as another
And the conclusion of one piece of magical evocation
By no manner of means means the end of anything at all.
Anyhow, what about the magician? The contrast in outlook and
    temper
Makes itself vividly felt in a prolonged listening
To the two. A long spell of Delius
Is enervating and relaxing like a muggy winter day in London,
While Sibelius charges his hearer with nervous energy
Almost as if he had performed some operations of *Prana* with him.
Back to the great music, you fools – to the classical Gaelic temper!
Out of the Celtic Twilight and into the Gaelic sun!

Of My First Love

O my first love! You are in my life forever
Like the Eas-Coul-aulin[1] in Sutherlandshire
Where the Amhainnan Loch Bhig burn
Plunges over the desolate slopes of Leitir Dubh.
Silhouetted against grim black rocks
This foaming mountain torrent
With its source in desolate tarns
Is savage in the extreme
As its waters with one wild leap
Hurl over the dizzy brink
Of the perpendicular cliff-face
In that great den of nature,
To be churned into spray
In the steaming depths below.
Near its base the fall splits up
Into cascades spreading out like a fan.
A legend tells how a beautiful maiden
In desperation threw herself
Over the cataract – the waters
Immediately took on the shape
Of her waving hair,
And on moonlight nights she is still to be seen
Lying near the base of the fall
Gazing up at the tremendous cascade
Of some six-hundred feet!

O my first love! Even so you lie
Near the base of my precipitous, ever lonelier and colder life
With your fair hair still rippling out
As I remember it between my fingers
When you let me unloosen first
(Over thirty chaotic years ago!)
That golden tumult forever!

---

[1] The beautiful Fall of Coul – the highest waterfall in Scotland – its name meaning, in Gaelic, tresses of hair.

The Wreck of the Swan

Even so – as a man at the end tries no more
To escape but deliberately turns and plunges
Into the press of his foes and perishes there –
I remember the lesson of the wreck of the *Swan*,
Within her own home harbour and under the lights
Of her crew's native city, swept to doom on Christmas Eve.

The lights were warm on happy family parties
In hundreds of homes. – One wonders
If a man or woman here and there did not part
The curtains to look out and think how black
Was the night, and foul for men at sea.

Few could know that quite near at hand, just beyond
The bald fisher-rows of Footdee, the crew
In the lifeboat *Emma Constance* were fighting to save
Five men in the wheelhouse of that trawler, the *Swan*,
That wallowed in broken seas.

It was not what a seaman would call rough in the channel
But there was a heavy run of broken water
Along the inside wall of the North Pier
And for some reason unknown the *Swan* grounded
Two hundred yards within the pier-head,
Swung round, held fast, and took to labouring
In a welter of breakers and spray.

Less than ten minutes later a gun
Fired a rocket from the Pier and a line
For the breeches-buoy was across the *Swan*.
Had it been accepted that would have ended the tale.
But the men of the *Swan* – who knows why? –
Refused that line of safety.

Meanwhile, with the celerity of firemen, the lifeboat crew,
Had assembled and tumbled into their powerful sixty-foot boat,
And she was off, and, in a few minutes, alongside the *Swan*,
Between that helpless ship and the pier.
Again the door of safety was wide open to the men of the *Swan*
And again they refused to pass through it.

The coxswain of the lifeboat roared at them,
Through his megaphone, to jump; but the five men
Of the *Swan* turned away and took refuge
In their doomed ship's wheelhouse instead.
There is a dark fascination in trying to appreciate
The spiritual inwardness of that strange situation.
Five men, for their own good reasons, refusing
To leave the shelter of their wheelhouse, while the lifeboat laboured
In the seas and the darkness, its crew dedicated to rescue,
Shouting to them in vain to come out and be saved.

A great wave hissing angrily came down on the lifeboat
And broke her adrift from the wreck.
Wielding the force of many tons it threw her
Against the foundations of the pier.
Along the length of 100 feet of solid masonry
She was flung like a piece of stick.

But the coxswain got her out again – a feat of seamanship
To hold the imagination in itself! –
And back alongside the *Swan* the *Emma Constance* went,
And again the lines were thrown,
But none of the men in the wheelhouse
Would come out to make them fast.

This time they had refused their last chance,
A sea of enormous weight broke over the wreck.
It carried away the upper part of the wheelhouse.
It swept the *Emma Constance* once more
Against the adamant wall of the pier.

This is the story of the men who wouldn't come out.
They were never seen alive again – and the coxswain and crew
    of the lifeboat
Carry the dark knowledge that up against
Something more formidable, more mysterious even,
Than wind and wave they battled largely in vain.

Four times they had gone back to that tragic wreck,
Manoeuvred with high skill in the cauldron 'twixt ship and pier,
Played the searchlight continuously on the battered bridge,
Cruised about for an hour,
But the men of the *Swan* refused to come out!

No dreamers these but hard-bitten men
Used to all the tortures of Old Feathery Legs
– The black villain who rides every crested wave
North of 65 degrees – he and his accursed legions,
The fog, the blizzard, the black-squall and the hurricane.

Up to their waists in water on the foredeck,
Gutting fish in the pounds, a black-squall
Screaming around, and the temperature 40 degrees below,
Working like automatons, 30...40...50 hours,
Grafting like fiends, with never a break or blink of sleep between.

A wave as high as the mast-heads crashing on deck
And sweeping all hands in a heap on the lee-scuppers,
Their arms and hands clawing up through the boiling surf
Still grasping wriggling fish and gutting knives.

And every now and then a message like this
Throbbing out of the black box.

   'VALKYRIE calling all trawlers!...He's got us...Old Feathery's
got us at last....We can see the rocks now...just astern....Another
minute, I reckon!...We're on!...Good-bye, pals....Say good-bye
to my wife...to my kiddies!...Good-bye, Buckie....Good-bye,
Scotland!'

In 31 years at sea, he'd spent less
Than four years ashore, mostly in spells
On an average of 36 hours
Between trips – that's the price
His wife and kids had to pay for fish.

Time the public knew what these men have to face.

Nearly 100,000 of them at sea.
Nor are they the only men concerned.
Shipbuilders, rope, net and box manufacturers,
Fish-friers, buyers, retailers, salesmen,
Railways and road transport,
Coal, salt, and ice industries,
– About 3,000,000 folk would have to look elsewhere
For their bread and butter
If there were no trawlermen – or fish.

'Stand by all hands!' Down below
The lads along the starboard scuppers,
Backs bent, hands clawing the net,
Long as the ship, wide as a street,
Keyed to high-tension point,
Every muscle tense and taut.
'Shooto!' Over she goes.

Off the South-East coast of Iceland,
The East Horns, a famous landmark,
About five miles off the port-quarter.
All along the coast the great, barren, sullen mountains,
Eternally snow-crested, and shaped
Like monstrous crouching animals,
Sweep down to the water line,
And many a brave ship lies
Under the lowering evil shadows
Of the terrible rocks.

The successful skippers read the 'fish sign'
In a thousand different ways.
The gulls, the wind, currents, tides,
The depth of water, the nature of the bottom,
The type of fish caught in certain patches,
The nature of the food in their stomachs
Exposed by the gutting knife,
These factors and a thousand others
Supply information to be had or read
Only after years of battle and bitter experience.

Trawling along the lip of a marine mountain,
Covered by 200 fathoms of water,
On what is veritably a narrow mountain pass,
Scooping up hard 'sprags' (cod)
And 'ducks' (haddocks),
Each net sweeping up fish in hundreds of thousands,
Towing for miles over an area wide as a town.

The skipper has been on the bridge
For nearly 60 hours on end,
Down below, in the fish-pounds for'ard,
The lads are reeling like drunken men,

The decks awash, swirling high
As their arm-pits, and icy-cold.

These men are no dreamers.

Rex est qui metuit nihil.

A true man chooses death as he can in no part lie to a girl
But will put himself conscientiously into the worst possible light.

Töten ist eine Gestalt unseres wandernden Trauerns...
Rein ist im heiteren Geist,
Was an uns selber geschieht.[1]

(Killing is only a form of the sorrow we wander in here...
The serener spirit finds pure
All that can happen to us.)

'Death is ugly.
Tomato is crashing to.'[2]

The Gaels never die! They either 'change' or 'travel'.

'Happy the folk upon whom the Bear looks down, happy in this
error, whom of fears the greatest moves not, the dread of death.
Hence their warrior's heart hurls them against the steel, hence
their ready welcome of death.'[3]

   'It was possibly the inculcation of these doctrines that moved
the Celtic warriors to hurl their bodies against cold steel – a charac-
teristic the world is only too familiar with in the conduct of our
Highland regiments. They can still listen to the battle-songs of a
thousand ages, with a susceptible mood nowise estranged amid
the crumbling foundations of a former sovereignty. A German
military authority – Clausewitz, I think – said that the Highlander
is the only soldier in Europe who, without training, can unflinch-
ingly face the bayonet.'

---

[1] Rainer Maria Rilke.
[2] Tio Nakamura.
[3] Lucan, *Pharsalia*.

For now I see Life and Death as who gets
The first magical glimpse of Popocatepetl,
Its white cone floating in the rare winter air,
Incredibly near, . . . incredibly unreal,
And its sister peak which the Indians call
'The sleeping woman,' like a great prone goddess,
Above her circlet of clouds,
Or like Mount Elbruz's mile-apart twin breasts of snow!

I don't look the kind of guy, do I,
Who aches to get away from the high truth
Of the passing mountains into the close heat
Of the Pullman again, and the company of his pals
– Into a small enclosed space where I can feel
Confident and important again?
I am accustomed to the *altura*, believe me.
I am what the guides call *schwindelfrei*.

This is not the poetry of a man with such a grudge against life
That a very little of it goes a long way with him.
No great barbaric country will undermine and ruin me,
Slowly corroding my simple unimaginative qualities,
Rob me of my conventions, of my simple direct standards,
Who have no undefeatable inner integrity to take their place.
I love this country passionately, expanding
To its wild immensity as a flower opens in the sunshine,
I am the last man in all the world to hate these great places
And depend for my only comfort on the theatres and cafés,
The wide, well-lit *avenidas*, the scandal and gossip of the cabarets,
The emotion and danger of the bull-ring.
I would not rather be sitting in the closed comfort of the Pullman,
A drink before me, surrounded by people I know,
And things I can understand.

I feel with Life
As a man might towards a little child,
But towards Death, as towards one of my own contemporaries
Whom I have known as long
As I have known myself.

The Caledonian Antisyzygy

I write now in English and now in Scots
To the despair of friends who plead
For consistency; sometimes achieve the true lyric cry,
Next but chopped-up prose; and write whiles
In traditional forms, next in a mixture of styles.
So divided against myself, they ask:
How can I stand (or they understand) indeed?

Fatal division in my thought they think
Who forget that although the thrush
Is more cheerful and constant, the lark
More continuous and celestial, and, after all,
The irritating cuckoo unique
In singing a true musical interval,
Yet the nightingale remains supreme,
The nightingale whose thin high call
And that deep throb,
Which seem to come from different birds
In different places, find an emotion
And vibrate in the memory as the song
Of no other bird – not even
The love-note of the curlew –
                    Can do!

Crystals Like Blood

I remember how, long ago, I found
Crystals like blood in a broken stone.

I picked up a broken chunk of bed-rock
And turned it this way and that,
It was heavier than one would have expected
From its size. One face was caked
With brown limestone. But the rest
Was a hard greenish-grey quartz-like stone
Faintly dappled with darker shadows,
And in this quartz ran veins and beads
Of bright magenta.

And I remember how later on I saw
How mercury is extracted from cinnabar
– The double ring of iron piledrivers
Like the multiple legs of a fantastically symmetrical spider
Rising and falling with monotonous precision,
Marching round in an endless circle
And pounding up and down with a tireless, thunderous force,
While, beyond, another conveyor drew the crumbled ore
From the bottom and raised it to an opening high
In the side of a gigantic grey-white kiln.

So I remember how mercury is got
When I contrast my living memory of you
And your dear body rotting here in the clay
– And feel once again released in me
The bright torrents of felicity, naturalness, and faith
My treadmill memory draws from you yet.

A Vision of Scotland

I see my Scotland now, a puzzle
Passing the normal of her sex, going erect
Unscathed through fire, keeping her virtue
Where temptation works with violence, walking bravely,
Offering loyalty and demanding respect.

Every now and again in a girl like you,
Even in the streets of Glasgow or Dundee,
She throws her headsquare off and a mass
Of authentic flaxen hair is revealed,
Fine spun as newly-retted fibres
On a sunlit Irish bleaching field.

Why

Concerned as I am with the West Highlands and Hebrides
Instantly to my hand is the fact
That the two greatest social and religious reformers
Of modern India – Dayanandi and Gandhi –
Were both born in the small peninsula of Kathiawar.
Gandhi was born at Porbunder.
It is on the sea-coast, jutting out into the sea,
And has all the infinite variety and charm
Of the expanse of ocean around it.
Mists of extraordinary beauty
Constantly rise from the sea
And encompass the land,
The sea itself is usually a brilliant ultramarine
With liquid green where the shoals lie.
The little town where Gandhi was born
Rises almost out of the sea
And becomes a vision of glory at sunrise and sunset
When the slanting rays beat upon it,
Turning its turrets and pinnacles into gold.
Morvi, where Dayanandi was born, lies inland
Not far away from the desolate waste
Of the Rajputana Desert which stretches to the north

Unbroken for hundreds of miles.
The land at Morvi is rocky
And the country is rugged,
The differences of their birthplaces are clearly seen
In the differences between Dayanandi and Gandhi.
We have Porbunders and Morvis enough
In Scotland: but they produce
No such outstanding characters
As Dayanandi and Gandhi.
Why?

My Songs are Kandym in the Waste Land

Above all, I curse and strive to combat
The leper pearl of Capitalist culture
Which only tarnishes what it cannot lend
Its own superb lustre.

Somewhere in its creative faculty is concealed
A flaw, a senseless and wanton quality
That has no human answer,
An infernal void.

Capitalist culture to the great masses of mankind
Is like the exploitative handling in America
Of forest, grazing, and tilled lands
Which exaggerates floods and reduces
The dry-season flow of the rivers to almost nothing.

A hundred million acres, which might have maintained
A million families, utterly destroyed by water erosion,
Nine million acres destroyed by wind,
Hundreds of millions of acres more
Yielding rapidly to wind and water erosion,
Forests slashed to the quick
And the ground burned over,
Grazing lands turned into desert,
The tragic upsetting of the hydrologic cycle
Which has turned into disastrous run-off

233

The water that should have been held in the soil
To support vegetation and percolate
To the lower levels and feed wells and springs,
Till now the levee builders try to race
The Mississippi and set it up on stilts
Whence sooner or later it must stumble.

Problems of erosion control, regulation of river-flow,
Flood control, silt control, hydro-electric power.
I turn from this appalling spectacle
Of illimitable waste; and set myself, they say,
Gad im ghainimh (putting a withy round sand).
The sand will produce a vegetation itself
If it is not interfered with. It will be a slow growth.
Nevertheless the vegetation manages to get a start
In the course of thousands of years,
And my poetry will be like the kandym
That doesn't advance step by step
But goes forward on the run, jumps through the air.
The little nut jumps along like a ball.
The sand comes along after, but the sand is heavier
And cannot catch up with the little nut
And bury it. But when the seed takes root
And the little shrub starts, the shrub
Cannot jump along like the seed ball.

How is it going to save itself
From the encroaching waves of sand?
It is not so easy to bury the kandym.
It doesn't have branches like those
Of the apricot and peach tree – its branches
Are slender and there are no leaves on them.
When the sand comes on the kandym doesn't try to stop it
But lets it go right through its branches,
Gives it right-of-way.

But sometimes the sand waves are so big
They bury the kandym nevertheless.
Then a race begins – the dune grows and the plant grows.
The dune grows fast but the plant grows faster still
And by the time the sand dune has attained its final height

The plant is found to have outstripped it.
Its little green bristles are waving in the wind
On the crest of the sand dune.
It has not only grown in height but has branched out too.
The whole dune is perforated with its branches.
The wave passes on, leaving behind
A good half of its sand.
So the little kandym has stopped the advance of the sand,
Turned the dune into a little hillock
Covered with vegetation.

But is there not one last danger?
The wind may blow the sand away
And leave the roots bare?
But the kandym knows how to fight with the wind too.
Lying flat on the sand it sends out extra roots
And holds the sand down with them.
In this way it gathers up the soil
And makes a foothold for itself.
My songs are kandym in the Waste Land.

from *Esplumeoir*

He's chain lightning. Brains count in this business.

It was an amazing discovery, like the inside of your head being painlessly scraped out. There was an amazing clarity, like the brilliant moon falling into it and filling it neatly.

But shairly, shairly, there maun be
Or sae, of course, it seems to you –
Some instinct o' black waters swirlin'
And dangerous images juist oot o' view
Ettlin' to spoil happiness and pu' apairt
Dreams that ha'e become realities?

I tell you, No! There's naething – naething o' the kind.
Nae ootward things, shapes, colours, soonds, or memories o'
    these
To strike in on and move and muddle the mind;
Nae *sombra do tempo* cast
By comin' events or present or past,
And least o' a' ony *Scheinprobleme* here!
I ken fu' weel for a man like you
To think o' this maun be as when
On the wa' abune your heid
Shiftin' prisms o' licht frae the water
May dance a fandango
Unutterably free and airy
In a squalid wee ship's-cabin
While you couldna hit the wa'
If you were locked in a wardrobe, you fool.
But as for me I canna mind a time
When the mere thocht o't didna mak' me
Licht up like a match!

'Aloof as a politician
The first year efter election'
You grumble, 'There's naething to see.
It's a' expressionless as tho' it micht be
Enamelled wi' an airbrush that tawnish grey

---

ettlin' trying   *pu' apairt* pull apart

Nae-colour sae common on motors – was't only yesterday? –
Yet bricht as when the stars were glowin'
Wi' sic a steady radiance that the lift
Seemed filled to overflowin' – I wadna hae't in a gift.
It mak's me feel upon my word
Like a fly on the edge o' a phonograph record.'
(A phrase divertin'ly *vergeistigt* here)

The Leisure State! Fell dreich, you think? Intelligence is
    characterised
By a natural lack o' comprehension o' life
But here intelligence is a', and a'thing devised
To favour 'life' and its expense excised,
Naething left in human nature cybernetics
Can ever delegate to electronic tricks;
Tint, clean tint, as gin it had never been
A' that could be touched or tasted, heard or seen.
Wi' nae mair expression than a china settin' egg.

The utter stillness o' the timeless world!
The haill creation has vanished forever
Wi' nae mair noise or disturbance than a movie fade-out,
The expression o' blankness which sae often
Distinguishes the profound thinker.

Naething to see – you sudna ha'e far to gang
For an analogy frae your Earth experience tho',
Sin' at winter's edge when a' thing's gone sere,
Emptied o' a' Simmer's routh and bare as a bane gey near,
Bacteriologists say the soil's teemin' mair thrang
Wi' life than at ony ither time, yet wi' nocht to show.
Like cricket's deceptive impression o' slowness
Tho' the split-second decisions sae often required
Ha'e to be made quicker than in ony ither game;
Or like the sleepy een o' a great detective
Wha misses nocht and canna be fooled
But's aye maist, when he looks least, alert.
Or as a day that was gaen to be

---

fell dreich extremely dreary   *tint* lost   *routh* plenty   *gey near* almost
thrang busy

Oppressively het wi' thunder later
Used to stimulate a'thing to live
Brimmin'ly afore the cataclysm
Till a'thing that ran or flew or crawled
Abune or aneth was filled pang-fu' wi' life
Like yon cicada shrillin' piercin'ly
Try'in to stert up the haill chorus.

He'd been underground an 'oor ago
And micht be doon a bird's throat by nicht.
That he was alive richt then was reason eneuch
For singin' wi' a' his micht.
Eternity's like that – a'thing keyed up
To the heichest pitch as if
A cataclysm's comin' – only it's no!

Eternity is like an auld green parrot
I kent aince. Its conversational range was sma'
Yet when it tilted its heid and cocked
A beady eye at you, you got the feelin'
That, if it chose, it could tell you a thing or twa;
That, as the French pit it,
Il connaît le dessous des cartes.
Eternity is like an obstinate jellyfish
That comes floatin' back as soon as you've scared it off
But, if you try to seize it, reverses its tactics
And jouks awa' like a muckle dawd o' quicksilver.

Or pit it like this – Eternity's
Twa doors frae the corner a'whaur
A sma', demure white biggin'
Wi' shutters and a canopy.
The canopy's royal blue
And it says *Eternity*
In discreet soap-glass letters
On ilka-side. Under the canopy
You walk up and the front door
Is a' mirror wi' a cool strip

---

pang-fu' crammed full   *jouks* dodges   *muckle dawd* big lump
a'whaur everywhere   *biggin'* building

O' fluorescent light on top.
You push the pearl button,
And listen to the delicate chimes
And adjust your tie in the mirror
And fix your hat – but the guy
Ahint the bullet-proof mirror
Sees a' that too,
Only you canna see him.
The guy ahint the mirror
Is Tutti-Frutti Forgle,
A muckle nigger wi' fuzzy-white hair
Wha kens his business.
Aince past Tutti, you check your hat
In a quiet soft-lit anteroom,
Syne the haill place is yours.

from *In Memoriam James Joyce*

– And all this here, everything I write, of course
Is an extended metaphor for something I never mention.

*   *   *

We have the privilege – or the great misfortune – to be present
at a profound, rapid, irresistible, and total transformation of all
the conditions of human activity and of life itself.[1]

So, like him, we cry *l'honneur des hommes: Saint Langage*'
Knowing even in the case of an excellent translation,
How the original French has the ring of Venetian glass
But the English of Waterford;
Papiemento, mixture of half the languages on earth,
The construction *Apo Koinou* in the Germanic languages,
Notando Jabavu and her native Xhosa;
And comment on the collapse of statecraft,
The special nature of French vowels,
The cultural significance of the Rhine,
The status of Paris as the 'capital of criticism,'
The ethics of dictatorship,
The white grapes of Thoméry –
Our object to counter in however small a degree
The general falling-off of first-hand intellectual effort;
For this decline, we realise, is far more dangerous
Than many an obvious disaster.

Hence this *hapax legomenon* of a poem, this exercise
In schablone, bordatini, and prolonged scordatura,
This *divertissement philologique*,

---

[1] Paul Valéry, in his address of July 1935, to the Collège de Sète. In this connection it is true of Joyce, as was said by and of another poet: ' "I will not leave a corner of my consciousness covered up, but saturate myself with the strange and extraordinary new conditions of this life." This willingness – and ability – to let himself be new-born into the new situation, not subduing his experience to his established personality, is a large part, if not the whole secret, of the character of his best work. It was his exposure of his whole personality that gave his work its quality of impersonality.'
'For there is nothing covered that shall not be revealed; neither hid that shall not be known.' (Luke XII.2.)

This Wortspiel, this torch symphony,
This 'liberal education,' this collection of *fonds de tiroir*,
This – even more than Kierkegaard's
'Frygt og Baeven' – 'dialectical lyric,'
This rag-bag, this Loch Ness monster, this impact
Of the whole range of *Weltliteratur* on one man's brain,
In short, this 'friar's job,' as they say in Spain
Going back in kind
To the Eddic 'Converse of Thor and the All-Wise Dwarf'
(Al-viss Mal, 'Edda die lieden des Codex Regius,' 120, 1f)[1]
Existing in its present MS form
Over five centuries before Shakespeare.
You remember it?

Let the only consistency
In the course of my poetry
Be like that of the hawthorn tree
Which in early Spring breaks
Fresh emerald, then by nature's law
Darkens and deepens and takes
Tints of purple-maroon, rose-madder and straw.

Sometimes these hues are found
Together, in pleasing harmony bound.
Sometimes they succeed each other. But through
All the changes in which the hawthorn is dight,
No matter in what order, one thing is sure
– The haws shine ever the more ruddily bright!

And when the leaves have passed
Or only in a few tatters remain
The tree to the winter condemned
                    Stands forth at last
        Not bare and drab and pitiful,
But a candelabrum of oxidised silver gemmed
By innumerable points of ruby
Which dominate the whole and are visible
Even at considerable distance

---

[1] Text, G. Neckel, Heidelberg, 1914.

As flame-points of living fire.
That so it may be
With my poems too at last glance
Is my only desire.

All else must be sacrificed to this great cause.
I fear no hardships. I have counted the cost.
I with my heart's blood as the hawthorn with its haws
Which are sweetened and polished by the frost!

See how these haws burn, there down the drive,
In this autumn air that feels like cotton wool,
When the earth has the gelatinous limpness of a body dead as a
      whole
While its tissues are still alive!

Poetry is human existence come to life,
The glorious energy that once employed
Turns all else in creation null and void,
The flower and fruit, the meaning and goal,
Which won all else is needs removed by the knife
Even as a man who rises high
Kicks away the ladder he has come up by.

This single-minded zeal, this fanatic devotion to art
Is alien to the English poetic temperament no doubt,
'This narrowing intensity' as the English say,
But I have it even as you had it, Yeats, my friend,
And would have it with me as with you at the end,
I who am infinitely more un-English than you
And turn Scotland to poetry like those women who
In their passion secrete and turn to
Musk through and through!

So I think of you, Joyce, and of Yeats and others who are dead
As I walk this Autumn and observe
The birch tremulously pendulous in jewels of cairngorm,
The sauch, the osier, and the crack-willow
Of the beaten gold of Australia;
The sycamore in rich straw-gold;
The elm bowered in saffron;
The oak in flecks of salmon gold;
The beeches huge torches of living orange.

Billow upon billow of autumnal foliage
From the sheer high bank glass themselves
Upon the ebon and silver current that floods freely
Past the shingle shelves.
I linger where a crack willow slants across the stream,
Its olive leaves slashed with fine gold.
Beyond the willow a young beech
Blazes almost blood-red,
Vying in intensity with the glowing cloud of crimson
That hangs about the purple bole of a gean
Higher up the brae face.

And yonder, the lithe green-grey bole of an ash, with its boughs
Draped in the cinnamon-brown lace of samara.
(And I remember how in April upon its bare twigs
The flowers came in ruffs like the unshorn ridges
Upon a French poodle – like a dull mulberry at first,
Before the first feathery fronds
Of the long-stalked, finely-poised, seven-fingered leaves) –
Even the robin hushes his song
In these gold pavilions.

Other masters may conceivably write
Even yet in C major
But we – we take the perhaps 'primrose path'
To the dodecaphonic bonfire.

They are not endless these variations of form
Though it is perhaps impossible to see them all.
It is certainly impossible to conceive one that doesn't exist.
But I keep trying in our forest to do both of these,
And though it is a long time now since I saw a new one
I am by no means weary yet of my concentration
On phyllotaxis here in preference to all else,
All else – but my sense of sny!

The gold edging of a bough at sunset, its pantile way
Forming a double curve, tegula and imbrex in one,
Seems at times a movement on which I might be borne
Happily to infinity; but again I am glad
When it suddenly ceases and I find myself
Pursuing no longer a rhythm of duramen

But bouncing on the diploe in a clearing between earth and air
Or headlong in dewy dallops or a moon-spairged fernshaw
Or caught in a dark dumosity, or even
In open country again watching an aching spargosis of stars.

*   *   *

– All dreams of 'imperialism' must be exorcised,
Including linguistic imperialism, which sums up all the rest.

from *The World of Words*

Ah, Joyce, this is our task,
Making what a moving, thrilling, mystical, tropical,
Maniacal, magical creation of all these oppositions,
Of good to evil, greed to self-sacrifice,
Selfishness to selflessness, of this all-pervading atmosphere,
Of the seen merging with the unseen,
Of the beautiful sacrificed to the ugly,
Of the ugly transformed to the beautiful,
Of this intricate yet always lucid and clear-sighted
Agglomeration of passions, manias, occult influences,
Historical and classical references
– Sombre, insane, brilliant and sane,
Timeless, a symbol of the reality
That lies beyond and through the apparent,
Written with the sweeping assurance, the inspired beauty,
The intimated truth of genius,
With natures like ours in which a magnetic fluidity
That is neither 'good' nor 'bad' is forever
Taking new shapes under the pressure of circumstances,
Taking new shapes, and then again,
As Kwang makes Confucius complain of Laotze,
'Shooting up like a dragon.'
But, taking my life as a whole,
And hovering with the flight of the hawk
Over its variegated landscape,
I believe I detect certain quite definite 'streams of tendency'
In that unrolling map,

Moving towards the unknown future.
For one thing I fancy the manner I have allowed
My natural impulses towards romance and mysticism
To dominate me has led to the formation
Of a curious gap or 'lacuna'
Between the innate and almost savage realism,
Which is a major element in my nature,
And the imaginative, poetical cult
Whereby I have romanticised and idealized my life.
In this realistic mood I recognise
With a grim animal acceptance
That it is indeed likely enough that the 'soul'
Perishes everlastingly with the death of the body,
But what this realistic mood, into which
My mind falls like a plummet
Through the neutral zone of its balanced doubt,
Never for one single beat of time can shake or disturb
Is my certain knowledge,
Derived from the complex vision of everything in me,
That the whole astronomical universe, however illimitable,
Is only one part and parcel of the mystery of Life;
Of this I am as certain as I am certain that I am I.
The astronomical universe is *not* all there is.

So this is what our lives have been given to find,
A language that can serve our purposes,
A marvellous lucidity, a quality of fiery aery light,
Flowing like clear water, flying like a bird,
Burning like a sunlit landscape.
Conveying with a positively Godlike assurance,
Swiftly, shiningly, exactly, what we want to convey.
This use of words, this peculiar aptness and handiness,
Adapts itself to our every mood, now pathetic, now ironic,
Now full of love, of indignation, of sensuality, of glamour, of glory,
With an inevitable richness of remembered detail
And a richness of imagery that is never cloying,
A curious and indescribable quality
Of sensual sensitiveness,
Of very light and very air itself,
– Pliant as a young hazel wand,
Certain as a gull's wings,
Lucid as a mountain stream,

Expressive as the eyes of a woman in the presence of love, –
Expressing the complex vision of everything in one,
Suffering all impressions, all experience, all doctrines
To pass through and taking what seems valuable from each.
No matter in however many directions
These essences seem to lead.

Collecting up all these essences,
These intimations coming willy-nilly from all quarters,
Into a complex conception of all things,
An intricately-cut gem-stone of a myriad facets
That is yet, miraculously, a whole;
Each of which facets serves its individual purpose
In directing the light collected from every side outwards
In a single creative ray.
With each of these many essences culled
From the vast field of life some part of one's own
Complex personality has affinity and resembles
When climbing on to the ice-cap a little south of Cape Bismarck
And keeping the nunataks of Dronning Louises Land on our left
We travel five days
On tolerable ice in good weather
With few bergs to surmount
And no crevasses to delay us.
Then suddenly our luck turns.
A wind of 120 miles an hour blows from the East,
And the plateau becomes a playground of gales
And the novel light gives us snow-blindness.
We fumble along with partially bandaged eyes
Our reindeer-skin kamiks worn into holes
And no fresh sedge-grass to stump them with.
We come on ice-fields like mammoth ploughlands
And mountainous séracs which would puzzle an Alpine climber.
That is what adventuring in dictionaries means,
All the abysses and altitudes of the mind of man,
Every test and trial of the spirit,
Among the débris of all past literature
And raw material of all the literature to be.

*   *   *

Where there are no graves, there can be
No resurrection.

I rejoiced when from Wales once again
Came the ffff-putt of a triple-feathered arrow
Which looked as if it had never moved.[1]

But now the bowman has fitted one more nock
To his string, and discharged the arrow straight up into the air
Partly as a gesture of farewell, partly of triumph,
And beautiful! – I watched the arrow go up.
The sun was already westing towards evening
So, as the arrow topped the trees
And climbed into sunlight,
It began to burn against the evening like the sun itself.
Up and up it went, not weaving as it would have done
With a snatching loose, but soaring, swimming,
Aspiring towards heaven, steady, golden and superb.

Just as it had spent its force,
Just as its ambition had been dimmed by destiny
And it was preparing to faint, to turn over,
To pour back into the bosom of its mother earth,
A terrible portent happened.
A gore crow came flapping wearily
Before the approaching night.
It came, it did not waver, it took the arrow,
It flew away, heavy and hoisting,
With the arrow in its beak. I was furious.
I had loved the arrow's movement,
Its burning ambition in the sunlight.
And it was such a splendid arrow,
Perfectly-balanced, sharp, tight-feathered,
Clean-nocked, and neither warped nor scraped.

---

[1] With acknowledgements to T.H. White, *The Sword in the Stone*. The reference here is to the author's friend, Dylan Thomas.

I was furious but I was frightened.
It is a very old and recurring portent in our history.
We remember the story of Valerius Corvus[1]
(Ah, would my bowman had been saved like Valerius
By a crow which hid him from the foe with its wings!)
And the famous episode in the great Irish epic of Ulster,
The *Táin Bó Cuailnge*,[2]
In which the goddess Morrigu attacks Cuchulainn,
Who scorned her love,
In the form of a crow.
(A like episode is depicted on one of the decorated faces
Of an Etruscan alabaster vase in the Florence Museum,[3]
Among scenes of the Trojan War.)
The crow is not a mere flight of fancy.
It is the creature which stands for battle
And the gods and goddesses of war.

But the crow cannot quench the light
With its outstretched wings forever
Nor break the law of gravity
Nor swallow the arrow.
We shall get it back. Never fear!
And how I shall rejoice when the War is over
And there comes from Wales once again
The fff-putt of a triple-feathered arrow
Which looks as if it had never moved!

from *The Snares of Varuna*

.....as I have often told
My angling friend Norman MacCaig
If I went fishing I could not be content
With salmon or brown trout.
My heart would be set on an oar-fish,

---

[1] Livy. VII, 26 (the campaign of 345); Dio Cass., fr. 34.
[2] The Cattle-Lifting of Cooley.
[3] Minali. *Studi e materiali di archeologia e numismatica.*

'King of the Herrings,' with its long tapering tail,
Continuous scarlet dorsal fin,
Scarlet erectile crest, and pelvic fins,
Placed far forward, transformed
In long slender oar-like blades.
And then[1] I'd have dorado,
The golden fish of the Alto Paraná,
The giant wels or sheat-fish which runs
To 600 lb in the Volga,
The African tiger-fish,
'The fiercest fish that swims,'
Sail-fish, marlin, wahoo, tarpon, tuna,
Sword-fish in New Zealand, and the great mako shark,
And largest of the true giants of the sea,
Largest of living animals indeed,
The blue rorqual... and even then
I'd remember with Herman Melville
That behind Leviathan
There's still the kraken,
And no end to our 'ontological heroics.'
And MacCaig has laughed and said
'Let me see you catch anything yet
Big enough not to throw in again.'

from *England is Our Enemy*

To distinctly English writers in England
Authenticity is never allowed;
The quality is perhaps
Not even known to exist.
There are too many vested interests.
In the United States Mark Twain
Could finally make headway
Against the Transcendentalists;

---

[1] *Vide* Goethe: *Dichtung und Wahrheit,* p.385. 'Weil meine Empfindung wie mein Urteil nicht leicht etwas völlig ausschloss' (Because my way of feeling, like my judgment, was not prone to exclude anything completely).

Poe could stand with his body starved
But his mind making its mark.
He had to fight many battles
Against many unscrupulous cliques,
And in the end his head became
Both bloody and bowed
But neither he, alive
Nor his reputation, he dead,
Have had to contend with the dead weight
Of dead, vested interests
And merely political disingenuousnesses
That have strangled
Most literary brightnesses
In England for a hundred years.
These tendencies work
Towards a wilderness of thumbs down.
It was Landor who first said
That every Frenchman takes a personal share
In the glory of his poets
Whereas every Englishman resents
The achievements of his poets
Because they detract
From the success of his own 'poetry';
And the remark was extraordinarily profound.
So the English literary world
Is an immense arena
Where every spectator is intent
On the deaths of those awaiting judgment
And every gladiator is intent
On causing the death of his fellow-combatant
By smiting him with the corpses
Of others predeceased.
The method, the mania, the typical
'Fair-play' of 'the sporting English'
Is really extraordinary in its operation.

Supposing, having no pet author of your own
Out of whose entrails
You hope to make a living,
No political bias,
No interest in a firm of publishers
Who make dividends out of other 'classics'

You timidly venture to remark
That Trollope, Jane Austen,
And the Mrs Gaskell of *Mary Barton*,
Are English Authors
Authentic in their methods.

'*But*' you hear the professional reviewers
All protesting at once
'Trollope has not the humour of Dickens,
The irony of Thackeray,
The skill with a plot of Wilkie Collins.
Jane Austen has not the wit of Meredith,
The reforming energy of Charles Reade,
The imperial sense of Charles Kingsley,
The tender pathos of the author of *Cranford*.
And as for Mrs Gaskell who wrote *Cranford*,
Well, she has not the aloofness of Jane Austen,
And Christina Rossetti had not
The manly optimism of Browning,
And Browning lacked the religious confidence
Of Christina Rossetti, or the serenity
Of Matthew Arnold. And who was Matthew Arnold?
Landor could not write about whist and old playbills
Like Charles Lamb.'
(*Saint Charles, Thackeray murmured softly!*)

No one who has paid any attention at all
To official-critical appraisements of English writers
Can gainsay the moral to be drawn
From these instances of depreciation
Or the truth of the projection itself.
Literary figures should, of course,
As is said of race-horses, be 'tried high,'
But to attach a Derby winner to a stone cart,
And then condemn it as a horse
Because it does not make so much progress
As a Clydesdale or a Percheron
Is to try the animal
Altogether too high,
And not fairly.

English official criticism has erected
A stone-heap, a dead load of moral qualities.
A writer must have optimism, irony,
A healthy outlook,
A middle-class standard of morality,
As much religion as, say, St Paul had,
As much atheism as Shelley had...
And, finally, on top of an immense load
Of self-neutralising moral and social qualities,
Above all, Circumspection,
So that, in the end, no English writer
According to these standards,
Can possess authenticity.
The formula is this: Thackeray is not Dickens,
So Thackeray does not represent English literature.
Dickens is not Thackeray, so *he*
Does not represent English literature.
In the end literature itself is given up
And you have the singular dictum
Of the doyen of English official literary criticism.
This gentleman writes...but always rather uncomfortably...
Of Dryden as divine, of Pope as divine,
Of Swift as so filthy
As to intimidate the self-respecting critic.
But when he comes to Pepys of course
His enthusiasm is unbounded.
He salutes the little pawky diarist
With an affection, an enthusiasm,
For his industry, his pawkiness,
His thumb-nail sketches.
Then he asserts amazingly:
'This is scarcely literature'
And continues with panegyrics that leave no doubt
That the critic considers the Diary
To be something very much better.
The judgment is typically English.
The bewildered foreigner can only say:
'But if the Diary is all you assert of it,
It must be literature, or, if it is not literature,
It cannot be all you assert of it.'
And obviously...

I once met a Peruvian who had come
To London to study English literature.
He said: 'Oh! but your writers, they pant and they pant;
Producing and producing! And then, as the type,
The Archtype, you have...
Charles Lamb *On Buttered Toast!*'
I said: 'Ah! That is because
You are not an Englishman!'

                    *   *   *

It is possible that a change may come.
In the general revaluation that is taking place
All the commercial considerations, the moral greasinesses,
The Professors of Literature, *Forschungen*, university curricula,
Honours examinations, all these phenomena commercial at base
Which stand in the way of the taste for
And honouring of literature
May be estimated at their true price.
To seek to abolish them is not much good,
For they are parts of the essential imbecilities
Of pompous men – of the highly refined imaginations
Of the More Select Classes.
They should be left isolated in little towns
But their existence should not be forgotten
Or they will come creeping in again.

from *Plaited Like the Generations of Men*[1]

Come, follow me into the realm of music. Here is the gate
Which separates the earthly from the eternal.
It is not like stepping into a strange country
As we once did. We soon learn to know everything there
And nothing surprises us any more. Here
Our wonderment will have no end, and yet
From the very beginning we feel at home.

At first you hear nothing, because everything sounds.
But now you begin to distinguish between them. Listen.
Each star has its rhythm and each world its beat.
The heart of each separate living thing
Beats differently, according to its needs,
And all the beats are in harmony.

Your inner ear grows sharper. Do you hear
The deep notes and the high notes?
They are immeasurable in space and infinite as to number.
Like ribbons, undreamt-of scales lead from one world to another,
Steadfast and eternally moved.
(More wonderful than those miraculous isles of Greece
'Lily on lily, that o'erlace the sea,'
Than the marvellous detailed intensity of Chinese life,
Than such a glimpse as once delighted me of the masterly and
    exhaustive
Classification of psychical penetrations and enlacements
On which Von Hartmann relied, giving here some slight dissection
Of the antinomies underlying ethical thought, discussing there
    the gradations

---

[1] 'The gods having placed Vishnu to the East surrounded him with metres (*chandobhir abhitah paryagrihan*); saying "On the south side I surround thee with the Gayatri metre; on the west side I surround thee with the Trishtubh metre; on the north I surround thee with the Jagati." Having thus surrounded him with metres, they placed Agni on the east, and thus they went on worshipping and toiling. By this means they acquired this whole earth (*tena imam sarvam prithivim samvindata*).' – Satapatha-brahmana.

   'When we have once penetrated the vaults of Nature's mysterious palace we can learn to speed our soul with the wings of speech, and it will chime away in ever more blossoming and sublime melody' (With acknowledgments to Ferruccio Busoni).

Of the virtues, the stratifications of axiology, with an elaborate
  power
And beauty – but there! – Oh, Aodhagán Ó Rathaille meets again
The Brightness of Brightness in a lonely glen
And sees the hair that's plaited
Like the generations of men!)[1]

All the knowledge is woven[2] in neatly
So that the plaited ends come to the hand.
Pull any of the tabs, and a sequence
Of practical information is drawn.

Each sound is the centre of endless circles,
And now the *harmony* opens out before you.
Innumerable are its voices, compared with which
The boom of the harp is a screeching,
The clash of a thousand trumpets a twitter.

All, all the melodies hitherto heard and unheard
Ring out in full number together, bear you along,
Crowd over you, sweep past you – melodies of love and passion,
Of the Spring and the Winter, of melancholy and abandon –
And they themselves are the spirits
Of a million beings in a million ages
Revealed as Krishna revealed his form
In the Udyoga-parva of the Maha-bharata

---

[1] Aodhagán Ó Rathaille, Irish Gaelic poet, 1670-1726. The reference is to O'Rahilly's
great *aisling* (i.e. vision poem), *Gile na Gile*.
[2] See also the third section of Professor R.B. Onians' *The Origin of European Thought*
(London, 1952), which is concerned chiefly with words connected with fate which
can be interpreted as terms connected with spinning and weaving and the use
of their product. The word *peirar*, often translated 'end,' means a bond or cord
which the gods can put on a person or an army (and Ocean is the bond round
the Earth, although here the bond is slipping over into the meaning of boundary
and so end); the image of binding is often used to express the power of fate or
the gods over men, and if we ask what these cords are with which fate binds
men, Professor Onians answers that they are the threads which fate or the gods
have spun, and that in certain phrases fate itself is thought of as a thread or bond
which is put upon men. A further very important chapter deals with *telos*. *Telos*
(which means 'end' in later Greek) in Homer 'covers a man's eyes and nostrils,'
and so seems also to be some sort of bond. *Peirar* even in Homer already has the
abstract meaning of boundary, but the boundary is doubtless still felt as a physical
rope. See also Professor Onians' remarks on the words *thymos, psyche, moirai,
phren* and *noos*.

Or like the Vision of the Universal Form (visva-rupa darsanam)
Before which Arjuna bowed with every hair on his body bristling
    with awe[1]
(Or like the tremendous vision
Which came to Buddha under the Bo-Tree
Or to Socrates when he heard, or dreamt he heard,
The Sybil of Mantinaea
Discoursing on mortal and immortal love
Or like Descartes' dream of November 10, 1619,[2]
Near the environs of Ulm
When there were presented to him,
Coming as an enquirer after truth,
A Dictionary, representing knowledge,
And the volume of the Corpus Poetarum,
Which he took to be the symbol of inspiration,
Or like the 'sudden illumination' that came
To Benchara Branford one night in his fortieth year:
'At once was born into vivid and enchanting consciousness
A new metaphysical calculus of sixty-four
Inter-related cardinal categories, of which thirty-six
Were the transmuted forms of the Geddesian concepts.'[3]
Or like the moment (not like it – it!)
By which as Kierkegaard says in *Begrebet Angest*
The individual is related to eternity,
The moment St. Paul refers to when he describes
Our all being changed 'in the twinkling of an eye.'
Because in that moment the individual chooses himself
And thereby all may be changed.
The moment partakes of eternity:
It is then eternity penetrating time.
How the moment can be made eternity
For the individual Kierkegaard shows
In 'Gjentagelsen' – it depends on repetition,
Kierkegaard's substitute for Plato's theory of reminiscence).

---

[1] In the Bhagavad-Gita. Compare also Matthew XVII. 6 and Luke V. 8.
[2] Chevalier, *Vie de Descartes*, pp.40-47.
[3] I.e. the concepts of the late Sir Patrick Geddes, Branford's collaborator.

If you examine one of them more closely you will see
How it clings together with the others, is conjoined with them,
Coloured by all the shades of sound, accompanied
By all the harmonies to the foundation of foundations in the depths
And to the dome of all domes in the heights.

Now you understand how stars and hearts are one with another
And how there can nowhere be an end, nowhere a hindrance;
How the boundless dwells perfect and undivided in the spirit,
How each part can be at once infinitely great and infinitely small,
How the utmost extension is but a point, and how
Light, harmony, movement, power
All identical, all separate, and all united are life.

Svaham aham samharami.[1]

*   *   *

Everlasting layers
Of ideas, images, feelings
Have fallen upon my brain
Softly as light.
Each succession has seemed to bury
All that went before.
And yet, in reality,
Not one has been extinguished...
The fleeting accidents of a man's life
And its external shows may indeed
Be irrelate and incongruous,
But the organising principles
Which fuse into harmony,
And gather about fixed pre-determined centres,
Whatever heterogeneous elements
Life may have accumulated from without,
Will not permit the grandeur
Of human unity to be greatly violated,
Or its ultimate repose to be troubled,
In the retrospect from dying moments,

---

[1] I myself will again bind the braid together. (See Bhatta Narayana's well-known drama, *Veni-samhara*, i.e., 'braid-binding.')

Or from other great convulsions.[1]
It is with me now, surveying all life
From the heights of Literature and the Arts, as it was
With Thomas de Quincey when he made
A symbology of the view he commanded
From the eminence of Everton.
Liverpool represented the earth,
With its sorrows and its graves left behind,
'Yet not out of sight nor wholly forgotten.'
The moving sea typified the mind.
Here was a respite, the tumult in suspense.
Here, cried de Quincey,
Are the hopes which blossom in the paths of life
Reconciled with the peace which is in the grave;
Motions of the intellect as unwearied as the heavens,
Yet for all anxieties a halcyon calm;
Tranquillity that seems no product of inertia
But as if resulting
From mighty and equal antagonisms,
Infinite activities, infinite repose.

*   *   *

All life's million conflicting interests and relationships,
Even as nerves before ever they function
Grow where they *will* be wanted; levers laid down in gristle
Become bone when wanted for the heavier pull
Of muscles which *will* clothe them; lungs, solid glands,
Yet arranged to hollow out at a few minutes' notice
When the necessary air shall enter; limb-buds
Futile at their appearing, yet deliberately appearing
In order to become limbs in readiness
For an existence where they *will* be all-important;
A pseudo-aquatic parasite, voiceless as a fish,
Yet containing within itself an instrument of voice
Against the time when it *will* talk;
Organs of skin, ear, eye, nose, tongue,
Superfluous all of them in the watery dark

---

[1] *Vide* Thomas de Quincey's *Suspiria*.

Where formed – yet each unhaltingly preparing
To enter a daylit, airy, object-full manifold world
They *will* be wanted to report on. Everywhere we find
Prospective knowledge of needs of life
Which are not yet but are foreknown.
All is provided. As Aristotle says,
'To know the end of a thing is to know the why of it.'
So with your work, vastly outrunning present needs
With its immense complication, its erudition,
(The intricacy of the connections defies description.
Before it the mind halts, abased. *In tenuis labor.*)
But providing for the developments to come. . . .

Even so long before the foetus
Can have either sensation or motion,
When, in fact, its cellular elements
First begin to differentiate themselves,
The various nerves which are to govern
The perceptions and reactions essential to life
Develop, as they shape themselves, a faculty
For discovering and joining with their 'opposite numbers,'
Sensory cell 'calling' to motor cell
By a force we may call Cytoclesis.[1]
Nor is this mysterious 'call'
A phenomenon of the nervous system only.
Throughout the body cell 'calls' to cell
That the elaborate and intricate development
Of tissues may proceed aright.
Thus in the case of the kidney tubules
The myriad secreting tubules are formed
In one portion of the primordial embryonic tissue
Budded out from the ureter.

---

[1] 'Mankind's improved lot will be conceived in the laboratories of research scientists. From this womb composed of glass, nickel, physical and chemical elements, higher mathematical equations and philosophical thoughts, science will present the future with giant and resplendent children of the Hindu Gilgames legend. The reason our modern world ranks lower, particularly in a moral sense, than the age of Pericles or Saint Thomas Aquinas is that we have awaited the birth of a nobler future from sterile wombs, degenerate dynasties, ambitious and empty-headed statesmen with their Councils of Five, white-gloved military officers, and so-called constitutional parliaments with their motley cohorts of venal representatives.' – Lajos Zilahy in *The Angry Angel*.

Nevertheless although these two entities
Are involved in the completion of all the kidney tubules,
There is the marvel that results in each secreting tubule
Meeting a collecting tubule
Accurately end to end.
Each complete duct is composed of two sections
Preformed from different embryological elements
But guided to meet each other by a 'call,'
A 'call' so wonderful that each kidney tubule
Meets each ureteric tubule end to end
And so completes the canal.

Ah, Joyce! We may stand in the hush of your death-chamber
With its down-drawn blind
But those who were on the other side
When you passed over would find
It (despite the general view: 'Another queer bird gone')
As when – no! Not the Metaphysical Buzzard!
(*C'est un numéro! C'est marrant* – in both senses!)
But the peacock flew in through the open window
With its five-foot tail streaming out behind,
A magnificent *ek-stasis*[1]
Counterpart of your great *Aufhebung* here,
Der Sinn des Schaffens[2] completely seen at last.
– The supreme reality is visible to the mind *alone*.

And so I come to the end of this poem
And bid you, Joyce – what is the word
They have in Peru for *adios*? – *Chau*, that's it!
                    Well, Chau for now.
Which, as I remember it, reminds me too
Of how in Chile they use the word *roto*
To mean a peasant, a poor man,
In Guatemala called *descalzado*;
And how a man will leave an impression
By the way he mushes his 'r's'
Or buzzes his 'y's' or swallows his 'd's'
So that you automatically think

---

[1] Breaking through to eternity.
[2] The Meaning of the Creative Act.

'Guatemala' or 'Argentina' or 'Colombia.'
They say *'bue-no'* in Mexico
When they answer the phone.
You can tell a Mexican every time
If you hear him using a phone.
And in Guatemala they use *'vos'* instead of *'tu,'*
As they would say *'che'* in Argentina.
And so, like Horace long ago,
'Non me rebus subjungere conor!'[1]
Sab thik chha.

---

[1] Which the Hungarian novelist, Lajos Zilahy, glosses: 'I won't let things get the better of me.' The final (Gurkhali) sentence means 'Everything's O.K.' This indicates that the author shares Werner Bergengruen's conviction of what the German writer calls 'the rightness of the world,' despite all that may seem to enforce the opposite conclusion.

To a Friend and Fellow-Poet[1]

It is with the poet as with a guinea worm
Who, to accommodate her teeming progeny
Sacrifices nearly every organ of her body, and becomes
(Her vagina obliterated in her all-else-consuming
Process of uterine expansion, and she still faced
With a grave obstetrical dilemma calling for
Most marvellous contrivance to deposit her prodigious swarm
Where they may find the food they need and have a chance in life)
Almost wholly given over to her motherly task,
Little more than one long tube close-packed with young;
Until from the ruptured bulla, the little circular sore,
You see her dauntless head protrude, and presently, slowly,
A beautiful, delicate and pellucid tube
Is projected from her mouth, tenses and suddenly spills
Her countless brood in response to a stimulus applied
Not directly to the worm herself, but the skin of her host
With whom she has no organised connection (and that stimulus
O Poets! but cold water!)...The worm's whole musculocutaneous
     coat
Thus finally functions as a uterus, forcing the uterine tube
With its contents through her mouth. And when the prolapsed
     uterus ruptures
The protruded and now collapsed portion shrivels to a thread
(Alexander Blok's utter emptiness after creating a poem!)
The rapid drying of which effectually and firmly
Closes the wound for the time being...till, later, the stimulus
     being reapplied,
A fresh portion of the uterine tube protrudes, ruptures, and
     collapses,
Once more ejaculating another seething mass of embryos,
And so the process continues until inch by inch
The entire uterus is expelled and parturition concluded.
Is it not precisely thus we poets deliver our store,
Our whole being the instrument of our suicidal art,
And by the skin of our teeth flype ourselves into fame?

---

flype turn inside out

[1] Ruth Pitter.

To My Friend the Late Beatrice Hastings[1]

(Who expressed the fear that a Communist anti-religious line might yet provoke a great swing back into the arms of the Church unless some substitute is provided, perhaps from Indian religious thought; and also to a friend in Manchester, who asks me to assist her young son in the preparation of a script on: 'What for youth today, if anything, is taking the place of the religion that so profoundly influenced former generations?')

Can historical materialism, which is only a historical method,
Be an adequate substitute, to the proletariat, for philosophy,
Always taken in its traditional meaning
As a universal and closed *Weltanschauung*
Into which all the currents
Of the natural and material sciences flow?

One meets here the well-known 'need for metaphysics'
Which rises up everywhere;
And it cannot be denied
That such a need exists
In the masses of workers.
Workers often develop a remarkably deep
Interest and understanding of philosophic problems,
The deeper, indeed, the greater the poverty
Out of which they labour to raise themselves.
Nor can it be doubted that the satisfaction of this need
Is a powerful and essential means
By which the working class makes itself more efficient and skilled
For the fulfilment of its historic tasks.

However, this 'need for metaphysics'
Has nowhere metaphysical roots.
And it would remain dissatisfied
Even though a new philosophy
Was brewed out of the holiest and costliest
Surrogates of the old philosophies.

It has, in every case, only historical roots
By means of which it is nourished
And with which it dies.

---

[1] A brilliant contributor under the pseudonym of Alice Morning to the *New Age* in its heyday, and authoress of *Defence of Madame Blavatsky*.

These roots, on one side, are the 'metaphysical stuff'
With which the brains of proletarian children
Are oppressed in the public schools
In the brutal and vulgar form
Of incomprehensible Bible texts
And hymns from the hymn books;
And, on the other side, the soulless character
Of modern mass-production, mechanical labour,
Which, by its eternal monotony,
Even anticipates the spirit of the worker
And leads him to philosophise
Over the meaninglessness of this existence
Which from infancy has been impressed upon him
As the work of a supernatural power.

A worker who has worked his way up
Out of the lowest depths of the proletariat writes:
'I wish to be free from the dogmas of dualism
Dictatorially commanded, free from servility.
My philosophy is the autocracy of the spirit....

'Is this civilisation, when the intelligence
Dies physically a horrible death?
Is this humanity
When the soul goes hungry?
When its desires thirst
Languishing for beauty and power.
I demand a remedy.
The plough, the chisel,
The trowel in the sinewy fist
– But this fist belongs to a man!
Watch over it!
The pen, the lyric, the telescope
Belong to the cycle of the spirit.
Do not forbid these!
For the suppressed talent bitterly avenges itself....

'Thought, in my world, is a cause of suffering,
Because through thought I know
How needy and unfortunate I am.
Were the veil of ignorance
Still over my spiritual eyes

Truly my heart would feel only half as much
The travail of my earthly suffering.
I have entered completely into the Marxist idea
That economic poverty is just as much
A basis for the degeneration of the spirit
As of the body of a people
And that only a life half-way free from worry
Will allow man to blossom
Into complete personality.

'How else could it happen that until now
Only the materially secure
(I will not say absolutely, but relatively)
Have formed the circle of the artistic élite,
Whilst much valuable talent has been murdered
Under the base pressure of economic calamity,
Or, better said, remained in embryo?
Man is matter, stuff; his spirit exists
In a material organisation,
And wherever physical nourishment
Necessarily has to be obtained
Only through externalised power,
Claiming everything, there falls away
The spirit-enlivening element which fructifies the soul.

'Such a person, naturally, is absorbed entirely
With the struggle round the ordinary problems of the stomach.

'He is, and remains, considered
From this point of view, the animal
In whom the spiritual personality is a farce.

'Here is found the great,
Ignominious and cardinal flaw
In the multitude of mankind today.'

One sees from this that modern workers
Understand how to philosophise very well,
But they wish to know nothing
Of a single philosophy
Whether it be the 'dualism' of philosophical idealism
Or of the 'ordinary problems of the stomach'
Of philosophical materialism.

What they have 'completely absorbed'
Is the 'Marxist idea' – historical materialism –
Which can in fact fully satisfy their 'metaphysical needs,'
Not through a new philosophy,
But through a history of philosophy
Written in accordance with the historical-materialist method.

It would not be difficult to write that history,
For, as Schopenhauer correctly says,
All previous philosophy revolves
About certain fundamental ideas
Which always return.
But *how* they return, out of what causes,
In what form and under what circumstances,
To determine this requires
An ever more precise scientific instrument,
And we will not be able to count on this
For a long time to come.

Therefore all the more
Ought we to avoid
Bringing philosophical speculation and playthings
Into the proletarian class struggle,
Whose metaphysical need,
In its dark impetus,
Knows much better the right road!

Old Wife in High Spirits

In an Edinburgh Pub

An auld wumman cam' in, a mere rickle o' banes, in a faded black
    dress
And a bonnet wi' beads o' jet rattlin' on it;
A puir-lookin' cratur, you'd think she could haurdly ha'e had less
Life left in her and still lived, but dagonit!

He gied her a stiff whisky – she was nervous as a troot
And could haurdly haud the tumbler, puir cratur;
Syne he gied her anither, joked wi' her, and anither, and syne
Wild as the whisky up cam' her nature.

The rod that struck water frae the rock in the desert
Was naething to the life that sprang oot o' her;
The dowie auld soul was twinklin' and fizzin' wi' fire;
You never saw ocht sae souple and kir.

Like a sackful o' monkeys she was, and her lauchin'
Loupit up whiles to incredible heights;
Wi' ane owre the eight her temper changed and her tongue
Flew juist as the forkt lichtnin' skites.

The heich skeich auld cat was fair in her element;
Wanton as a whirlwind, and shairly better that way
Than a' crippen thegither wi' laneliness and cauld
Like a foretaste o' the graveyaird clay.

Some folk nae doot'll condemn gie'in' a guid spree
To the puir dune body and raither she endit her days
Like some auld tashed copy o' the Bible yin sees
On a street book-barrow's tipenny trays,

---

rickle o' banes rattling frame of bones
dagonit colloquial expletive cf. American doggone it   *syne* then
dowie feeble   *ocht sae souple and kir* anything so supple and free of care (cured)
lauchin' loupit up laughing leaped up   *skites* darts through the air
heich skeich crazy and irresponsible
crippen thegither wi' laneliness and cauld all shrivelled up with loneliness and cold
gie'in' giving   *dune* done   *tashed* spoiled

A' I ken is weel-fed and weel-put-on though they be
Ninety per cent o' respectable folk never hae
As muckle life in their creeshy carcases frae beginnin' to end
As kythed in that wild auld carline that day!

Facing the Chair

Here under the radiant rays of the sun
Where everything grows so vividly
In the human mind and in the heart,
Love, life, and all else so beautifully,
I think again of men as innocent as I am
Pent in a cold unjust walk between steel bars,
Their trousers slit for the electrodes
And their hair cut for the cap

Because of the unconcern of men and women,
Respectable and respected and professedly Christian,
Idle-busy among the flowers of their gardens here
Under the gay-tipped rays of the sun,
And I am suddenly completely bereft
Of *la grande amitié des choses créés*,
The unity of life which can only be forged by love.

---

muckle much   *creeshy* fat and greasy   *kythed* appeared
carline old woman

Credo[1]

As a poet I'm interested in religious ideas
– Even Scottish ones, even Wee Free ones – as a matter of fact
Just as an alcoholic can take snake venom
With no worse effects than a warming of the digestive tract.

The Ross-shire Hills

What are the hills of Ross-shire like?
Listen. I'll tell you. Over the snow one day
I went out with my gun. A hare popped up
On a hill-top not very far away.

I shot it at once. It came rolling down
And round it as it came a snowball grew,
Which, when I kicked it open, held not one
But seventeen hares. Believe me or not. It's true.

---

[1] 'Credo' appeared, untitled, embedded in the text of *In Memoriam James Joyce* in 1955. But it deserves its own integrity. – Eds.

Appendix 1

Glossary for 'On a Raised Beach'

In assembling this glossary I have expanded upon the glossary made by Nancy K. Gish, which is appended to her book *Hugh MacDiarmid: The Man and His Work* (London: Macmillan, 1984). I have also referred to *Chambers Twentieth Century Dictionary*, which MacDiarmid was using at the time of composing 'On a Raised Beach' (in the edition edited by Thomas Davidson, although MacDiarmid uses words in the poem which did not appear in the *Dictionary* until the later edition, edited by Miss A.M. Macdonald). MacDiarmid's use of *Chambers* and other sources such as Dr Jakob Jakobsen's *Etymological Dictionary of the Norn Language* and *Two Popular Lectures* (Lerwick, 1897), on Shetlandic dialect and place-names, is discussed by Ruth McQuillan in her invaluable essay 'MacDiarmid's Other Dictionary', published in *Lines Review* no. 66, September 1978, pp.5-14. – A.R.

Adamantine: Made of or resembling adamant (an imagined rock with fabulous properties); as hard as diamond, unbreakable, impenetrable.
Aesthesis: Feeling, sensitivity, sensual perception.
Angle-titch: Earthworm.
Arris: An external angle, sharp edge, or ridge.
Ataraxia: Impassiveness, freedom from passion, calmness, stoical indifference.
Auxesis: Enlargement or exaggeration; amplification; gradual increase in intensity of meaning; hyperbole; growth in size.
Ayre: Low-lying strip of land, usually between loch and sea; a beach.
Bakka: Banks or steep rocky ridges.
Bead-proof: Of such proof or strength as to carry beads or bubbles after shaking, as alcoholic liquors *(Chambers)*.
Bistre: A warm brown colour, made from the soot of beechwood.
Braird: (Scots) To sprout; to appear above ground like the first shoots of corn.
Bricole: A medieval engine for throwing stones.
Burr: A rough ridge or edge; any impediment or inconvenient knot.
Caaba: Venerated shrine of Mecca, enclosing a sacred black stone, said to be a ruby brought from heaven.
Cabirian: Ancient, secret mystery rites.
Cadrans: A wooden instrument by which a gem is adjusted while being cut.
Caen-stone: A lightish-yellow building-stone (from Caen, Normandy).
Cairn: Mound or heap of stones erected for a memorial or mark.
Carpolite: Fossil or petrified fruit.
Catasta: A place of torture; a block on which slaves were exposed for sale.

Cavo-rilievo: A style of relief in which the highest portions of the figures are on a level with the plane of the original stone, which is left around the outlines of the design.

Celadon: A pale shade of green.

Chatoyant: Having a changeable, undulating, or floating lustre, like cat's eyes in the dark.

Chiliad: A thousand.

Christophanic: Pertaining to the appearance of Christ after his death. The 'Christophanic rock' rolled away from Christ's tomb.

Coigns: Corner-stones.

Corbeau: Very dark green.

Crusta: A hard coating; a layer of the earth; also, a cocktail served in a glass, its rim encrusted in sugar *(Chambers)*.

Cyathiform: Cup-shaped.

de Bary: A nineteenth century German botanist.

Deictic: 'Proving directly', from Greek *Deiktikos*, to show; demonstrating.

Diallage: Rhetorical method of argument, whereby various points of view are all brought to bear upon one point.

Duss: (From Old Norse *dyss*) A thrown-up heap (of stones).

Ébrillade: A check of the bridle which a rider gives a horse, by jerking one rein, when it refuses to turn.

Eburnation: The process by which bone becomes hard and dense like ivory.

Écorché: Flayed; a figure on which the muscles are represented stripped of the skin, for the purposes of artistic study.

Enchorial: Of the country, as used in a particular country; used by the people; demotic.

Encrinite: Fossil crinoid (lily-shaped echinoderms), like a starfish, sea-urchin or sea-lily.

Energumen: A 'possessed' person, a demoniac.

Enfouldered: Charged with thunderbolts and lightning; 'mixed with lightning or fire' *(Chambers)*.

Engouled: In the mouth of a beast, in reference to crosses or bars with ends which enter the mouths of animals.

Entrochal: Pertaining to entrochi (wheel-like plates of which some crinoids are composed).

Epanadiplosis: Rhetorical figure wherein a sentence begins and ends with the same word.

Faculae: Small bright spots on the sun.

Fescue: Straws or twigs used to point out letters for children learning to read; a blackboard-pointer used in teaching; but also a genus of grasses, including many valuable and fodder grasses.

Fiducial: Firm, a fixed point from which measurements are made or to which positions are referred; confident, sure and certain.

Foraminous: Pierced with small holes; porous; cf. the 'foraminifera' in the poem 'On the Ocean Floor' (small crustaceans whose shells are perforated with pores).

Foveoles: Small hollows or pits, depressions.

Futhorc: The Runic alphabet.

Glaucous: Sea-green; greyish-blue.

Glout: To look sullen; a sullen or sulky look.

Gloss: To elucidate; to explain; also to glow, to have a fair and lustrous appearance.

Gorgonises: Turns to stone; petrifies.

Haecceity: 'Thisness'. Duns Scotus's word for that element of existence on which individuality depends, hereness-and-nowness.

Haptik: Pertaining to the sense of touch (to lay hold of, touch, grasp). Haptiks (or haptics) is the science of studying data obtained by means of touch.

Hellya: (Possibly from Icelandic 'hella') a flat stone.

Hellyina bretta: A flat stone turned upwards; the steep rock (place-name).

Hellyina grø: Rubble; broken stones; the grey rock (place-name).

Hellyina wheeda: The white rock (place-name).

Hoar: White or greyish-white, esp. with age or frost.

Hraun: A rough place; bare rocks in the sea; a rocky wilderness.

Hurdifell: A rocky hill, covered in fallen boulders.

Hvarf: Turn around; reject; slip away from (as hay is turned).

Klett: A rock; a cliff; a low rocky shore.

Kolgref: A charcoal pit; 'to lay onyting in kilgref' is to prepare the ground roughly, leaving it in an uneven state.

Kollyarun: The round-topped cairn.

Lithogenesis: The process of the production of rock.

Lochia: Watery discharge following childbirth. But the word is associated with metaphors of parturition (or 'the act of bringing forth') in Nietzsche and Soloviev, and may refer to the evolution or 'second birth' of consciousness.

Millya hellya: Between the smooth rocks.

Omnific: All-creating.

Optik: Pertaining to sight, or to the eye; visual.

Pegasus: The winged horse that sprang from Medusa's blood, associated with the Muses: hence, an embodiment of the power that raises a poet's imagination above the earth. Also a constellation in the northern sky.

Queedaruns: White cairns.

Ratchel: (Scots) Broken stone.

Røni: A cairn.

Ruderal: Growing on or among stone or rubbish (rudera are fragments or ruins of a building); growing in waste places or among rubbish.

Rugas: Folds or wrinkles.

Rupestrine: Composed of rock or inscribed on rock.

Schwendener: A nineteenth-century German botanist responsible for the theory that a lichen is not an individual, but a composite plant made up of an algal host body and a parasitic fungus.

Slickensides: Polished and scratched or striated rock surfaces, produced by friction.

Striae: Narrow streaks, channels, or ridges; the furrows or flutes of a column.

Tesserae: Small quadrilateral tablets of stone or glass; the fragments of a mosaic; tokens, tickets or passwords.

Truité: Having a delicately crackled surface.

Appendix 2

A Note on MacDiarmid's Use of Sources

Increasing critical attention has been paid in recent years to MacDiarmid's practice of creative transcription, taking obscure passages of prose from journals and books and transforming them into verse. While he was engaged in this practice as early as the 1920s, it became a characteristic method of his later work, and *In Memoriam James Joyce*, for example, applies this mode of composition on an epic scale.

Some key critical texts in this area of MacDiarmid studies are:

Edwin Morgan, 'MacDiarmid and Sherrington', *Notes and Queries* 10:10, October 1963.

Kenneth Buthlay, 'Some Hints for Source-hunters', *Scottish Literary Journal* 5:2, December 1978.

Alan Riach, *Hugh MacDiarmid's Epic Poetry* (Edinburgh: Edinburgh University Press, 1991).

There follows a select list of some of the most important sources for a number of the poems included in this volume.

'Empty Vessel': The traditional ballad, 'Jennie Nettles'.

A Drunk Man Looks at the Thistle: The traditional ballad, 'The Twa Magicians'; Richard Church, a review of *Dostoevsky Portrayed By His Wife*, *The New Age* (20 May 1926), pp.25-6; D.S. Mirsky, *Modern Russian Literature* (London, 1925). And *passim*.

'To hell wi' happiness': J.N. Duddington, 'The Religious Philosophy of Vladimir Solovyov', *Hibbert Journal* (April 1917), pp.434-47.

'Dytiscus': J.S. Martin, *Orchardford* (London, 1924).

'On a Raised Beach': F.R. Leavis, *New Bearings in English Poetry* (London, 1932).

'Island Funeral': J.B.S. Haldane, 'Some Consequences of Materialism', in *The Inequality of Man and other essays* (Harmondsworth, 1932).

'Scotland': e.e. cummings, 'N&: seven poems', in *Complete Poems*, I, 1913-35 (London, 1968).

'Dìreadh III': J.S. Martin, *Orchardford* (London, 1924); H.J. Muller, *Out of the Night: A Biologist's View of the Future* (London, 1936).

'In Memoriam James Joyce': L.A. Waddell, *The British Edda* (London, 1930); J.S. Martin, *Orchardford* (London, 1924); 'Yeats' Inner Drama', *The Times Literary Supplement* (4 February 1939), p.72.

'The World of Words': J.C. Powys, *Autobiography* (London, 1934); John Buchan, *A Prince of the Captivity* (London, 1933); T.H. White, *The Sword in the Stone* (London, 1939).

'The Snares of Varuna': Herman Melville, letter to Nathaniel Hawthorne, 17(?) November 1851.

'Plaited Like the Generations of Men': Ferruccio Busoni, *Letters to His Wife*, trans. Rosamond Ley (London, 1939); 'De Quincey's Retreat: The Uncharted Lands of Dream', *The Times Literary Supplement* (10 June 1939), p.340; Sir Charles Sherrington, *Man On His Nature* (London, 1940).

'Happy on Heimaey': R.M. Lockley, *I Know an Island* (London, 1938).

Appendix 3

Sources for 'Perfect'

The poem 'Perfect' was first published in *The Islands of Scotland* in 1939, but almost all of the words of the poem were written by the Welsh writer Glyn Jones in prose, in a short story entitled 'Porth-y-Rhyd'. When this was revealed in the correspondence columns of *The Times Literary Supplement* in January 1965, MacDiarmid claimed that 'any plagiarism was certainly unconscious' and immediately made the 'necessary explanations and apologies' to Jones.

It was with the generous concurrence of Glyn Jones that the poem was included in *The Complete Poems of Hugh MacDiarmid*, in 1985, with an explanatory note.

'Perfect' is a small masterpiece, and as the critic Kenneth Buthlay has shown in his essay, 'Some Hints for Source-Hunters' (*Scottish Literary Journal* 5:2, December 1978, pp.50-66), MacDiarmid has made exemplary use of source-material in this poem. The relevant extract from Jones's story runs as follows:

> Tudur held her wrist, wet, and cold as iron, and drew her to the window, and on her palm lay the small frail skull of a seagull, white, and complete as a pebble. It was lovely, all the bones pure white and dry, and chalky, but perfect without a crack or a flaw anywhere. At the back, rising out of the beak were twin domes like bubbles of thin bones, almost transparent, where the brain had been that fixed the tilt of the wings, with the contour of the delicate sutures inked in a crinkled line across the skull, and where the brow-bone sloped down into the beak were two dark holes like goggles where the eyes had shown out of the feathers.
>
> – *The Blue Bed and Other Stories* (London: Jonathan Cape, 1937)

Buthlay has also pointed out that practically every other word in the poem has come from particular sources. For example, the Spanish epigraph (which means 'The dead open the eyes of those who live', but also suggests 'The dead open their eyes on those who live') comes from the play *La Celestina*, by way of a biography of R.B. Cunninghame Graham:

IN MEMORY OF GABRIELA CUNNINGHAME
GRAHAM OF GARTMORE
DIED AT HENDAYE, FRANCE
8 SEPTEMBER. A.D. 1906. AGED 45
LOS MUERTOS ABREN LOS OJOS A LOS QUE VIVEN.

This is an inscription from a bronze plaque in the ruined priory on Inchmahone Island, in the Lake of Menteith, where Cunninghame Graham's wife is buried; it is quoted in A.F. Tschiffely's biography of Cunninghame Graham, *Don Roberto* (London: Heinemann, 1937), p.344.

Even the *situation* of the poem may be sourced in the naturalist Seton Gordon's book *The Immortal Isles* (London, 1926, p.7), where we find: 'Along the western seaboard of South Uist...in the green machair...' What MacDiarmid has made of these sources remains, of course, a matter for judicious critical appraisal.

Index of Titles

Index of First Lines

Chronology

1927	Founded Scottish Centre of PEN. Member of Scottish National Convention. Declined adoption as Labour candidate for Banff county. Adopted as Nationalist candidate for Dundee. Son Walter born.	1927	*Albyn, or Scotland and the Future.*
1929	Left Montrose to work on *Vox* in London. Delegate to the PEN Congress in Vienna.		
1930	Public Relations Officer in Liverpool with the Organisation for Advancing the Interests of Merseyside. Separated from Margaret Skinner.	1930	*To Circumjack Cencrastus.*
1931	Delegate to the PEN Congress in Vienna.	1931	'First Hymn to Lenin' published in *New English Poems.*
1931-32	Divorced Margaret Skinner. Married Valda Trevlyn. Moved to Thakeham, Sussex, and then to Longniddry, East Lothian. Son Michael born.	1932	*Second Hymn to Lenin. Scots Unbound and Other Poems.*
1933	Moved to Whalsay, Shetland. Expelled by National Party of Scotland for communism.		
1934	Joined the Communist Party of Great Britain. Mother died.	1934	*Stony Limits and Other Poems. Scottish Scene, or the intelligent man's guide to Albyn.*
1935	Nervous breakdown. Hospitalised. Edinburgh University Rectorial Election – bottom of the poll.		
1936	Public testimonial of support presented.	1936	*Scottish Eccentrics.* Routledge refused to publish *Red Scotland: or, what Lenin has meant to Scotland.*
1937	Expelled from the Communist Party for nationalism, but reinstated on appeal to the National Conference.		
1938	Expelled from the Communist Party for nationalist deviation.	1938	*Scotland; and the Question of a Popular Front Against Fascism and War.* First number of *The Voice of Scotland. Dìreadh.*

		1939	*The Islands of Scotland.* 'Cornish Heroic Song for Valda Trevlyn' published in *Criterion.*
		1940	*The Golden Treasury of Scottish Poetry.*
1942	Left Shetland Islands. Found work as a fitter with Mechans Ltd, a munitions factory, in Clydeside. Rejoined Scottish National Party.		
1942-48	Member of the National Council of the Scottish National Party.	1943	*Lucky Poet.*
1944	Merchant Service with M.F.V. *Gurli* on the Clyde. Rejoined Scottish National Party.		
1945	Stood as Scottish Nationalist candidate for Kelvingrove. Lost his deposit. Unemployed in Glasgow. Short spells as post-office sorter and staff member of the *Carlisle Journal.*	1945	Revived *The Voice of Scotland.*
		1946	*Poems of the East-West Synthesis.*
		1947	*A Kist of Whistles.*
1948	Left the Scottish National Party.		
1950	Civil List pension. Visited Russia with Scottish-USSR Friendship Society. Stood as Independent Scottish Nationalist for Kelvingrove. Lost his deposit. Moved to Strathaven, Lanarkshire.		
1951	Moved to Brownsbank Cottage, Biggar, Lanarkshire.		
		1953	*A Drunk Man,* 2nd edition.
		1955	*In Memoriam James Joyce.* 'Third Hymn to Lenin' published in *Voice of Scotland.*
1956-57	Rejoined the Communist Party. Awarded Honorary LL.D. by Edinburgh University. Visited China with British-Chinese Friendship Society. Made Honorary Member of Scottish PEN.	1956-57	*A Drunk Man,* 3rd edition. *The Battle Continues.*

287

1958	St Andrews University Rectorial Election – bottom of the poll. Edinburgh University Nationalist Club presented Andrew Fletcher of Saltoun Medal.		
1959	Visited Czechoslovakia, Bulgaria, Rumania and Hungary giving Burns Bicentenary lectures.		
1960	Aberdeen University Rectorial Election – second to Peter Scott.		
		1961	*The Kind of Poetry I Want.*
1962	Critical recognition and 70th birthday celebrations. Presentation of R.H. Westwater portrait.	1962	*Collected Poems. A Drunk Man*, 4th edition. *Hugh MacDiarmid: a festschrift.*
1963	Received 1962 William Foyle poetry prize. Refused freedom of Langholm.	1963	*Aniara.*
1964	Visited Canada. Stood as Communist candidate for Kinross and West Perthshire against Conservative Prime Minister Sir Alec Douglas-Home. Lost his deposit.	1964	Kenneth Buthlay's critical monograph, *Hugh MacDiarmid* appeared in the 'Writers and Critics' series.
		1966	*The Company I've Kept.*
1967	Visited the USA. Became President of the 1320 Club. 75th Birthday Exhibition, National Library, Edinburgh.	1967	*A Lap of Honour.*
1968	Visited Italy. Elected Honorary Fellow Modern Language Association of America. Awarded £1,000 by Scottish Arts Council.	1968	*The Uncanny Scot.*
		1969	*A Clyack-Sheaf. Selected Essays.*
		1970	*More Collected Poems. Selected Poems* (Penguin).
1971	Visited Italy and met Ezra Pound.		
1972	Symposium at Edinburgh University. Exhibition in Edinburgh University Library. Created Governor of the Academy of Pure Malt Scotch Whisky.	1972	*The Hugh MacDiarmid Anthology* (Open University Set Text). *Lucky Poet* reissued.

1973	Visited Ireland. Participated in Rotterdam International Poetry Festival.	1973	Translated Brecht, *The Threepenny Opera.*
1974	Elected Honorary Member Royal Scottish Academy as Professor of Literature.	1974	*Direadh I, II and III.*
1975	Received the Freedom of the Burgh of Cumbernauld.	1975	*Metaphysics and Poetry.*
1976	Visited Canada.	1976	*Contemporary Scottish Studies* reissued.
1978	Awarded Honorary Litt. D. by Dublin University. Died 9 September in hospital in Edinburgh. Buried in Langholm on 13 September.	1978	*The Complete Poems of Hugh MacDiarmid, 1920-1976.*